## Praise for Art Cullen and *Storm Lake*

### An Honoree of the Society of Midland Authors Literary Awards

"[Art Cullen] has become sought after as one of the nation's leading progressive voices on rural life and politics. . . . Presidential candidates are contacting him, personally. And national media outlets call on him to explain the way rural Americans perceive national political developments." —*Des Moines Register*

"He is tall, with a shock of white hair and a horseshoe mustache. He looks startlingly like Mark Twain, and writes like Samuel Clemens, too: sometimes folksy, sometimes eloquent, frequently mocking, and customarily outraged." —*The Christian Science Monitor*

"Cullen's book demonstrates the important role that local editors play in standing up and speaking to power in America. . . . *Storm Lake* is an engaging, folksy read about how a small-town newspaper editor copes with existential threats to a way of life and an industry vital to American democracy in a state known for its extremes of weather, economics, and politics. [Cullen] tells good stories and writes with a journalistic flair that prefers punch to polish. . . . The pages of *Storm Lake* clearly demonstrate why Cullen won journalism's most revered prize." —*The National Book Review*

"Art Cullen's story of what had happened to his home town echoed [Elizabeth] Warren's story of what had happened to the country in many ways—rural Iowa, in his telling, had itself been transformed for the worse by unchecked capitalism. Part of what has distinguished Warren's story is that it has a different frame of reference, in which politics is not an argument over the cultural aftermath of the sixties but over the influence won by wealth in the eighties, which from certain vantage points—the consumer-bankruptcy courts, Art Cullen's Storm Lake—can seem the only American story worth telling." —*The New Yorker*

"With a self-effacing, homespun honesty . . . Cullen makes an eloquent case that community newspapers are integral to the fabric of small towns . . . [and] that diversity is keeping Storm Lake alive. Many Latino, Laotian, and Vietnamese families work in the packinghouses. Cullen argues that these families have thrown a much-needed life preserver to Storm Lake's economy."
—*Minneapolis Star Tribune*

"An engaging storyteller, Cullen recounts the deeds (and misdeeds) of youth, but his writer's passion shines when he discusses the events that led him to write the prize-winning editorials. . . . The moral, economic, and social history of a small town in Iowa might not seem like much of a story, but in Cullen's hands, it is." —*Booklist*

"*Storm Lake* is a must-read, and it is a great read." —WBUR

"An impassioned, significant book from a newsman who made a difference." —*Kirkus Reviews* (starred review)

"[A] memoir that gracefully illuminates the challenges facing the American heartland. Composed of political history, tales of civic controversies, and human interest stories, the subject matter is elevated by Cullen's passion into parables relevant to all Americans. . . . A window into small-town America." —*Publishers Weekly*

"Read this book and you will understand why Art Cullen's courageous writing—sensitive, challenging, sometimes abrasive—helped build Storm Lake into, as Cullen phrases it, 'a community, not just an unrelated gathering of people.' Cullen captures, in prose that is almost poetry, the ethos of small town, rural Iowa, the heart and soul of the 'good America.'" —Tom Harkin, former U.S. senator from Iowa

"Mechanization may have driven out small farmers, smothered the lake, and helped push the town paper to the edge of starvation, but Storm Lake has persevered, clutching its social fabric against the forces that have torn so much of the rural Plains asunder. If you care about the future of the Republic, Art Cullen's thoughtful, clear-eyed ode to his western Iowa hometown is not to be missed."

—Colin Woodard, author of *American Nations: A History of the Eleven Rival Regional Cultures of North America* and *American Character: A History of the Epic Struggle Between Individual Liberty and the Common Good*

"Art Cullen does not believe in the notion of flyover country. He knows that Storm Lake is a place where hardworking and community-minded people live, work, and play. He believes strongly that Storm Lake is worth writing about and fighting for, and you will, too, after reading *Storm Lake.*"

—Tom Vilsack, former governor of Iowa

"Pulitzer Prize winner Art Cullen embodies what community journalism is all about, which is an understanding—even love—of place and people, a determination to make things better, and the backbone to challenge powerful interests. Cullen knows Iowa and a lot more. This book will delight you and inform you and surprise you. It will also give you hope. At a time when press freedoms are threatened and facts are in dispute, it is good to know that Cullen and his compatriots are standing guard."

—Dan Balz, chief correspondent of *The Washington Post*; author of the *New York Times* bestseller *Collision 2012*

"This is a cry from the heart from the heartland, and it is for those people on the coasts who think nothing important happens in the middle of the country. In fact, everything important that is happening pretty much anywhere in the country happens there—right there, around Storm Lake, in Iowa."

—John M. Barry, author of *The Great Influenza* and *Rising Tide*

PENGUIN BOOKS

STORM LAKE

Art Cullen is half the ownership and 25 percent of the news staff of *The Storm Lake Times* (founded by his brother John) and the winner of the 2017 Pulitzer Prize for Editorial Writing for his editorials taking on corporate agribusiness for fouling the state's water and despoiling its soil. His commentaries on politics, immigration, and the environment have been published by *The New York Times*, *The Washington Post*, and *The Guardian*, along with regional newspapers and news sites. Cullen has been profiled by National Public Radio, Katie Couric, and CNN, and has served as a guest political analyst on MSNBC. This is his first book.

# Storm Lake

Change, Resilience, and Hope
in America's Heartland

# ART CULLEN

PENGUIN BOOKS

PENGUIN BOOKS

An imprint of Penguin Random House LLC
penguinrandomhouse.com

First published in the United States of America by Viking,
an imprint of Penguin Random House LLC, 2018
Published in Penguin Books 2020

Map illustration by Dolores Cullen

ISBN 9780525558897 (paperback)

THE LIBRARY OF CONGRESS HAS CATALOGED THE
HARDCOVER EDITION AS FOLLOWS:
Names: Cullen, Art, author.
Title: Storm Lake : a chronicle of change, resilience, and hope from
a heartland newspaper / Art Cullen.
Description: New York, New York : Viking, [2018] |
Identifiers: LCCN 2018025006 (print) | LCCN 2018034055 (ebook) |
ISBN 9780525558880 (ebook) | ISBN 9780525558873 (hardcover)
Subjects: LCSH: Storm Lake Times—History. |
American newspapers—Iowa—Storm Lake—History. |
Journalism—Iowa—Storm Lake—History.
Classification: LCC PN4899.S76 (ebook) | LCC PN4899.S76 C85 2018 (print) |
DDC 071.77/18—dc23
LC record available at https://lccn.loc.gov/2018025006

Printed in the United States of America
1  3  5  7  9  10  8  6  4  2

Set in Bell MT Std
Designed by Cassandra Garruzzo

*This book is dedicated to the memory of my friend Jim Benson, Poland Township, Iowa, farmer (February 20, 1947–December 10, 2017). Jim died of complications from ALS (Lou Gehrig's disease). His sage advice: "Keep 'er between the ditches, Art!"*

# Contents

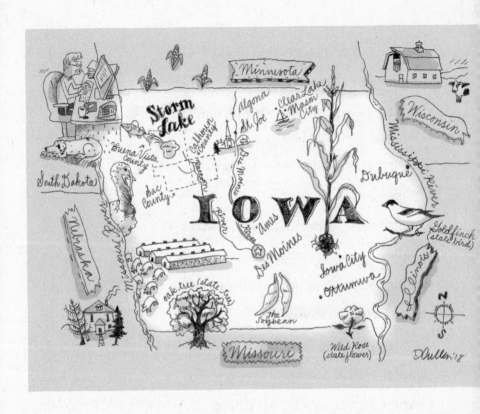

# Author's Note

Never did I seriously think of writing a book. Editing a country twice-a-week newspaper in my hometown of Storm Lake, Iowa, was plenty for me. But about a week after I won the Pulitzer Prize for editorial writing in April 2017, a couple of New York publishers asked me on the same day if I would like to write a book. I laughed at the first caller and took the second more seriously but still thought it ludicrous. I could not write much more than seven hundred words at a time. But a third and most important publisher, my big brother John of *The Storm Lake Times*, told me to call them back. I always listen to John.

We struck up a conversation with editor Wendy Wolf at Viking. I suggested a series of essays and personality sketches that would paint a picture of how rural Iowa had morphed since my career humbly launched thirty-eight years ago in Algona, Iowa. She wanted to know more about the family story, of how the second smallest newspaper (we think) in the Pulitzers' 101-year history won for taking on corporate agriculture over pollution and local government secrecy.

So it became the story of a hometown newspaper founded in 1990 by John in a tempest, joined by his little brother as editor, and how we interpret this place on the broken prairie with a pretty (but polluted) lake. A patchwork expanse of corn and soybeans, peppered by industrial-scale hog and poultry confinement buildings, surrounds us while the steady slice of the meatpacker's cleaver occupies us. People stream in from around the globe, from Cuba to Myanmar, speaking thirty languages, searching for the first rung on the American ladder to a dream. While much of rural Iowa is emptying out of people and aspirations, our little town is revitalized by immigrants to whom we introduce you. Some of us blame the newcomers for problems as old as the railroad, and succor it with a brand of radical politics steeped in resentment that finds voice in Donald Trump and our congressman Steve King.

The story goes back to Algona in a 1980s rural depression that saw farmers hanging themselves in barns. Could the rural places we loved survive? It goes back to Mexico in 2005 to find Storm Lake's twin city and font of our new neighbors praying for a shot at freedom. In the people we find the spirit that draws us to them, and which eludes so many others building a political pitch on running them off.

Our story dwells mainly in the here and now of Storm Lake—buffeted by the currents of corn markets and wind and rain and political sleight of hand. We explore how we can maintain the world's most productive agricultural complex without destroying ourselves and the people downstream. The challenge is even greater with climate change bearing down on Iowa's—and everyone's—way of life. Change is underfoot against that horizon that should sustain our special little place. That's a story of hope, which is what farming and family newspapering are all about.

My thanks to the staff of *The Storm Lake Times*, especially John and my wife, Dolores, for supporting me while I was off writing a book. Also, thanks to Todd Case of Iowa City, Martin Case of Minneapolis, Minnesota, and Michael Gartner of Des Moines for helping to guide me. And of course to the readers of *The Storm Lake Times* for getting me this far.

# Storm Lake

# CHAPTER 1

# The First Question: Why?

A good reporter's first task is to ask questions. It's a family habit of ours, learned early on.

My first memory is of waving good-bye to Dad on our sun-drenched lawn one Sunday morning a hundred yards north of the sparkling lake. I was two. Dad piled into a car bound for Madison, Wisconsin, where he would be a guinea pig for a potential cure for tuberculosis. The year was 1959.

Why did he leave me there? Where was he going? Would he come back?

A childhood friend of his from Whittemore, Iowa, Lloyd Roth, head of the department of pharmacology at the University of Chicago, was working on this project at the Veterans Administration hospital. Roth was also a physicist and had worked on the Manhattan Project, which developed the atomic bomb.

Dad had picked up TB during World War II while stationed in Sicily with the Army Air Corps. He was a captain in charge of a supply depot at an air base; it's a wonder the planes could fly, because he didn't know a screw from a screwdriver. The disease didn't fully manifest itself until after the war. When it did, more than a decade later, our family was in quarantine in Storm Lake, Iowa, a meatpacking town of about seven thousand with a small college and, yes, a lake.

There we were, Mom alone with six kids, I the youngest.

Brother Bill let loose hamsters in the basement that spread throughout the house.

Brother Jim and I painted the basement red—including the clothes and bedding drying in the furnace room.

Brother Tom, the eldest, tore the screen doors off the Corral Drive-In theater with a beery buddy.

Brother John wanted to run away.

Sister Ann was taking care of me, after a fashion.

Mom called Dad in the hospital hoping for sympathy. He laughed.

They took out a lung and he wasn't supposed to last more than a few months. He made it fourteen years, just long enough for me not to understand him.

Meantime, Mom had been battling the VA ever since the war ended, trying to get him promised benefits. The records building in St. Louis burned down and with it the evidence that Dad contracted TB while in service.

She had been through an endless siege for information before. Her first husband and father of my oldest brother, Tom, Omer Kelly, was shot to death in a Chicago bar when Tom was about two. Mom spent years trying to find out how he died. Her father, Art Murray, traveled from Bancroft, Iowa, to Chicago with his lawyer, Luke Linnan, to find justice. Linnan had an old friend who was a judge there. The judge told them to go home, and to quit asking questions.

She never quit asking.

Our mother reared us to do the same.

Sometimes your questions get answered. Which means, of course, that often they don't. I have been a reporter and editor for Iowa newspapers for thirty-eight years, and I've spent a lot of that time asking questions about little towns and about quiet people who also ask the same questions amid a patchwork of corn and soybean rows.

I didn't mean to wind up in Storm Lake at all. I was driving to the big city and bright lights but took a U-turn to come back home where brother John had just started a weekly newspaper, *The Storm Lake Times*. I did not want to go back. But the journey led me to the story of a lifetime, to a Pulitzer Prize in 2017 for taking on corporate agriculture over river pollution, and down a road to a place where I finally realized that I belonged.

Worlds are built and worlds are buried amid the tall grass here in Iowa. You plunge your finger into the soft black soil and expose a seed, a kernel of knowing where you are, a story, an idea, a myth of who you are, and it grows out here against all the odds. It persists against the hail that comes sideways. It preserves itself frozen in a January gale out of the northwest that makes you wonder how you ever survived. It gets flooded and scorched and comes back. No matter what you do for the next ten years, it comes back. It demands you pay heed to it, heel to it, nurture it, and hope for it. It's the land, the story, an impulse to take a rough first draft of history, a drive to divine some truth in a place that lays it bare, by asking and listening. To love a place and be its chronicler, to commit yourself to it, to prick its conscience and make it aware that we have bucked up against its limits, and to leave your mark for posterity. The seed becomes a song, its verses written in this expansive green garden, and you are left to discern them and write one anew. To be a friend to the place and not to spoil it.

These are the questions I start with.

Who came first, and where did they go?

What is our place?

When will I live up to him?

How do we live against that horizon?

Why am I drawn or pushed here?

Where are we going?

Into the pink sunset, down Buena Vista County blacktop C-49, as the combines spew dust and corn stover, you can almost see the lights eleven miles west as dusk enshrouds Varina, home to St. Columbkille Catholic Church and a grain elevator outpost with a smattering of weathered frame houses.

Home beckons.

Storm Lake, Iowa.

## CHAPTER 2

# The Next Question: Why Not?

The phone rang where I sat for another hot and dank August evening in 1990 at the Mason City, Iowa, *Globe Gazette*. I was the night editor. The job and life were everything the glamorous title suggests. I was the one responsible for getting the paper put to bed before a 1:00 a.m. press time.

I had just finished my supper of a cold sandwich; I was sitting in the break room in the basement, where you could hear an ancient press hulking on the other side of that gray steel door.

It was John on the other end of the line. Again. He said it was too much, this new little tabloid weekly. He needed me.

John had been publicly relating for Buena Vista University, a Presbyterian college of about one thousand students on the lakeshore campus in Storm Lake. But he, too, had been a newspaperman, though he'd been out of it for six years, and he missed his editorial soapbox. He walked into his old office at the Storm Lake *Pilot Tribune* in 1989 and asked if he could buy it. The publisher, a pup in his twenties and son of the chain owner, told John, a seventeen-year veteran of community journalism, that he didn't quite understand business.

That got his Irish up. There was no happy handshake. The moment he walked out the door he knew he was launching his own paper.

With daughter Bridget, a toddler, and son Justin, an infant, John told his wife, Mary, that he wanted to start a weekly. *The Storm Lake Times*, "Buena Vista County's Hometown Newspaper." She must have told him he was nuts.

I for certain told him he was nuts.

I was a reporter and editorial writer miscast to run a news desk and copyediting operation for the *Globe Gazette*, a twenty-seven-thousand-circulation, seven-day regional paper "Making All North Iowans Neighbors." I hated it.

Copy editors can save your career and maybe your life. They can make you sound like Yeats. And they can take the fun out of the Cubs winning the World Series because they get no credit for it. And you do not know grammar.

But when John called me, not long after his meeting with the pup, and asked me to come home to help start a weekly, I told him he was out of his mind. The *Pilot Tribune* was the oldest business in Storm Lake, older than prostitution. Take your TIAA-CREF college pension and hide amid the ivy vines, I advised.

He didn't listen. John is stubborn.

Eighteen months before, I had moved up I-35 from the *Daily Tribune* of Ames (home of the Iowa State University Cyclones) to Mason City (home of the former brick factory) on my way to Minneapolis. I was determined to get back to the *Minneapolis Tribune*, where I got my start. I was making steady progress up my path, even if I was at the point of a nervous breakdown. If I could just hang in there at Mason City another year or so, maybe a Twin Cities door would crack open. Maybe I could get back to reporting. Maybe I could get at that big story.

We had two children. Son Joe was two and daughter Clare was a newborn. I worked nights while they slept. I slept during the day when they played with Dolores.

I was having my midlife crisis about eighteen years early, at thirty-two. I resisted the urge to buy a red Corvette soft top for lack of funds. We had a red Plymouth K-Car station wagon that rattled tie rods over railroad tracks. My fantastic notions of being a national correspondent for a great American newspaper were being revealed as just that. I was a hack night editor wearing a bow tie to work that even the gay copy editor sneered at, not to mention the sports slot man from northern Minnesota who made racist comments out loud. You couldn't fire him because he whipped out the sports agate pages with the standings and late scores so fast.

I quit going to church. I even started reading the Bible looking for some truth. That was a first. Armageddon scared me off (I always begin at the end to see how everything turns out). I wasn't writing anything worthwhile. People at work didn't especially like me. The editor who hired me left for another paper in the chain two weeks after I was seated. The future didn't exactly beckon. I didn't believe in much of anything anymore. I wanted to do a special reporting project assisted by Iowa State University on post-Soviet agricultural reconstruction in Russia. The grant fell through. I begged for a job at the *Des Moines Register* as an ag or business writer. No luck. But I still thought I could make it up to Minneapolis.

The human resources department at chain headquarters in Davenport ran the Mason City paper, in perpetual fear of a union. Strangely, it ended up that they could not fire anybody because of the threat of a union that did not exist, and they didn't want anyone to start one. It was impossible to get a fire going on a mossback. Sometimes they referred to our paper in the corporate newsletters as a "profit center," not a newspaper for a community of people who wanted to be neighbors.

What was I doing there?

And John was on the phone.

*The Storm Lake Times,* his new baby, had a big appetite. Way bigger than he expected. People in town were aching for a home-owned, hometown paper by a homegrown boy. It hit four thousand paid circulation in no time in a town that had grown to nearly ten thousand people.

"I need your help," he said. When big brother asks baby brother for help a second time, it's a charm.

Why not?

I told Dolores that we should move home to Storm Lake and forget about my corporate climb. She thought I was crazy, just like my brother.

"Sounds pretty risky," said her farmer father in a pair of fifteen-year-old bib overalls.

I wrote my first "Editor's Notebook" column for *The Storm Lake Times* on September 28, 1990.

"I'm out to prove Tom Wolfe wrong. He said you can't go home again. I'm home after 15 years and it feels good."

That was the lede.

"I left with a laundry bag over my shoulder in 1975 bound for St. Paul and swearing never to look back. Funny how the years, a few gray hairs and a couple of little children clear one's vision."

I talked about how John got me my first job in Algona, Iowa, and how I came home with a new identity. I explained that I grew up in Storm Lake being called Jerry but switched my byline to Art because I never liked Jerry. Jerry Lewis: goofy. Art Buchwald: goofy but clever.

"A tornado destroyed much of Algona. Then a flood. My brother John left me as editor, and a farm depression brought Kossuth County to its knees. Fifteen percent of the county's population was ushered out over the past decade, including me. Often I miss it, and often I worry about that old home.

"In Ames, where I edited *The Daily Tribune*, one could see a state determined to rebuild itself. A great story was building around research parks, business incubators, new agricultural product development centers, biotechnology complexes and an Extension Service that was writing a gospel on diversification just as fervent as the message of planting maize on ISU's 'Corn Train' 100 years ago. . . .

"Such musings came back to me as I drove down the Varina blacktop on Sunday evening. I thought of where I had been and where I was going the next day.

"I thought of the Indian trails along Storm Lake and Buena Vista College, the dam at pretty little Linn Grove and the Saturday livestock auction at the sale barn, Sunday band concerts and meatpacking.

"Not a whole lot had changed, but my Storm Lake vanished with me 15 years ago. It still is a progressive town with wide streets and a cold winter wind. It still depends too much on pork slaughter and the college, and it still seems somewhat content as things are.

"This has changed: I look at Storm Lake and Buena Vista County through an adult's eyes today. I see an opportunity to help build a community around all those old, abiding graces that once sent me out with a sense of wonder. That's what *The Storm Lake Times* is all about—building a community, building a newspaper and building a business.

"What a priceless opportunity, what a comforting town. It's great to be home."

We bought a home on Irving Street, just a block west of John and Mary's house on Cayuga Street (named after a New York Finger Lake, along with Seneca and Oneida streets). Old maple trees were in full fall blaze when we moved in. St. Mary's School, where the Cullens learned to write, was just three blocks away.

John grows a mustache, I grow a mustache. John goes to work at a newspaper, I go to work at a newspaper. John gets married, I get married a year later. He buys a house near Lover's Lane along the lake, I buy a house near Lover's Lane along the lake.

The Cullen Brothers opened a new chapter in the history of Storm Lake. Print the truth and raise hell.

## CHAPTER 3

# "And Ye Shall Have Dominion over the Land"

The lake was gouged by the final retreat of the Des Moines Lobe of the Wisconsin glacier fourteen thousand years ago, a three-thousand-acre prairie pothole. The government surveyors found it in 1854, an azure jewel of clay bottom and water mirroring a blue sky nestled in a sponge of bog and big bluestem tall grass.

Herds of five hundred thousand elk came to drink from banks lined by granite cobblestone. Balls of fire reputedly three stories high rose from the tall grass in autumn. The grass grew so thick and high it could envelope a man on his steed. The Dakota patrolled the region of northern Iowa and southern Minnesota, engaging in marginal turf wars with the Sac and Fox in what was known to the white pioneers as the Upper Des Moines region, spanning from one rim of the Des Moines Lobe on the east pocked by Clear Lake, and on the west by Storm Lake. Twenty-five miles south of Storm Lake is Black Hawk Lake, named after the Sac chief, which is the southernmost glacial lake in the United States. The golden dome of the Iowa Capitol shines from a hill that is the southern tip of the Des Moines Lobe, where the Raccoon and Des Moines rivers join on their way to the Father of Waters, the Mississippi.

Lewis and Clark just missed us in 1804. They stopped off near Sioux City on the muddy Missouri, not realizing what lay seventy miles east.

This is where the West begins.

The wind never stops, twenty miles per hour strong out of the west. It propels North America's largest wind turbine complex along Buffalo Ridge, a couple of miles into the sunset from Storm Lake. The ridge is the western edge of the Des Moines Lobe. It rises up to the horizon as the golden hour draws over a lake with six boats floating on a June evening, blades silhouetted against the orange sky.

Inkpaduta, the Dakota chief, could not have imagined this.

Neither could Henry Lott, a white settler in the valley of the Des Moines River near Boone, a whiskey and gun trader who arrived in the winter of 1846 and shortly would set one Native American against the next.

Boone County history suggests that the Dakota leader Sinamindota met with Lott near Boone. Accounts differ on what their rub was, but Lott convinced neighbors that the Dakota posse robbed him, scalped his family, and raped his wife. The story was good enough to attract a group of rival Pottawattomie native people into the fray to go after the Dakota. They learned that the family wasn't scalped but had scattered. It is believed that Lott's wife and son later died as a result of the incident.

Lott reputedly loaded a barrel of pork and a barrel of whiskey with an undescribed blend of nastiness up the Des Moines River from Boone into Dakota territory. At first he started trading with the natives. He was able to track down Sinamindota and assure him that all hard feelings had washed down the river. Lott suggested a nice place for a round of shooting elk, and Sinamindota agreed to join the hunt with two of his men. Lott sent them out to circle the elk, then tracked each of them down and killed them from behind.

For emphasis he followed it up by murdering Sinamindota's family in 1853. Their blood ran into the creek, known today as Bloody Run, on the border of Kossuth and Humboldt counties in northern Iowa. Seventy-five Dakota people died from an "epidemic" inspired by sampling Lott's pork barrel.

Lott was charged in Polk County (Des Moines), Iowa, with first-degree murder. The sheriff might have let him get away. Lott fled, they say to the Pacific slope for mining, where he was ultimately lynched by other miners for "misdemeanors."

The Dakota chief Inkpaduta retaliated in 1857 by murdering the Gardner family in their cabin at Spirit Lake, sixty miles north of Storm Lake. It went down in Iowa legend as a hospitality issue. They say he would come upon a house and, finding it unlocked, leave the white settlers inside alone. Trouble came with the locked door, and a nasty fate befell the unwelcoming Gardners, as the lore goes. A garrison of fourteen soldiers chased the chief through all the sloughs around from their outpost at Fort Dodge and another just over the border in Minnesota. Two of them separated from the unit and froze to death in Palo Alto County, about thirty miles northwest of Bloody Run. Their bodies were found eleven years later, so remote a swamp it was.

But Inkpaduta never was found. Not that he wouldn't stand out. He was big, his face was pocked from smallpox, and he had red hair. That's what his name means: red top.

The whites would hear about him popping up around the region and wreaking havoc. That he killed somebody over there, and robbed a place over here. Not sure where. Nobody ever was. There were stories in the papers. They said he was at Little Big Horn for Custer's Last Stand. That one of his twin sons killed Custer and kept his horse. There is an argument that the stories of his exploits were planted in the papers by the *federales* to keep the white man whipped up into aiming for a red man, like they do today with Mexicans, except we say they are brown.

People would ask about Inkpaduta. Sitting Bull said he was in Manitoba. But everyone knew Sitting Bull was covering for the last Dakota to stand up to the blue soldiers in the Upper Des Moines territory. So who knew where Inkpaduta ended up? Probably not on the reservation where the Dakota were herded, in Sisseton, South Dakota. They said he died in Manitoba.

They say the spirit of Inkpaduta lives. That he lives. That he is still out there. That he belongs here. He was a hero to the Dakota people in many ways because he was the last man standing in his world. He was villain to Abby Gardner, who testified to her account of the family massacre in a then-popular book.

The question: If we cannot effectively record the past or the present, how can we ever agree to step forward together when all times demand it?

We peer into the myth and search for a fact on the way to a truth. It makes us wonder if we understand what we are up against.

Inkpaduta might have. Lott didn't.

And they say this:

A maiden was forbidden by her chief to marry a suitor from

another tribe. The two young lovers attempted to elope, starting out across the lake in a canoe. A storm upset the boat and the two drowned. The saddened chief cursed the waters as the cause of his sorrow and in his grief christened the waters "Storm Lake." At night along the lakeshore some can hear their plaintive cries, calling each other home.

A bner Bell, a fur trader with a full black beard and a long pipe, was the first white man in Buena Vista County, settling along the Little Sioux River about fifteen miles north of Storm Lake. He came in 1856 not far behind the surveyors and Henry Lott, just as the Dakota were driven up to a reservation along the Minnesota River. All was clear in the Fort Dodge / Upper Des Moines territory.

While Bell was building a cabin near the Little Sioux River, my ancestor Kieran Mulroney and his brother, a great-something-grandfather of mine, Patrick, had just fled the famines in Ireland. They got their wagon stuck in the West Fork of the Upper Des Moines River near Cylinder, Iowa. They stayed there for a blizzard and nearly froze to death like the soldiers chasing Inkpaduta.

Kieran declared himself to be the Judge Roy Bean of Palo Alto County, whose seat was Emmetsburg. He was sheriff, magistrate, and hangman, if need be. It is not clear from which constitution he derived authority. Not far from where the Mulroneys got stuck, the Cullens set up shop on Cullen's Corner along the main wagon trail (now U.S. Highway 18). The place must have reminded them of Ireland: sloughs and rocks not fit for a German farmer.

At least there were no Brits in the neighborhood.

Our people had made their way over from the lead mines on

the Mississippi at Dubuque. They came west from Chicago (my great-grandmother watched the city burn sitting on a bluff as an indentured servant to publisher Marshall Field) and up from New Orleans, these dirty Irish papist immigrants.

Great-grandpa Joe Murray came from Sinsinawa, Wisconsin, just across the river from Dubuque, to found a granary in the outpost of Bancroft in Kossuth County. His son, Art, my grandfather, built it into a grain elevator empire with eleven farms created by draining sloughs surrounding the East Fork of the Upper Des Moines River and Plum Creek. To the innovator goes the profit. The granary was built just as the prairies and sloughs were conquered. It was the only game in town. The Murrays were growing grain, reaping it, buying it, and storing it for haul. They were vertically integrated, as the economists say, decades before Cargill.

Art Murray called Bancroft, population eight hundred, "the garden spot of Iowa." He was the town patriarch. He built the baseball field and the church. He sponsored the town team that went to the national American Legion tournament. He lost his son, Tommy, who was scouted by the big leagues, to a sniper in the Philippines in World War II. Art was never the same. It killed him in his fifties. The doctor said he had a brain hemorrhage.

But not before creating that fortune, built on drainage and storing bootleg liquor for the whiskey runners during Prohibition. The trains would come to the elevator and load up on corn and cornpone, bound for Duluth on Lake Superior and Chicago, where Art made "friends" on the Board of Trade who helped him make the "trades."

He bought farms during the Great Depression from the insurance companies and let the tenants live there on a crop share until they died. He hosted high-stakes poker and craps games at the elevator.

"He would never take an IOU for a farm," a woman from Lone Rock, near Bancroft, once told me. But he would take everything else fair and square. It was a family occupation. They would have to pull teenager Tommy out of the craps games to suit him up for the baseball games.

During the Depression the hoboes would hop off the trains at the elevator and the boys at the scale would tell them about Grandma Bessie, Art's wife. They were told she would feed them. My mother, Eileen, the oldest of six, served them through the back door when she was a little girl. They were on their way to somewhere. Mom remembered them all as good men.

My mother adored her father. She adored her brother, the carefree Tommy. She knew what her mother, Bess Murray, was about. Eileen would be a woman of sophistication. She was sent off to the College of St. Catherine, an all-women's school near the river in St. Paul, Minnesota. She studied English and had a choice: become a secretary, an English teacher, or a nun. One of her chums was a girl named Abigail, who married a young St. Thomas English professor named Eugene McCarthy. He went on to become a U.S. senator from Minnesota and the peace candidate during the torrid summer of 1968.

Eileen Murray became the executive secretary to the CEO of Bankers Trust in Des Moines. Iowa still banned selling liquor by the drink in bars, a hangover from Prohibition. She was in a speakeasy called the Blue Moon where a call came from a mole at the sheriff's office saying that a raid was coming. The women went into the restroom, where they were safe from male arresters. In bounded a young sportscaster from WHO Radio named

Dutch Reagan. He didn't use his real first name, Ronald, yet. He divided the sea of women and made his way out the bathroom window, reputation intact except with her. Every time she saw him on TV she would say: "That sonofabitch."

Eileen was slender and comely and witty. She met a Notre Dame football player named Omer Kelly from Algona, just eighteen miles down Highway 169 from Bancroft. His father ran the Algona Municipal Utilities. Omer matriculated to the Great Lakes naval team with his enlistment in the service during World War II. He was assigned to the Office of Strategic Services, predecessor to the CIA. They married and had a son, Thomas Omer Kelly.

As I mentioned, Omer was shot to death in a Chicago bar. They said Omer and his brother had hurled epithets at a Jewish bartender. You could believe that, a drunken football player defending his flap-jawed brother from Iowa. Mom didn't believe it. She said Omer knew too much from the OSS. She said he knew something about organized crime. She asked a lot of questions, and said she got mysterious calls telling her to stay calm. To remain quiet. To not ask all those questions. Late at night I heard one of those calls from my bedroom in the basement. She was sitting at the top of the stairs in the kitchen. I heard her crying.

Art Murray wanted to know. Luke Linnan was the best country trial lawyer around. Better drunk than any other was sober. So they went to Chicago and looked up that judge that Art and Luke knew, probably from Art's trading days during Prohibition. The judge told them both they were in over their heads.

That's all we ever knew. Rummaging in a box in the basement when I was about twelve, I found a clipping from the *Bancroft Register* about Eileen Murray marrying this man about town,

Omer Kelly. We never knew about her previous life. Mom was making Chef Boyardee pizza. "Who is Omer Kelly?" I asked. She dropped the pizza on the kitchen floor.

"Go outside and don't ask about that. And comb your hair."

Mom mourned Omer's death from the comfort of Bancroft, where they still grieved Tommy falling in the Philippines. Another handsome young man, a clothier from Algona named Pat Cullen, found her and young Tom. He was just back from the war, a captain with a couple of years of football in at Emmetsburg Junior College, twenty miles west. Before the war he drove a Lincoln Zephyr, no slouch. He left it in the safekeeping of his brother Maurice, a mechanic in Fort Dodge. Maurice's wife was certain nobody was coming home from that damn war and sold Dad's Zephyr. He came home to find his car gone, but he also found Mom. She never did like Maurice's wife. The feeling, no doubt, was mutual.

Ultimately, the Murray elevator went broke. Uncle Joe got sick with a bad heart and Uncle Don got busy with politics in the state senate. Dad said that if Art Murray's estate had been handled properly none of the Cullen children would have had to work a day in their lives. More than half the money went to the federal government. The Murray heirs, or at least some of the in-laws, squabbled over it, but what was gone was gone. Overalls to overalls in three generations, the saying goes, but not quite this time. Mom inherited a 320-acre farm despite the estate debacle. She sold it for about seven hundred dollars per acre in the early 1970s, knowing she would need the cash with a sick husband and a large brood. When she died in 1989 each of the six Cullen children inherited sixty thousand dollars. John poured it into starting the newspaper. When I came on board, I started pouring mine in, too. So did our other brothers and sister, with no promise of ever getting back a dime. For a long time, they didn't.

The irony is that the spoils of drainage were used to found a newspaper that made national waves by questioning the pollution that the drainage system enables. Grandpa Art was too good at his job. They drained too much. It is choking our rivers and lakes today.

# CHAPTER 4

# Bringing Home the Bacon

Down at Storm Lake, they plowed under the tall grass and drained the sloughs that protected the lake in order to plant row crops. They ripped out all the shoreline cobblestones in the late 1800s to build foundations of the town on the north shore of the lake, where the *Pioneer* statue peers over the waves with a salute. The mud rushed into Storm Lake, which God built with no inlet or outlet, but which man later improved. A drainage ditch called Powell Creek facilitated the drainage and the freshly freed sod's journey to the lake bottom.

The lake went from twenty-six feet deep to seven feet deep in a matter of twenty years or so, by 1900. Iowa black gold fed the fish with algae and slowly strangled them. The northern pike died from lack of oxygen. The perch disappeared with the suffocated reeds and cattails. The water went from blue to brown and green. By 1915 the Iowa Highway Commission, which was in charge of lakes, warned that Storm Lake was filling in with farmland and needed a good cleaning. Nothing was done until the 1930s.

Small farms populated by Swedes and Germans popped up from government land grants sold off by the railroads. The corn grew and the hogs wallowed and the cattle took over where the buffalo once roamed around these little farms on the broken prairie. That boundless blue sky with the cumulus clouds was the limit.

Old Fred Schaller came up from neighboring Sac County and started a bank in Storm Lake: Citizens First National Bank. His son George was on the Federal Reserve Board in Chicago in 1934. Riding the Illinois Central's Hawkeye train home, George Schaller struck up a conversation with a man from Nash Brothers Packing out of Chicago. He was riding to northwest Iowa to scout a site for a new pork and beef packinghouse in partnership with Kingan and Company of Indianapolis, a growing regional meat player. He was thinking Spencer, thirty-eight miles up Highway 71, which was a four-letter word to town builder-banker Schaller. He told the Nash man that he should stop briefly in Storm Lake for lunch. They sat on the red bricks at the depot eating cheese sandwiches and making a deal for a packinghouse in Storm Lake. Nash and Kingan opened its plant a half mile north of the lake as Storm Lake Packing Company in 1935, with Tom Nash as the first manager.

No place in the world is better suited than Iowa to growing maize, the most-used crop ever known. The thick black soil holds water. Summers are hot and humid. The growing season is perfect for one-hundred-day maize lines.

Corn, we call it. Oats. Alfalfa. Horses. Cattle. Hogs. Later soybeans to replace the oats and alfalfa. And tractors to replace the horses. The Waterloo Boy, the Johnny Popper. The twelve-row combine and the twenty-four-row planter. Now we have forty-four-row planters. You can sow a thousand acres in a week. Tell the hired man to see if he can hook up with the custom harvesters working the wheat from the Dakotas down to Kansas, because Iowa just doesn't need him anymore.

Iowa grew to be called the Tall Corn State. The tall grass was all gone.

When there really were family farms—before the farm crisis that set in as a pall over the state in the mid-1980s—they would come to the old wooden sale barn with the round show ring. Boys carved their names in the wooden bleachers with pocket knives, and fathers with their fathers in overalls would get rid of an old sow for slaughter or look over and maybe lay in a few fancy feeder calves. Every Saturday morning the cook wagon would fire up as the pickups rolled in with a rack of hay or a trailer full of bleating lambs in tow. The buyers would come in from the meatpacking houses in Sioux City, South St. Paul, Omaha, and Chicago to view the critter on the hoof and bid for slaughter. The livestock would ship by rail to the city stockyards awaiting the cleaver, losing weight every mile of the trip. The meat bosses realized that they should move their plants closer to the livestock. The livestock were where the corn grew. Kingan found Storm Lake and expanded but wasn't breaking in with the big meat companies, where the bigger money and market leverage were.

Hygrade, based in Detroit, bought Kingan in the early 1950s as the packers fed on one another trying to get bigger. The Kingan purchase put Hygrade in the big four along with Swift, Armour, and Cudahy. By the time Hygrade took over, the plant had dropped beef and processed only pork in Storm Lake. Hygrade was making money. The union was strong in the 1960s and 1970s. Everyone seemed happy enough.

Hogs were the mortgage lifters for small farmers. Year in and year out, if you had thirty sows farrowing and you finished out those litters for slaughter when they got to 250 pounds, you would make money. The men who farmed and worked nights at Hygrade might buy a few feeder pigs from the friend who laid in the sows, and finish them out for beer, bread, and boat money. They would move the fat hogs to the packinghouse via the sale barn or through a hog buyer directly at the plant. It was a system that worked pretty well for Storm Lake: A diverse network of independent producers, both full- and part-time farmers, fed corn and soybeans to hogs that were processed by six hundred union workers.

Iowa is the Hog State, too. Number one.

Maybe wages and livestock producer profits got too fat in Storm Lake. At least it looked that way from Hygrade headquarters in Detroit. Meatpacking traditionally operated on 1 to 2 percent profit margins. The unions were finally making progress after World War II in building wages, benefits, and job security. Hygrade expanded the Storm Lake plant, its most productive and profitable one, by 60 percent in the early 1970s. Nobody quite appreciated that the postwar window of prosperity was about to close.

Iowa Beef Packers (IBP) had entered the game.

Two cattle industry veterans, Currier Holman and A. D. Anderson, founded IBP on the premise that the meatpacking industry was antiquated and inefficient. If a path had been cleared to rural meatpacking decades earlier by the likes of Kingan, IBP paved the way out of the jungles of Chicago, South St. Paul, Kansas City, Sioux City, and Omaha, where stockyards and packinghouses stood beside one another, and into small towns like Storm Lake, Denison, and Columbus Junction, Iowa, where the corn was harvested and stored. Rather than ship the livestock on a train from Storm Lake to Chicago, we cut the hogs right here. IBP took it a step further.

Starting in 1960 in Denison, Iowa, fifty miles southwest of Storm Lake, IBP revolutionized the meat industry with the introduction of boxed beef. Before, the old-line, established meatpackers like Hygrade shipped whole carcasses or quarter carcasses to big-city butcher shops, which then whacked the ribs and pulled the loins and sheared the shanks and displayed them behind glass for meat shoppers. IBP upset all that by cutting the pieces in the plant, vacuum packing them, freezing them, and shipping them directly to the meat counter. They wanted to automate processing to take the skill out of the job, the founders declared. Their company color would be green, they said, because it was the color of money.

IBP knocked out the neighborhood butcher shop, the unions, and the Mob to control urban meat distribution. Holman and IBP were convicted of bribing the Mob in a dispute with New York butchers and the Amalgamated Meat Cutters union. The judge fined IBP seven thousand dollars and levied no penalty on Holman, saying it was the way business was done in the New York Meatpacking District.

"Business, as we conduct it, is very much like waging war," Holman once said.

IBP knocked out the sale barn, too, as a market intermediary when livestock production became contracted directly with the packinghouse. They changed the way markets worked across America. And IBP tamed the union as conflicts led to wildcat strikes in Denison and Sioux City. Cars blew up. Wages went down. This outfit was tough. They prided themselves on it. A company that came out of nowhere—not Chicago or Detroit but Denison, population 6,000—had taken the cattle world by storm. The company announced in 1979 that it wanted to get into pork.

The Amalgamated Meat Cutters, who negotiated wages of forty-four thousand dollars, including overtime, in 1975, smelled the end. Hygrade was developing a nasty cough as its patriarchal ways—by IBP thinking—were getting blown out by a radical new industry model. Hygrade in 1979 wanted the union to take a three-dollars-per-hour pay cut. The union refused. IBP was circling Storm Lake smelling blood in the water.

The Hygrade plant closed in 1981. Most of the union Hygrade workers looked elsewhere when the plant remained dark for a year. A lot of them got union jobs twenty-two miles west at the Wilson meatpacking plant in Cherokee. (It closed down in 2015.)

Storm Lake was on edge. The entire town was built around meatpacking. Hygrade had six hundred men working. They sent their kids to the Catholic school and gave the church enough money that there was no tuition fee until our later years in school. They bought new pickups every other year, and boats. And now they were out of work. It was the Reagan era. They were freed from the union, and from employment.

IBP bought the shuttered plant using state and local tax incentives, which was also something of a new thing. It aimed to turn the hog industry on its ear, as it had done with cattle. Storm Lake was its first foray into pork. The union boys were replaced by nonunion help, some left over from Hygrade and, for starters, a contingent of about three hundred Laotian refugees from the Vietnam War. The Tai Dam community of Laos and Vietnam situated around Dien Bien Phu had been transported intact from Thai refugee camps to Iowa at the invitation of Governor Bob

Ray. He called it the Iowa SHARES program. Two of the biggest beachheads were Storm Lake and Des Moines. Lakeside Presbyterian Church, the old money in town, was the first to sponsor a Tai Dam family and the Southeast Asian Christian Ministry. Iowa embraced them out of compassion and shame about our dirty little war. Plus they worked like nobody had seen anyone work. They fed their families by scooping unwanted carp out of the lake down below the dam at Outlet Creek, which feeds the Raccoon River. Grandpa worked the day shift while the son worked the night shift and shared a house with another family. They kept their heads down. They had a Christmas party every year and invited everyone in town. The egg rolls were delicious. The new workers never let anybody down.

The Tai Dam developed a patronage system, whereby they located jobs for Lao speakers who were not Tai Dam or Christian but Buddhist. The Buddhists came by word of extended family and converged on the IBP pork plant. Storm Lake has a gorgeous gold-leaf Buddhist temple, one of the few in Iowa.

Some of the displaced union workers called them gooks. People would insist that they were overfishing the lake although the conservation officers never thought so. Some thought we were coddling the people we had been fighting. Actually, they were our displaced and dispossessed fighters. The Laotians never minded. They just kept working. Storm Lake got used to it and rolled with newcomers. A lot of the union guys were sore about the Laotians, but they also knew the gig was up. IBP was the new boss in town. They saw how the union got handled. It was a huge shift: from union to nonunion, from all white to a large contingent of Asians who were here, after all, because of their service to us in the Vietnam War. Storm Lake was on the cusp, in the late 1980s, of changing in even bigger ways.

Family networks from Laos increased their ranks at IBP. But as the plant expanded, there still weren't enough. The farm debt crisis of the mid-1980s drove off legions of farm boys on whom IBP had depended to fill out its roster. Along about 1990, the same year *The Times* was launched, IBP started recruiting in San Antonio, East Los Angeles, and, ultimately, rural Mexico to fill the turnover churn and the growth in job numbers. Young, single men, many from the agricultural state of Jalisco, were drawn over the Rio Grande and through the desert and up through Kansas along the old cattle trail to this oasis of freedom from poverty and five hundred years under somebody's boot. And since 2000 they have been coming from all over the world, from Africa to Samoa, to get a job in meatpacking.

Tyson bought IBP in 2002. Tyson, king of the chicken broiler industry, was to the Southeast and poultry what IBP was to the Midwest and red meat. Tyson practically invented vertical integration, where Tyson owns the livestock from birth to slaughter. The birds are reared and fed in barns owned by the farmer on contract with Tyson. The packages of chicken you buy in the grocery store cooler carry the Tyson brand name. Tyson saw the same possibilities with IBP and pork. They could buy hogs that were fattened on contract indoors by a regional producer that delivered a hog of consistent size and fat content to fit automation. They could then package it across all the several Tyson market lines. Efficiencies are leveraged up and down the supply and marketing chains. When Tyson bought IBP it became the biggest meat processor in America. It has ninety-seven thousand employees across the country. It is number one in the U.S. for chicken production and beef, and number two in pork behind

Smithfield Foods of Virginia, which is owned by a Chinese company.

Storm Lake also long was home to turkey production. Years ago the gobblers were reared seasonally on pasture for holiday consumption. As white meat demand increased in the 1970s and 1980s, turkey production moved indoors and slaughter was conducted year-round. When I was a kid, Mexicans would come to work in the plant while it was open for the season and move on. We called them gypsies. At first it was under the ownership of the Vilas family of Storm Lake. The Vilases sold out as the meat industry consolidated. The turkey company eventually ended up with Sara Lee/Hillshire Brands, which used the turkey for sausage and deli meats. A complex with hundreds of turkey barns surrounds Storm Lake thirty miles in any direction. Again, Tyson spotted Hillshire Brands as a stellar marketing company in prepackaged foods through which it could move its multiple meat products, from Canadian bacon to chicken nuggets to beef rib eyes. Tyson bought Hillshire in 2014. Storm Lake became pretty much a Tyson town. It employs more than two thousand men and women, about a third of the city's labor force.

Sixteen miles up Highway 71 is Rembrandt Foods, one of the largest liquid egg companies in the world, with three hundred workers and millions of laying hens, owned by Minnesota businessman Glen Taylor. It opened in 2001, as the egg industry moved from Arkansas to Iowa to be closer to the corn.

With all that livestock packed into one locale, when the flu comes around it can be the plague. In the spring of 2015 a highly pathogenic flu virus swept in from China, over the U.S. Northwest and down over the Great Plains to Storm Lake.

Birds keeled over by the flock virtually overnight. Rembrandt Foods was cleared of hens. The poultry—7 million carcasses—was burned and composted. The barns were fumigated. Rembrandt Foods' biosecure facility was shut down. So was the Tyson turkey processing plant. Crews came in from across the country and lived in the Buena Vista University dorms while they worked through all the cursed barns.

It took two years to get back into production and get over an estimated $1.2 billion loss. Tyson workers, laid off for a year, were paid by the company. The community feared that those families would leave Storm Lake for foreign points whence they came, primarily Mexico, and so did Tyson. It caused Rembrandt Foods' CEO, Dave Rettig, to reconsider any expansion in the Buena Vista County radius of production. The newest layer facility went to South Dakota.

Swine flus also are common and can wipe out the population of a confinement building in no time. Pork integrators are trying to spread out their production to avoid one another, but they are running out of places to hide. Disease comes on weather's wings and it is not at all clear whether such critical masses of livestock can be sustained under existing confinement technology. The USDA would have us believe that waterfowl spread the bird flu, but it has not contemplated in its formal research whether population density itself gives rise to the virus. Few waterfowl were found with it in Iowa or Minnesota. Outdoor chickens raised within sneezing distance of infected turkey barns were healthy, not even a sniffle.

More hogs and turkeys are paced through every day. The plants get more efficient, more automated, to increase speed and reduce workplace injury, the main one being repetitive stress injury on the hands, wrists, and forearms. A $30 million chilling expansion was just put in place in the Storm Lake pork plant. In

Waterloo, the Tyson pork plant is growing, too, with 245 workers added in 2017. State and local governments in 2017 doled out more than $200 million in incentives to attract Prestage Farms of North Carolina to depopulated Wright County in north-central Iowa, where it will slaughter twelve thousand hogs per day. Few manufacturers are adding jobs in Iowa other than food processors.

To see Storm Lake today, look through Dan Smith's eyes. Smith has watched Storm Lake morph from a white farm and meatpacking town of seven thousand in 1950, the year he was born, to a small city, by Iowa standards, of fifteen thousand, where some thirty languages are spoken. Smith, sixty-seven, retired after thirty-three years in the pack, on and off. When he called in sick on his final day of work in April 2017 he was making $15.30 per hour as a forklift driver. He had been making twice as much, relatively speaking, nearly four decades ago as a union packinghouse worker.

When Hygrade shut down in 1981, he was making $11.75 per hour union pay. Had his wages kept up with inflation, he would have been pulling down $115,000 per year when he hung up his hard hat. That's what the city manager and school superintendent make nowadays.

Everybody knows Dan, the guy with the sunburst tattooed above his ankle. He would wave and smile when he went by, in and out of the giant coolers, from 6:00 a.m. to 3:00 p.m. every day carting boxes of pork. The chicks dug him when he crooned in a rock-and-roll garage band with a full head of blond hair in high school. At his retirement party at Brewsters bar, the ladies still gathered around the guy who might be the one man in town without an enemy. He is a lover, not a fighter. Sure enough, there were Asians and blacks and Latinos along with the whites wishing Dan the best fishing. It made him feel so good he ran for the city council. He knows what the workingman and -woman are up against.

"When Reagan broke the air traffic controllers, that started the whole thing tumbling down," Dan recalled. "They got this town to where everybody was living week to week. And it takes two of 'em to do it."

Joe Smith, Dan's dad, had saved up thirteen thousand dollars to build a new house in Storm Lake in 1962 on a meatpacker's check. He had a bar and pool table in the basement. All the union boys did. If one guy gets a camper, the other guy has to get one. Or a boat. Buck Hott played steel guitar in a country band at Puff's White Cap Inn. Buck's boy Bill and Dan rocked at the Cobblestone Inn on Sunday nights at the teen hop.

Most of that halted and turned seemingly overnight while I was away from Storm Lake. IBP, when it opened the shuttered Hygrade plant, offered Dan half the pay he made through the union with Hygrade. His wife at the time had a job and they were able to squeak by, raising three daughters. You could see it in the homes surrounding St. Mary's School that used to house Hygrade union families. The paint was peeling. They were starting to get run down. It was all about wages. Everybody in town felt it.

"We would get a quarter raise and inflation or health-care expenses would eat it right up," Dan said. "They know how much they can pay."

Tyson around 2010 started gradually increasing wages beyond the rate of inflation to reduce a chronic turnover rate that often reached 100 percent annually in the early IBP days of the 1980s.

Dan gets it. He doesn't blame the immigrants. He doesn't blame Tyson, necessarily. It's battling in the world marketplace for protein share with JBS of Brazil and Smithfield Foods. He knows Tyson could just as easily move everything to Mexico if the cost gets too high in Storm Lake.

"I don't begrudge anyone the right to make a living," he said.

Employees voted down joining the United Food and Commercial Workers, merged successor to the Amalgamated Meat Cutters—a union with a sharp knife—a couple of times since Hygrade folded. The union IBP workers in Waterloo, across the state, were getting the same deal as Storm Lake, so why join? The union International out in Washington wanted to protect the contracts it still had left. Consumers demand cheap food, which came from cheap corn and hogs slaughtered by cheap workers who got paid just enough to get by. Why raise trouble? Especially if you think they might call in the *federales* to ship you out. Hygrade's closing was a pungent memory. People still argue about it thirty-eight years later. A third union drive that appeared like it might sail was called off in the dark of night by untold bosses. So you go with the flow, everybody, the boys out in Washington and the ones with low-laid heads back here and the folks downtown on Lake Avenue with crossed fingers.

Dan lives with Louise Schmeling, who was until recently a regional manager for Casey's General Stores. Casey's is the main business and social gathering spot for many small towns that can barely support a post office. They are everywhere. The convenience-store chain was founded by Don Lamberti, the son of immigrant coal miners who never graduated from high school, near Des Moines. Lamberti gave millions to

Buena Vista University, and earned a Beavers degree by building the students a fancy new rec center with an indoor track.
Casey's sells you breakfast, dinner, and supper along with a gallon of milk and gasoline. Louise is fluent in Spanish. She was
advancing in the company. She left her job following a disagree-
ment with a boss.

Casey's may be everywhere, but Walmart is the new general
store in the twenty-some regional trade centers of Iowa, like
Storm Lake. The Coast-to-Coast hardware store on Lake Avenue
is gone. So is Lake Hardware. And Lake Apothecary. And Varen-
horst Fabric. And Iowa Feeder's Supply. And Norm's Livestock
Supply, your Kent Feed Dealer. All gone. All victims of corporate
integration and mature markets seeking efficiency as people move
on to greener concrete pastures. All were advertisers with *The
Storm Lake Times,* and their spaces remain blank. John Cullen
and Dan Smith were classmates at St. Mary's. John played key-
boards with The Gladiators, which Dan, in tight pants, fronted
with vocals. John's mother, Dorothy, prayed at Mass every day
that *The Times* would find success because she could see the business model fraying. We all were shoehorned into a big box, and it
happened before our eyes without any of us being able to do a
damn thing about it.

Walmart came to Storm Lake in 1990. Later it expanded into
a super center, adding groceries to compete with two existing
Iowa-based chain supermarkets in town. It sucked up customers
and blew out Lake Avenue downtown businesses. You can get
things now that you couldn't buy before in huge quantities all in
one place. The parking lot is packed 24/7. The main crime reported by *The Times* is shoplifting at Walmart. The culprit is
often someone from twenty-five miles away who doesn't notice
the cameras.

Mom-and-pop businesses have figured out over the past twenty-five years how to survive in Walmart's shadow. They offer niches: nursing uniforms, *quinceañera* dresses, Mexican baked goods, health food, and handmade candy. Immigrant businesses come and go monthly, short on market research or cash. Downtown has more bars and restaurants than before. The three locally owned, strong banks anchor the main downtown intersection, Fifth and Lake, known as the Bank Corners. Three blocks south of downtown on Lake Avenue are the Church Corners, featuring the iconic Lakeside Presbyterian Church with its clock and bell spire, the Baptist church that has attracted a sizable Hmong contingent, and St. John Missouri Synod Lutheran Church (Missouri Synod Lutherans, much more conservative and rural than the Evangelical Lutheran Church in America, are huge in northwest Iowa), which was the first church to sponsor South Sudanese civil war refugees here. A block east sits the Methodist church, and a block south of that, St. Mary's Catholic, home to most of the Latinos. There are evangelical and Pentecostal churches of all degrees and in multiple languages. We are not unchurched here, but although we are proud of the Buddhist temple, we lack a synagogue or a mosque.

Go south on Lake Avenue and you run into the lake, where parks line its whole north shore and young Latina mothers parade strollers on a glowing summer evening.

Up on North Lake Avenue, near Walmart, the baseball and softball diamonds at the Field of Dreams fall strangely silent most days while the soccer fields are packed on evenings and weekends with players from around the world. On Sundays the police occasionally are called to calm down some of the more excitable men during the adult league games. The police chief was a certified soccer referee and used to mow the fields. During the winter they have soccer leagues in the gyms. The high school soccer team has been state runner-up twice in the past five years. Fathers shout coaching instructions from the stands in Spanish. Mariachi music booms at tournament tailgates. One Anglo student is on the team, two Sudanese, one Hmong, and the remainder (twenty) are Latino.

Immigrants comprise 90 percent of the elementary school enrollment.

They live in decrepit mobile homes, in newer apartment complexes funded by low-income housing tax credits to Omaha developers, in tiny cottages near the railroad tracks, and in nicer owner-occupied homes in upscale neighborhoods near the lake. The housing stock is chock-full. But we don't make enough money here, with an average working wage of fifteen to eighteen dollars per hour, to sustain much new single-family housing. Lots just five hundred yards from the lake go vacant for years for want of an executive to build on them. Neighborhoods are skeptical of more apartment complexes going up near them. Tension over housing is on a slow simmer. Storm Lake was a town of single-family houses. The change to multifamily is starting to get complaints at city public hearings. Research tells city hall that Storm Lake needs at least six hundred more housing units now, but they simply are not built because the income base won't support housing without a subsidy. That bothers people in Storm Lake.

The city has become a regional center for primary health care organized around Buena Vista Regional Medical Center, a county-owned hospital managed by UnityPoint Health of Des Moines. UnityPoint also operates two of the family clinics. Mercy Health Network of Des Moines has a third clinic. The fourth clinic is United Community Health Center, seeded by the federal government to help serve the working poor and underinsured. That's a large share of the immigrant population. Storm Lake also is home to Methodist Manor Retirement Community, which offers senior citizens options from assisted-living apartments to end-of-life care. It has enough critical mass of monied elderly to launch a $30 million lakefront upgrade to its long-term care unit and survive the buffets of the state's managed-care Medicaid clampdowns. Iowa Central Community College can't crank out nursing aides, licensed practical nurses, and registered nurses fast enough.

Opiates are a big and growing problem across rural America. Not so much in northwest Iowa, where physicians have been traditionally conservative about prescribing pain medication. This is meth country. It's the poor man's cocaine. In the 1990s stories were routine of hazmat teams raiding motel meth labs or finding portable lab remains in road ditches. Iowa restricted pseudoephedrine sales in stores and knocked down domestic meth production. Most of it now comes from Mexico. Local police are just starting to see an uptick in opiate trading, but nothing extraordinary. The drug of choice remains Busch Light. Almost all domestic disputes and violent crime such as assault involve alcohol, not meth or heroin.

D an and Louise have made it work. He helped her attend Buena Vista University while she reared her two children and worked. He manages some housing rentals for a friend that provides a little cash. Dan gets by.

Dan's little brother Jerry made it. He worked his way out of the county road crew by laying sidewalks and driveways under moonlight. He has a big crew with bigger machines laying streets and parking lots now. Jerry's son Matt works with him; Jerry and Anne have a place on the lake.

A guy who wants to bust his hump like Jerry Smith can make it in Storm Lake.

Dan never wanted to work like that. Storm Lake may be boring but it is an easy place to be. It's cheap. Rent costs six hundred dollars a month for a house. You can drive from the northwest corner of town to the southeast corner in seven minutes at twenty-five miles per hour, unless there is a train on the tracks bifurcating the town north and south. A Busch Light at Brewsters during happy hour is two dollars, all other times three dollars. Dan likes easy, cheap, and familiar.

He swore he would go to church and never leave Storm Lake as long as his mother was alive. And he didn't, despite his weakening position to the rest of the world. He could have taken off along with all those other young Iowans. He had trade skills in heating and air-conditioning, even had his own business long enough to lose weight at it. He claims no regrets.

"I love this town. It's a feeling, not a definition. It's heart. It's upbringing. I can't picture myself living anyplace else. How do you picture that? I am the last little bit of old school that raised this place up."

Dan campaigned for the city council in 2017 on the theme of getting the party started. He won one of two seats; the top vote getter was Jose Ibarra, thirty, who ran as a voice for immigrants. Dan wants to bring people together. Get that old loose lake town feeling back. He knows he can't solve all people's problems with streets, property taxes, or fireworks late at night. He can do without the phone calls.

"There are periods of my life where I don't give a flip about the politics of this country. How does my life change? I don't make any more money. My life is on an even plane. I just go on."

Yet he thinks he can do some good on the council. He thinks

the cops are a little heavy on their bar checks. Go easier on the public intox stuff—you don't have to bust that college kid stumbling home. When asked at a council candidates' forum what he would do for downtown, he replied, "I like it the way it is."

He wants answers on housing that no one can provide.

Others at the forum acted like anything but politicians. Regarding diversity, mayoral candidate John Crampton, a Storm Lake native in his thirties who moved back to town because of its relatively low crime, said: "The only minority here is Iowa State fans." Which got all the University of Iowa Hawkeye fans laughing, and Jose Ibarra laughed right along. Latinos soon will be the majority in Storm Lake.

# CHAPTER 5

# Lessons for Life

In 1958 Mom packed brother Tom off to military school in St. Paul, where he could march in the morning with a fake gun and sword at St. Thomas Academy. That left five of us at home, 216 Geneseo Street, a brick house with a big backyard abutting a gravel alley.

The family moved to Storm Lake from Algona in 1956. Dad and his brother Ed bought a hardware store together in Algona to get Ed off the road as an appliance salesman. Ed enjoyed a drink now and again. One morning Ed sat in the back of the store nursing a hangover. A farmer walked in. Ed told the stock boy to go up front and see what the guy wanted.

"Just lookin' around," the farmer said.

The boy went to the back and reported it to Ed. The boy sat down. Ed mustered himself up. He went out to the farmer, who repeated that he was just lookin' around.

"See that water tower over there?" Ed said, pointing out the window onto State Street. "Go climb it. You can look around the whole damn town from there."

Algona wasn't big enough for Mom and Ed's wife. Mom and Dad looked at moving to Colorado to favor his lungs, because he was wheezing from the TB, but they couldn't leave Iowa. They couldn't be that far from Bancroft, Whittemore, and Algona. From that land or the people it shaped. Moderate people. Prosperous people. Good roads and clean fields. Diligent people up here in northern Iowa. Honest people. And friendly people, pretty much, if you play the game the Iowa way.

So they checked out Storm Lake.

They found a hardware store to buy. Ed would run the Algona Our Own Hardware while Dad ran the Storm Lake Our Own Hardware.

The TB was taking its toll on Dad. Ed's wife wanted to move back to Wisconsin, where she was from. Ed gave up his interest in the stores and moved. One morning after Ed had been out all night again, they found his body. He had shot himself to death.

Dad unloaded the hardware stores. He was sick. They probably were giving him up for dead. But he then heard from his old friend Lloyd Roth. They attended Whittemore Presentation Academy together. They went to Emmetsburg Junior College together, then Dad went into clothing sales at Zender's, a men's store in Algona. Lloyd went off to study science: physics, math, biology, pharmacology. When they enlisted in the army, Dad was sent off to officer training school in light of his advanced education. Roth was secretly sent to New Mexico to work on the atomic bomb. Nobody knew where he was.

When Dad was on the ropes Lloyd Roth reappeared. Who'd

think that a town of eight hundred would produce a kid who might cure TB? Dad left for Madison.

Dad called my brother Tom into his hospital room. Dad told Tom the story about how he adopted him as his son. He told Tom that he could change his name to Kelly. Tom declined, or so the story goes as I like to remember it.

I don't know how Mom survived our juvenile terrorism or how she got all the hamsters out of the house. I doubt my brother Bill was much help.

D ad and I would play catch on the south side of the house. Mom would watch from the kitchen window. It must have been anguishing to watch him huff with his ten-year-old youngest son. "Oh, that one had some pop on it," he would tell me.

Bill was his great white hope. He was a lanky lefty like Dad. He threw a natural screwball that could barely break a tissue. But it would curve and dive and confound a plowboy who always looked dead-red.

Bill was a decent high school southpaw for St. Mary's. I was the batboy. Bill was on the mound the only time St. Mary's played Storm Lake High School in any sport. St. Mary's had about 150 students. SLHS was five times that size. At one time in Iowa, Catholic schools were not allowed to compete in the state tournament, either by church or by state. Times changed with the boomers. People were coming together and putting aside those old divisions, thank goodness.

Baseball was the one sport where St. Mary's could compete— we didn't have enough boys or money to field a football team. But Storm Lake High had Ron Kennedy on the mound. He was

six feet eleven inches and 285 pounds, and he could step halfway
to home plate while delivering a ninety-miles-per-hour fastball.
That's all he needed to throw.

We all wished that Kennedy attended St. Mary's, but he
wouldn't fit into our wooden desks. His humble parents sent Ron
and his six-feet-nine-inch brother, Randy, to the public school,
where the college scouts might see them. They won the state
basketball championship in 1968, an undefeated year in which
the Tornadoes beat the Des Moines Roosevelt Roughriders—
the biggest school in the state—in the state title game that still
goes down as one of the great days in the town's history. Really.

Bill was pitching the game of his life against Storm Lake. Dewey
Christiansen, the cagey little leadoff man, was stepping out of the
box chasing Bill's screwball.

With a runner on base in the late innings, Kennedy stepped
up to bat.

"Low and away," Dad prayed.

Bill gave him the high heat. Kennedy's eyes exploded and so
did the ball as it sailed over the National Guard Armory and
landed near Dubuque.

Just when you think you have reached the mountaintop comes
the avalanche.

In baseball, I couldn't get past the foothills.

"Looks like he runs in a gunnysack," Dad told his brother Joe
as he watched me try to beat out a grounder to short in Little
League. He would retire to the living room to sit in the chair
with a Grain Belt beer and listen to Herb Carneal and Halsey
Hall call the Minnesota Twins game on WCCO-AM, the fifty-
thousand-watt clear-channel "Voice of the Upper Midwest."

After his stay in Madison the doctors hoped Dad might live

for six months or so. He was the first man to be treated with the new TB cure. Nobody knew what would happen.

T he hardware business was in other hands. Dad had to do something. So he ran on the Kennedy ticket in 1960 for the Iowa legislature. An Irish Catholic Democrat didn't stand a chance. There were still isolated cross burnings in northwest Iowa over the Kennedy nomination. A guy in Sioux Rapids ground Dad's card under his heel.

"Fish eater."

Dad campaigned like a champion. He prided himself on getting more votes in Buena Vista County than JFK did. He was a proud New Deal, New Frontier Democrat. He had worked on the railroads during the Great Depression in the Civilian Conservation Corps. He believed in the power of people coming together against powerful interests. He cursed the Farm Bureau. And he lost to incumbent representative Fred Jarvis, who served in the House as long as he cared to. They even named a blacktop stub after Jarvis near his Alta home.

Dad got a consolation prize as a federal crop insurance agent through political connections. The job was supposed to be immune from politics; it wasn't. But Dad was always either the top or near the top county agent in the nation in sales. It was his protection from politics, his sales gift. Every Christmas we would drive the dark gravel roads delivering bottles of whiskey to farm customers. We would dodge the dogs through the mud and snow while he sat in the 1959 Chevy station wagon with the heater on, working on his daily allotment of three packs of Marlboro Reds.

He didn't say that much. He would tell me how Denis Menke from Bancroft, playing with Pete Rose for the Big Red Machine in Cincy, did that day. He would ask how school was going. I would grunt and shrug. He knew what I was up to. I would hang out at the pool halls where the old men spat into coffee cans. I didn't realize all his friends and crop insurance customers were spitting into those cans and watching me smoke cigarettes I stole from Dad.

"Stay out of The Wheel and Northside," he warned me.

Then he would bust me on a snitch. Grounded for a week. Two weeks. A month.

I would tell Dad, in junior high, that Notre Dame was ranked high in the preseason polls.

"Where did you pick that up? *Playboy?*"

But that's all he would say. He could whip you into line with just one sentence.

Warren Buffett's father would not give him dessert until he said something bad about Roosevelt at supper. Not at the Cullens'. "We'll let the Republicans take care of you, after I kick you from here to Sac City, you little pup," Mom would say when I smarted off about politics, which I knew was their sensitive spot. You could make fun of the church, but not of FDR or JFK. You would be put out on the street.

Sunday post-Mass dinner inevitably involved Mom and Dad picking apart Monsignor Ivis's sermon and making fun of his constant begging for money and exhortations against damnation if you didn't give enough. Then the conversation would turn political. It could go on for more than an hour or until Dizzy Dean and Pee Wee Reese came on the TV for the Falstaff big league game. Your head could be as mushy as Mom's greasy fried eggs and as beaten as the bacon when the youngest had his ears boxed by parents and siblings over the execution of the Vietnam War.

Mom wanted each of her children to be an orthodontist or a U.S. senator. Or a priest.

"Jesse James rode a horse," she reminded my orthodontist after she got the bill.

I tried to stay away from Mom and Dad. I got a driver's license and an antiestablishment attitude. A rebel without a cause in 1974, the year Dad died, and the year the war started winding down.

I worked nights running projectors at the Vista Theatre and the Corral Drive-In. I slept at home. That was it. He was trying to reach me, probably, but it was pointless. He died when I was a junior in high school. I managed it by drinking. So did Mom. We were each going our own way and we were so much alike, both victims of frustrated passions.

Her coda was the Prayer of St. Francis: "Make me an instrument of your peace."

She said that if women ruled the world, wars would be rare. Margaret Thatcher, Joan of Arc, and Hillary Clinton notwithstanding, I believe she is right. We should try it someday.

She cussed at the sight of William Westmoreland, Henry Kissinger, and, yes, Lyndon Johnson. She defended Harry Truman. They killed her brother, after all. And he ended the war. There was Korea. We didn't win that one. We are dealing with it today but the guns went quiet. And there was Vietnam. If JFK had lived, things might have been different, she said. She listened to Bobby Kennedy and supported Eugene McCarthy, the other peace candidate. Dad was sort of with Humphrey. HHH knew a practical way out. We talked about it every day and every night, it seemed. One night Dad sat us down and said he would help any of the boys get to Canada. All of us avoided getting The Letter. We were just lucky. I was so lucky to have been born in 1957: Boys born that year were not required to register for the draft, as it was abruptly canned after all the protest and unrest.

The Kennedys were shot dead. Martin Luther King was gunned down in Memphis. Mom would not allow a gun, not even a BB gun, in the house. She cursed the military industrial complex along with Ike. She despaired over the nuclear arms madness.

Late at night, once or twice, she would drink and talk about Omer Kelly. After she died we found the prayer cards for Tommy. I think Ann has them. And Mom talked to me one night, while she lay in bed and I sat on its edge, about Dad with honesty I never imagined. I can remember only the moment, not what she said.

She tried to find some peace amid pain and loss. She found it in sarcasm. Strangely, in cursing the darkness of war and violence. And in hoping that one day somebody might say something about it.

Every morning five of us would walk the six blocks down the gangplank to school. Ann would start out, about five minutes late, and then each of us would follow five minutes later. I came up last, about a half hour late, ready to wrestle with the Sisters of the Presentation of the Blessed Virgin Mary.

However much we dreaded and feared them at the time, those Irish nuns taught us how to write. We published our first newspaper when I was in junior high. Our government teacher at St. Mary's, Sister Mary I Can't Remember Her Name PBVM, told us about the First Amendment. She said we were free to express ourselves. Dan Statz, Charlie Dick, Guy Golvin, and I decided to push the envelope and see how far the Constitution would stretch in a dictatorship. We commandeered brother Jim's mimeograph machine, on which he published *Ampersand*, an underground newspaper that was tolerated but not encouraged at St. Mary's High School. We started in junior competition by launching *Schizophrenia*. I was the editor, Charlie was the senior writer, Dan was our ace columnist, and Guy was the art director.

Our first issue broke all newsstand sales records. We spent the proceeds on a carton of smokes. A classmate revealed our identities under duress, and we were first called into the principal's office under the stairwell where we were met by a stern Sister Maureen, who sent us over to the rectory—No. Lord, not the rectory, please; a thousand years in Purgatory but not the dark recesses of the rectory—where we were tried by Monsignor Sweeney for heresy, libel, poor taste, and treason against the Holy Roman Empire. He told us to give the money back from our ill-gotten sales. We had to admit we had smoked it. He said he was going to put a red note in our file that would stay with us forever.

I went home that night ready for the whipping of my life.

I found Mom and Dad settled in with a highball laughing like Red Skelton.

Anything in defense of satire and iconoclasm. That was the message I got.

Sister Ruth Marie, knowing I was marked with the cardinal letter, told me in high school that I had "a way with words" but I consistently failed to apply myself. I used an Alford defense and got out of town pledging never to return.

My big brother John, seven years my elder, wanted to see the world and make movies. He had a plan. He knew when the Hawkeye was coming to the Illinois Central Railroad depot to take him away to Chicago. He would fold his clothes neatly in a suitcase and walk six blocks up Geneseo Street. He would sit on the red bricks and wait. I don't know how many times he tried. But each time a 1959 Chevy station wagon with fins would float up with Dad behind the wheel to bring ten-year-old John home.

He went off to Notre Dame on that train and came home ready to start a movie-producing career. Dad asked when he intended to start. John said he would take the summer off.

"The hell you are," the old man replied.

Dad told him to get a job, which he did, as sports editor of the Storm Lake *Register* and *Pilot Tribune*, then locally owned by J. B. Anderson. John went off for a while, to report for lumberjacks in Washington State at a weekly in the woods, and then to our ancestral haunt in Algona, where old family friends invited him to join the *Algona Upper Des Moines* and *Kossuth County Advance*, twin weekly newspapers.

I told Mom I was going to attend the University of Iowa so that I might perfect beer drinking with John Johnston, John McKenna, and Ab Tymeson. "The hell you are. You're going to St. Thomas." St. Thomas was the family school, brother academy to St. Kate's. All men. I protested, but Mom told me if I left for Iowa City I shouldn't bother to return to Storm Lake. You did not question Eileen Cullen's declarations, so I packed for St. Paul.

M usic would be my major. No, they said, you can't play the piano. How about theater? You must read large volumes of history. Okay, then, business. I flunked accounting because I never did the worksheets. (Never applied myself.) With an

Ireland Hall eviction notice on the way, I had to recover fast. I went through the college catalog in a haze and landed on journalism. It was the Watergate era. Journalism was hot. It ended the Vietnam War and brought down Richard Nixon. The only requirement was to type twenty-five words per minute. I could do twenty-six, thanks to St. Mary's typing teacher, Rose Sessions.

Father Whalen, a Madison Avenue ad man before donning the collar, sized me up and tamped his pipe during his Persuasion in Writing lectures and shook his head, thinking: "Kid, you have no panache."

This college thing wasn't for me. I went home on break whining about how I was broke and how could I possibly afford to add to my Schmidt decorative beer can collection. Big brother John told me to get off the couch and get a job.

Shooed back to St. Paul, I whined to my journalism adviser, Professor Norm Larson, about how mean my big brother was. The professor told me to get a job, too. He knew just the person to call, Gary Heer, supervisor of the copyboys, as Norm had worked at the *Minneapolis Tribune* as a copy editor.

There was no way out. I had to get a job. Heer was nice enough to hire me.

That's where I got my real Introduction to Journalism 101—ripping teletypes, jumping when assistant city editor Terry Murphy (who had my number) yelled, "COPY!," occasionally fetching coffee, and hanging around to eavesdrop while big decisions were made by the sharpest minds in the Twin Cities.

We had just put the Friday paper to bed and raced across the street for last call at the Little Wagon when the bar phone rang. It was the Associated Press in New York calling. "Hey, the pope died," the bartender said. "What pope?" the night managing editor, Steve Ronald, said. "We just got a new pope a month ago. Is there some other pope?" The bartender gave him the phone and started pouring our drinks into Styrofoam cups in violation of Minneapolis city ordinance. It was trumped by the call of the First Amendment, which says that Congress shall not violate last call.

We ran back across to the *Trib*. I was told to find everything I could in the clipping morgue on Pope John Paul. They ripped up the newspaper in no time, remade it, and called back the fleet of teamsters rolling out to St. Cloud with the paper.

"Stop the presses!" somebody must have cried.

Right then and there, I decided this was for me.

My time was up. St. Thomas had enough of me. Father Whalen had done everything he could. I was twenty-two and an adult in any state in 1980. I went to the authorities at the *Trib* and told them that I had to leave unless I could get a job as a reporter. They told me to inquire in the human resources office, where I sat down for a lovely exit interview. I think they stamped my file "drunk, disorderly, disheveled." Fortunately for me, big brother John came to the rescue and got me a job at the papers where he worked, in Algona.

# CHAPTER 6

# A Tornado and an Implosion

## LISTEN TO THE WIND

*Algona, Iowa, September 15, 1984*

White clouds brushed a blue sky, and the hot September wind swept across dry, swaying fields.

Dust billowed over the gravel road, instilling a gritty taste of rain to come. In the corn fields, green plants were spewed through the air from choppers to wagons. Silage was in the making.

Four men worked. Fifty years ago it would have been 12 or better to do half as much. They worked for pay, asking for no help, when 50 years ago neighbors pitched together about this time of year to see each other through.

Bean fields were turning yellow, soon to be a golden tan. Pods were ready to burst. That is, in those fields that rain didn't wash away in summer torrents, or in fields that didn't sit dry and barren for spring seeds.

Other beans, green and struggling with small pods, were racing against prospects of a frost, a younger generation facing a deadline.

These pliable pods couldn't be cracked. They were fuzzy in the mouth and when smashed released a taste of strong iron, protein for millions. Together they stand alone, waiting in the wind, while silage is chopped across the cloudy gravel road.

There would be celebrations afterwards, years ago. Barn dances under harvest moons, even in hard times. This year the dust will settle under snow, and the fields will wait for the roar of machinery, alone until next spring.

Stalk, leaf, cob and ear of corn shot into the red gravity wagon. Kernels were doughy and cracked easily, leaving a sweet taste, from starch to sugar in seconds. It's quick energy and efficient feed.

Will there be stomping, dancing and neighbors pulling together?

Years ago they talked about the weather, about how those clouds, winds and rains would settle the dust, and about how the sun in its waning days would bring the oats, wheat, rye and corn to their fruition.

Today beans and corn grow while cattle mingle around a gray, weathered barn. They are prices and products.

Prices for those products between 1978 and 1982 increased 23 percent for the farmer. But the cost of those hogs, cattle and corn by the time they reached the dinner table went up 35 percent in the same period. In 1984, his products brought him 6 percent less income than the year before while his costs climbed 4 percent.

Buy him a cup of coffee and talk about the weather. He'll talk about his bank balance in accountant's terms.

Look at his wrinkled, soiled, thick fingers. Ask him about the rain, while he thinks of the climate in Washington. Ask him how he is doing.

Look at his moist eyes.

He stood alone in the field, licking the grit from his teeth and kicking the sandy soil around the papered stalks.

A 3-year-old, a blonde little Dutch boy, proudly told him that he rounded up the hogs. He lifted the boy.

Make acerbic comments about the man. Tell him what he did wrong. He knows. He's not crying for help, just "yelling ouch," he said. In 1982 the federal government paid $1.5 billion in direct subsidies to farmers. That's 2 percent of total farm receipts. Yet some say subsidies are handouts.

Rain might come after the wind. He'll stand in the field alone, letting it wash the ink on the 2-column page into indiscernible blotches.

Clear the dust and see that in 1979 farmers paid $12 billion in interest and earned $32 billion, while in 1982 they paid $22 billion in interest and earned $20 billion. Farming is business, and figures say the business is going broke.

But the figures are all different, the situations unique. Calculators spell a hard-to-define message in varied terms, a fogged barometer. Some are locked into confinement buildings, some chained to machines to roll across the grain carpet they had to lay, millions in debt.

While he stood in the field, looking at the clouds, they looked for those clouds elsewhere in the world, starving alone. Tell him to cut back his production, to cull his herds, while 450 million people fall asleep hungry, by the day. Though it is the essence of life, it doesn't seem vital.

Speak of a lifestyle, juxtaposed against first liens and cold December prices. It is a business, the biggest in the nation, spurring 20 percent of U.S. jobs, opening Main Street doors in Algona, Bancroft, West Bend and Swea City.

While the dust blows and the rain comes, talk to him about the weather. Buy him a cup of coffee and listen to the wind rustling the dry corn.

John worked as a photographer and my personal trainer at the *Kossuth County Advance* and *Algona Upper Des Moines,* where I made my soft landing from the Twin Cities in January 1980. They were twin weekly newspapers, vestige titles of when they competed against each other before they merged. The *Kossuth County Advance* was the Protestant, Republican weekly published by the Dewell family. The *Algona Upper Des Moines* was the Catholic, Democrat paper published by the Waller family.

It was at Algona where I learned about local banker Gardner Cowles, who became one of the biggest family names in newspaper publishing and broadcasting nationally. Cowles's editor friend Harvey Ingham at the *Algona Upper Des Moines* moved downriver to edit the Des Moines *Register and Leader,* which was faltering in its battle with the *Des Moines Daily Capital* and the *Des Moines Tribune*. He implored Cowles in 1903 to buy the *Register and Leader*, which Cowles did. They turned it into the juggernaut that was to become the *Des Moines Register* and the *Des Moines Tribune*, the *Minneapolis Star* and the *Minneapolis Tribune*, WCCO in Minneapolis and KCCI in Des Moines, and *Look* magazine.

"Print the truth and let the chips fall where they may," Harvey Ingham told a young reporter.

I learned to read with the *Des Moines Sunday Register* comics section. Dad's cousin Maury White, whose roots are in Whittemore, wrote the lead sports column for the Big Peach Sunday sports section. When they asked Maury for press credentials at the Rose Bowl he blew past the gate, saying: "Don't you know who I am?"

It was the "Newspaper Iowa Depends Upon."

The *Register* flew its "Good News" airplane to Whittemore for my uncle John Cullen's ordination as a priest. It had correspondents in every county and bureaus in the four corners of the state. I was one of those stringers. When a story was too hot to handle in Algona, I would phone it over to a young state editor named Randy Evans, who would publish it under the byline "*The Register's* Iowa News Service." Then I could run the story in the Algona paper with the defense that the *Register* had already blown the cover, never revealing that I was the ghostwriter.

*Sunday Register* circulation was more than five hundred thousand. Gardner Cowles campaigned to "Get Iowa Out of the Mud" so he could get his Sunday paper delivered by his motor force to every RFD box in Iowa on every secondary road. It resulted in the most developed farm-to-market road complex in the world, with a gravel intersection every mile. The *Register* saturated Iowa Sundays, and so did the *Minneapolis Tribune* in Minnesota.

Gardner "Mike" Cowles Jr. took what his father and Ingham had done and grew it into a national media company with newspapers throughout the Plains and the Upper Midwest, complemented by TV and radio, and even a daily newspaper in New York for a time. Mike Cowles had become a major media presence in the Big Apple.

There I was in Algona sitting in Harvey Ingham's chair in 1984. I was twenty-seven. I liked to imagine that the ancient black L. C. Smith typewriter I used was his. It sits in the front of *The Times* office today.

Algona and Kossuth County were booming. Grain exports were exploding, and so were Iowa farmland prices. They rose to around four thousand dollars per acre at Ottosen in Humboldt County, which was the record in the early 1980s. Iowa State University economists were issuing cautions but nobody listened. Farmers bid up sales and rents, thinking that grain prices and yields were on a boundless plane up. They forgot the first law of physics and economics: gravity.

Prices went down.

Federal Reserve Board chairman Paul Volcker decided to "Whip Inflation Now" (Gerald Ford's campaign slogan) and forever by jacking up interest rates to 22 percent.

All those young farmers who borrowed money to bid up land found it coming back to bite them. The tight money policy strangled farm lending, whipped inflation, caved corn prices, and caused land prices to drop in half or worse, depending on the neighborhood, over a two-year period.

We called it the farm crisis.

Kossuth County was the epicenter. It had the highest-quality land in Iowa. Its entire economy was built around farming.

The crash came. We covered it in intimate detail. The shoe store lady crying as the shop closed on State Street. The former head of the Iowa Pork Producers who went under and started a sandwich shop. The mayor of Bancroft, another leader in the Iowa hog industry, got out of hogs and into the moving business with his sons. Farmers hanged themselves in barns. They moved equipment in the middle of the night so the repo man couldn't find it the next day. White crosses cropped up on courthouse lawns. Those were the darkest days of Iowa since the Great Depression, in many ways more tragic because the stakes were so much higher. The falls were harder.

The harvesting of farmers went strong for five years. This one has assets that are ripe. Pluck that farmer and send him off to town.

The farm crisis knocked out whatever confidence rural Iowa had. Young people fled. The same factors that hurt farmers were killing manufacturers: high interest rates and a strong dollar that strangled export sales. Inflation was whipped, but so was Algona. The motto became "Will the last one leaving town turn out the lights?" And the state policy became jobs, any jobs, no matter the wage, no matter the cost.

What would be the next shoe to drop? The Lone Rock Bank failed. Other banks teetering on the edge with huge farm loans were bought up by the chains and inherited accounts that they found were too big to fail. Strangely, they became the survivors because the banks had bet too heavily on them in the first place.

We were calling Snap-on tools in Kenosha, Wisconsin, once

a month to ask about the latest layoff rumors. Snap-on is still there. But the Hormel plant shut down in Fort Dodge. Algona has a Hormel plant—that pepperoni on your pizza likely was sliced there. There was a big strike on Hormel. We had no idea what could happen next.

The post–World War II ag boom had ended.

Smelling a bargain as farm assets imploded, Wall Street started to invest in pork in the late 1980s the same way it had invested in concentrated, integrated poultry production. It discovered that you could make pretty decent money using cheap corn and cheap help in a building built by the farmer with his own debt to raise hogs on contract for the meatpacker. At the same time, the farms that had been selling were moving into stronger hands. It was a triple whammy: The cattle left Iowa because the land was too valuable, hogs moved indoors and out of open markets, and the stronger landowners could use chemicals to manage ever-larger acreage inventories.

Ethanol made from distilling corn was reaching commercial scale after a strong decade of experimentation spawned by the oil crisis of the 1970s. Farmers long besieged by corn price swings saw energy demand as a way to stabilize corn markets and sow a new base outside traditional livestock feeding. Ethanol and the corn sweetener industry developed simultaneously based on the zeal of midwestern corn farmers who came to see it as their salvation from just making do feeding corn to hogs, cows, and chickens. Ethanol came to be politically sacrosanct as it grew to consume a third of Iowa's corn crop. In 2017, more than 4 billion gallons were hooched from forty-three distilleries in the state. It was a bipartisan purchase of the rural vote by Democrats and Republicans. The golden cap came with energy legislation in 2007 that established the Renewable Fuel Standard—requiring 15 billion gallons of ethanol to be blended with gasoline nationally to reduce smog in big cities.

These developments—bankrupted farmers, Wall Street investing in livestock for the first time and moving them off the landscape, and betting on the corn-ethanol game—ushered in the specialization of agriculture in the late 1980s and squeezed out on-farm diversity and unneeded people. It suited the Big Ag players—the seed and chemical companies could deal with fewer customers who were bigger and could be locked into their supply chain. The corporate players didn't need the retail feed stores or the local general veterinarian in the county seat town anymore. The pork integrators had their own feed mills and vets on retainer.

The result was a steady drain on rural life. The impression was indelible in physical and psychic terms: Had the sun set on the place we cherished?

The owners of the Algona paper were the Waller family, longtime friends of my parents. It was a hard-bitten newspaper bunch that seldom walked away from a donnybrook. The Waller brothers and the Cullen brothers were a great wrestling tag team.

"They'd rather fight than eat," said my dad's best friend, Joe Bradley, about the fraternal coalition.

Denny Waller was the dynamic young publisher. He got his start with *Look* magazine, owned by the Cowles publishing dynasty in Des Moines. He struck off for Washington State with brother John hoping to buy his own newspaper and get out from beneath his father's imposing shadow. The purchase didn't work out and Denny found his way back to Algona with John in tow. He bought the majority interest and set out to make the newspaper the best of its class in the country.

My first real story was covering the tornado that destroyed much of Algona on June 28, 1979, when I was a summer intern. Denny's dad, Russ, a grizzled old publisher who wore plaid shirts with striped ties before it was fashionable, served as my personal editor as I cut my teeth in spot news reporting. "This is crap. Get out of the way and get the news up front. Rewrite it, and fast!"

John shot a dramatic photo of a person running in front of the tornado as it was about to destroy the Chrome Truck Stop. The twister came within about one hundred yards of John, who had jumped into a crawl space beneath Van's Café across the highway from the truck stop. The photo went around the world via the Associated Press. He was considered by his peers to be one of the best press photographers in the Midwest. It's because he is fearless in his perfectionism and absolutism when it matters.

I owe the Wallers and big brother John everything in my career. They taught me from the ground up.

"How long should the story be?"

"As long as it needs to be."

They were hard-news people. Old Russ Waller was shooting photos at the Kossuth County racetrack when there was a fatal crash. Little Jack Waller, then about ten, was roaming the infield and found the driver's burned shoe. He showed it to a proud father, who photographed the shoe and ran it in the newspaper.

That's the sort of paper it was.

When someone came in to pick a fight with one Waller, all the Wallers would gather to put up a united front. They fought off Duane Dewell with his *Kossuth County Advance*, and

eventually bought it. They fought off the *Algona Reminder*, a free
shopping guide, by containing it. They fought the county engineer and the board of supervisors, some of whom were indicted
by a grand jury for bid rigging on county road projects. They
fought the county attorney. And they sold papers. We had the
highest household penetration of any newspaper in Iowa, with
eighty-eight hundred circulation in a county of twenty-two
thousand.

We covered seventeen high schools with one sportswriter.
We published huge, gorgeous, full-width front-page photos of a
deer or a farmer standing by a weathered shed or clouds over the
Upper Des Moines River.

I covered a murder trial of a kid who ran over a cop because
he thought he was in *The Dukes of Hazzard*. A story about a man
who was accused of welding a chastity belt onto his girlfriend, a
waitress at the Back Door Diner downtown. A couple of local
boys put a bomb in the back of a police car. After they did their
time, they decided to smoke a joint at Ambrose A. Call State
Park. The ranger nabbed them. We ran a brief on the front page.
They walked into the office wanting to blow me up. I told them
all I wanted to do was to get their side of the story. I had a full
pack of smokes in my shirt pocket. Three hours later, the pack
was smoked and so was the interview with the "Men Who Are
Misunderstood." Everyone in town bought a copy and shared
the outrage that we would print that story in our nice little town
of six thousand.

There was always a fight into which the newspaper could insert itself. One of the city fathers of the burg of Lakota put me
over the hood of a car in a dispute over school reorganization in
which I unwittingly misrepresented his position. Denny Waller's
wife, Mary, who was like a big sister to me because she was the

daughter of my dad's best friend, was the president of the Algona Library board. There was a big fight over the historic Carnegie library, which was too small, and whether it should move. I wrote a column about it that Denny didn't like, and he suggested nicely that I should rewrite it or not run it. I argued. He pulled out a pair of scissors and clipped up the story in front of my face.

"It's not running," he said.

Lesson learned. That's what "publisher" means on the masthead on page 2.

And when there wasn't a fight they got into one anyway. The paper was making good money. Denny owned a majority interest. His dad regretted that he sold and his brothers weren't happy and there was a lawsuit filed among the family. While they were off litigating, John and I were in charge of getting the paper out, along with the ad manager, John Shaw. Brother John was named editor. We worked all hours, well past midnight, for chicken scratch. But the gift was mine: I got the editorial page. I was writing editorials for the state's largest weekly at age twenty-six. We were the first paper in Iowa to endorse Tom Harkin in his bid to unseat U.S. senator Roger Jepsen. Harkin never forgot. It paid off in Storm Lake twenty-five years later.

Denny was done in by high interest rates that killed off so many Kossuth County farmers. Michael Gartner and Gary Gerlach had just been fired as the editor and publisher, respectively, of the *Des Moines Register* for trying to buy the paper from the Cowles trust heirs. It was a complicated deal, but it ended up that Gannett bought the *Register* and the Minneapolis operations were sold and a lot of hearts were broken. Gartner and Gerlach bought the Algona paper. The Wallers all moved away.

# CHAPTER 7

# Lust at First Sight

John and I lived in a mobile home together just outside of Algona. Dancers from the local strip club would sun themselves across the drive as I emerged on a Monday. I would wave and go to work.

That single-wide wasn't wide enough for us two tall toothpicks. John tired of it, and of me, maybe even of the tanning strippers. He evicted me from the mobile home for just cause, being his brother. And then he decided to truck that home down the road to Storm Lake in search of a mate. He found one in Mary Tolan, a schoolteacher at Our Lady of Good Counsel School in Fonda, twenty miles east of Storm Lake.

That left me as editor in Algona, alone.

John was Iowa's top community newspaper photographer. We filled his hole with a friend, Tom Wallace, a portrait specialist with whom I dined every evening at the local restaurant. We agreed that we would be working monks in Algona, where the state of romantic play was limited by the fact that single women mostly had left town.

I ached for a girlfriend growing up in Storm Lake. I longed for love in college—all my roommate's girlfriends liked me just fine but I stayed on the top bunk. I looked in every corner for combustion in Algona but could find nothing that sparked. So I gave up on it. Poetry, too. "Love . . . hid his face amid a crowd of stars" was for people who couldn't sleep at night. Journalism and scotch would have to do. I made love to ten-point type on a thirty-six-inch web of newsprint. We lived for the newspaper. We were paid to nose into other people's business and then tell them what we thought about it. Not a bad substitute for carnal knowledge.

J ust a few miles up from Bloody Run Creek, in the valley of Upper Des Moines, a man in dirty striped overalls and an engineer's cap shoveled ears of corn from a weathered crib alongside Kossuth County Road P-56.

Ernie "Junior" Gales was the last of the corn shellers with his rusted old Minneapolis-Moline. He emptied out the crib—a barn sided by spaced slats that let air flow through to naturally dry the ears—for one of his last custom shelling customers who still insisted on using a picker. Everyone else had converted to combines that roll the kernel off the ear in one swoop, then into a wagon bound for a bin where the corn would be dried from 24 percent moisture down to 17 percent using natural-gas flames and fans. The old corn picker puts his full ears in the crib to let the incessant wind do the drying nature's way.

They used to pick with a horse pulling a wagon. The man would walk beside the wagon and pick by hand with a hooked glove. He would throw the ear against the wagon's bangboard. We still call it that in Iowa basketball, not a backboard.

Ernie worked alone. His sons had moved off, one to be a stockbroker in Mason City, another a mergers-and-acquisitions lawyer in Phoenix, the third an engineer (an educated son of the tinkerer father) in Pennsylvania. The girls were all in the helping professions: teacher, nurse, occupational therapist, physical therapist, journalist, and counselor to migrants.

Ernie's wife, Helen, was at home shaping perfect dinner rolls standing on orthopedic shoes in a flower-print dress.

I had a camera. I said nothing. He said nothing. I shot photos. He did not smile. Then I shook his hand. A couple of fingers were stubs from when he got his hand caught in the sheller's conveyor that ran to the crib. He smiled. I wrote down his name. I didn't know what to ask, he didn't offer. We published the photo in the newspaper, a working farmer on a September afternoon.

A couple of years later Ernie's daughter joined us as a summer reporting intern. Carol Gales attended the University of Notre Dame.

Just a week or so after Carol came aboard her sister Dolores walked into the newspaper office. She had bicycled fifteen miles up from the farm near St. Joe. Carol brought her back to the composing room, where we pasted up galleys of type onto layout pages. I was pasting up the editorial page. Dolores came around the corner wearing spandex riding shorts.

It was lust at first sight. I asked her out on a date.

We went for a cup of coffee at the Chrome Truck Stop at the intersection of highways 169 and 18—the four corners that were destroyed by the 1979 tornado and rebuilt.

She was on the rebound from working as a slave potter on a farm in north-central Iowa. Young artists would throw pots in the day, sleep in a barn at night, and go on the road on weekends selling the pottery. They got paid fifty dollars a week. She figured out the scam after a year and bagged it for a life of bike riding in Sherman Township, Iowa, where you can see the end of the world unobscured by trees. Just you on the bike with grasshoppers and corn and the wind in your face.

She did artwork by day in the abandoned farmhouse where Ernie was reared. It sat on a hill looking east down the slope to the banks of the Upper Des Moines River. Ernie would kill entire days down there fishing and dreaming, until his dad, Ernie Senior, turned forty-six and Ernie turned eighteen. Ernie Senior sat down in the shade under the catalpa tree and told Junior that he was working the farm now. Senior remained seated in the shade while Junior developed back problems hauling slop. He hated working with horses. They were the last family to get plumbing or electricity around St. Joe. Theirs wasn't the best ground. But the Galeses had everything they needed along the river.

What directed me to him that day?

What brought her into the office that day?


I came to the house to pick her up for our second date. This one was a movie at the Algona Theatre. Her brother, as I took him, stood on the back stoop with a .22 rifle shooting at the garden à la Jethro Bodine. Damn rabbits. I sat at the kitchen table where Helen served me snacks and drinks and tried to make me feel welcome. I was from good stock in Whittemore and Bancroft. Good Catholic people like the Galeses. Plus Helen liked that I had a position in town, as the editor.

Ernie came in from shelling corn. Helen served him salad. He wolfed it down without saying a word. I noticed that a baseball bat propped up the stove door. I asked Helen, "Why the bat?"

"That's what we used to drive off the last boyfriend," Ernie said.

Those were among the first words he spoke to me.

Dolores explained to me that the stove door was sprung. Ernie didn't see the need to spend money on a new spring or, heaven forfend, a new stove when an old baseball bat was handy. This despite the fact that Ernie and Helen owned five hundred acres of prime ground free and clear, and he paid cash for each of his nine children to attend four years of Catholic college: Notre Dame, Marquette, St. Catherine's, you name it. He wrote a check to all of them. But not to North Iowa Appliance.

For our third date I bought broasted chicken at the Hy-Vee grocery store. With baked beans and potato salad. We sat under the catalpa tree and ate as the sun set over the ridge to the west where the foxes holed up. We went inside where the light faded against the faded wallpaper. Nobody was there but us and the ghost of Grandma Gales, who indicated no disapproval.

Lust had turned to love.

On that third date, we decided to marry. We had known each other about two weeks.


We talked about how Algona and St. Joe were falling apart around us, about how the farms were going broke. We knew we had to get out. There was no bottom we could see while immersed in it. We also agreed that we would not stray too far from this place. She needed to be near the river, close to the spirit of that abandoned farm on the hill, where the dreams of that place and her grandmother could be fresh every night. They still are.

The place on the hill was not like her square farm home plopped down on flat ground with the trees removed to accommodate wider machinery. Its rooms were built in angles. Its lawn played shady host to Fourth of July parties where scores of cousins came together, all from nearby farms. Dolores would sit in her room on the second floor of the square house and draw pictures of the horses she could never have. She imagined her own up on the hill. She escaped the isolation of the farm—never going camping up at Lake Winnie in Minnesota like the cousins, seldom going to the movie theater except for a biblical epic, fishing in the ditch for tadpoles—through art and two wheels on a blacktop.

We married in St. Joe along the river the Saturday after Thanksgiving in 1985. It started snowing as we walked into church. By the time we came out it was a full-on prairie blizzard. The entire wedding party was stuck for three days in the bound-up deep freeze.

The abandoned farmhouse on the hill decayed over time. There were holes in the roof. You wouldn't want to walk inside. There are places like it every couple of miles or three. Places where there were parties in the yard and chickens, too.

Rural Iowa was emptying out. Kossuth County's population has dropped by a third since I met Dolores. Sixty-seven of Iowa's ninety-nine counties have lost population every year since 1920. The *Algona Upper Des Moines* newspaper nameplate was retired. The *Kossuth County Advance* survives as a weekly that has less than a third the circulation it did when I got there in 1979. The owner lives in Charles City, an hour's drive away, where he publishes that town's small daily. The *Des Moines Register*'s Sunday circulation is just north of a fifth of what it was at its peak. The Mason City *Globe Gazette*, which had twenty-seven-thousand circulation when I was there, in 2017 had a daily press run of nine thousand copies, according to the Iowa Newspaper Association.

G artner called Algona the "flagskiff" of their chain, which came to include the *Daily Tribune* of Ames and, briefly, the *Daily Globe* of Worthington, Minnesota. They packed me off for Ames in 1986 when they got the keys, and our photographer Tom Wallace went down with me. Tom is now a photo editor at the Minneapolis *StarTribune* and is godfather to my oldest son. I was managing editor of the Ames paper while Gartner was president of NBC News. The newspaper had been on snooze for several years and I was brought in to wake it up. Gartner was big in New York media circles. I was in a Big 12 college town running an afternoon daily with eleven-thousand circulation. It was my chance to get into the passing lane.

One of our first stories was about a man living under a bridge in Ames. They hadn't seen quite that type of story before; most of the newspaper was about how tremendous Iowa State University and the Ames parks system were. The paper had always done a spectacular job covering sports. Its editorial page was conservatively silent.

We got the rock band started with young graduates from Iowa State looking for a rocket launch with Gartner's help. They would go off after a year or two to the *Kansas City Star*, the Associated Press, even the *Wall Street Journal*. But often the rock band van broke down when our city hall reporter was sacked out with bottle flu on Monday. Or we missed our deadline by a half hour again. Or the university president tried to get the paper to muzzle its reporter for detailing safety issues in university-owned airplanes.

I walked into the newsroom at six-thirty a.m. and learned that Sam Mack, an Iowa State Cyclone basketball star, had been shot while pulling an armed robbery at the Ames Burger King. They identified him from the team photo behind the joint's cashier counter. The cops showed up and mowed him down. "We put so much lead in his ass he'll never jump again," the Ames police chief told me.

Coach Johnny Orr, a god in Iowa, told the Story County district court jury that Sammy was a good man but misdirected. That damn football player who was with him must have talked Sammy into it. The jury let him off. Mack went on to play with the Houston Rockets in the NBA. He was jumping again.

I was about to jump, too.

I was sitting in another one of those endless meetings that seemed to entertain publisher Gerlach, a Harvard-trained lawyer who could squeeze the copper from a penny between two long, craggy fingers. I got into an argument with the ad manager about having to put out too many special sections with too small a news staff, and I was told that arguments were not appropriate. I thought a little debate livened things up. So I told those who were awake that I would be heading back down to the newsroom because we had a paper to get out. It was, in retrospect, too direct an approach to the truth. These are things you learn the hard way.

Overlooking the capital city from the Des Moines Club up there in the air is intoxicating, but when you sober up you realize you don't really belong there. If you go up there into the ether enough, it can affect your thinking and you can lose your direction.

It wasn't long after that changing breezes propelled me to a hitch in Mason City, and then back to Storm Lake in 1990 when big brother John called me home. He knew that rural Iowa was deflating. He knew that Storm Lake was challenged, but it deserved a newspaper like the one we published in Algona.

We learned the formula together: Print the truth, let the chips fall where they may, pay the IRS and the bankers first, then the printer and yourself last. And the most important lesson: Pick your fights carefully. Comfort the afflicted and afflict the comfortable, but not to the point where they will cancel their subscription or kill an ad. You can make better money selling shoes. That's what Gerlach told me. But if you work like a dog and kiss the right behind you can stay in business another week to tell them most of what you think.

John told me to put up an editorial page that would be the soul of the newspaper and the conscience of the community. And that's how we merrily set on our way twenty-eight years ago. John wrote the editorial for the first edition on June 28, 1990. Nothing fancy. Just a clear statement:

## WHAT WE BELIEVE
### *AN EDITORIAL*

"We hold these truths to be self-evident, that all men are created equal, that they are endowed by their Creator with certain unalienable Rights, that among these are Life, Liberty and the pursuit of Happiness."

With these immortal words, the founders of our nation declared their independence and set about to build the most glorious nation in history. Today, more than 200 years later, these noble words continue to inspire us as we embark on what we hope will be a grand journey of our own with the founding of *The Storm Lake Times*. This newspaper is dedicated to the timeless principles espoused by our forefathers.

The foundation of our freedom is the First Amendment to the Constitution, that other great document of our republic, which guarantees all Americans the right to speak and write freely, to worship as we please, to assemble and to criticize the government.

The key, we believe, to maintaining our democracy is to let the light of truth shine upon all that we say and do. Whenever truth is limited, tyranny takes root. We must be ever vigilant in the search for truth. As the Gospel of St. John notes:

*"Ye shall know the truth, and the truth shall make you free."*

Guided by these sacred words, The Times humbly begins publication.

We Americans, heirs of the longest-running democracy in history, often take our freedoms for granted—until we see our brothers and sisters in Poland, China, South Africa and elsewhere fighting and dying for these same treasured principles.

The mission of this newspaper is to be a mirror of life in this wonderful community. We hope that when you look in this mirror, you will like what you see.

There is much to praise about life here, and that is what makes publishing this newspaper worthwhile. We enjoy a high standard of living, honest government and good friends. But we must not become complacent.

We are troubled by those who put narrow self-interest above the common good. We are disgusted by intolerance and injustice. We are saddened by suffering. And we are frightened by attempts to limit our rights. We are all members of the family of man. And so we will speak for those who are silenced; we will laugh for those who rejoice; and we will cry for those who suffer.

We believe in free enterprise and the right of people to hold a job, earn a decent wage and raise a family free from want and fear. We believe in government that is honest with its people; that is willing to care for those who are unable to care for themselves; and remembers that its role is to serve, not enslave, the people.

We believe in Buena Vista County, its heritage and its future. We believe in a sense of humor and optimism that tomorrow will be even better than today. We believe in one nation, under God, with liberty and justice for all.

# CHAPTER 8

# The Newspaper Is the Family

My first story for *The Storm Lake Times* covered former president Jimmy Carter's lecture at Buena Vista University. I welcomed him to Storm Lake and asked him how Iowa can pull back from becoming a second-world economy: We export raw products and people and we mine the natural resource base.

Carter disagreed with the premise.

But I say the questions are crucial. How can rural Iowa meet its potential and make itself whole? What should be one of the richest places in the world is fast becoming poor. "Iowa has become a sacrifice state," said Bill Stowe, who manages the Des Moines Water Works (DMWW). "We and our land are collateral damage for industrial agriculture."

We provide the raw content of what becomes food. But many of the workers making that food live in trailer homes not as hospitable as a hog house. Half of Iowa's newborns depend on Medicaid. We grow the corn that feeds the cattle that feed your grocery stores and the beans that feed the hogs that make your bacon. But the Storm Lake food pantry regularly runs out until an appeal brings in more for the working poor.

The farmers were driven out in legions as efficiency wrenched them out. The snow-filled ditches are black from bare fields giving up their ransom to the constant wind and turn of the disk. Rural communities try to figure out what to do with grand old brick school buildings whose enterprise has long been vacated. Sioux Rapids just up Highway 71 is tearing down abandoned buildings on its main street over delinquent taxes, hoping that someone will find the razed property attractive.

But who? The school superintendent is beside himself over budget cuts wrought by five straight years of declining enrollment. Who will shop at the new store you build off Highway 71 in Sioux Rapids when everyone's gone to Minneapolis? If Pocahontas County continues to lose population at its current rate there will be nobody left to turn out the lights by 2050. It has become a vast field of corn and soy, corn and soy, soy and corn, dotted by hog houses and turkey barns.

Bill Stowe himself is the story of Iowa. He was born to a Story County farm of five hundred acres near Ames in 1959 and grew up around small towns and farms, the youngest of three. Neither the brother nor the sister wanted to farm. The siblings moved to Newton (where the Maytag repairman rested until they moved him to Mexico) for jobs. Bill went to college and got an advanced degree in engineering and a law degree. The parents died and three brothers, cousins to Bill, rent the farm on contract with about five thousand more acres. That's ten or twenty Old MacDonald farms run by one farm corporation. One of the cousins has a Harvard MBA. He knows what a hedge is on the Chicago Mercantile Exchange. They don't speak much, Bill and his cousins.

Stowe believes that The System, as it were, destroyed the Iowa he once knew. The integrators, the chemical companies, the seed complex, the food processors—it's all wrapped up in the same cord. On a sweltering July day in 2017 he was monitoring nascent algae blooms approaching toxicity in the two rivers, the Raccoon and the Des Moines, from which he draws water. He was frustrated. His attempt to sue over Iowa surface-water pollution had been thrown out a few months earlier. He thinks the state legislature might sink his operation because it sued over what he sees as industrial agriculture polluting our state. If that happens, he'll bail out of Iowa just like all those others before him and go where it seems his talents might be wanted. Maybe Madison, Wisconsin.

What can you do to grow a place that has become something other than a pretty little town? A place that has become an industrial protein center—red meat, white meat, eggs and soy, high-protein corn oil extruded in the ethanol process—for the nation with a workforce that comes from around the globe speaking more than a score of languages? A place that attracts second-world workers for a step close to a first-world life?

Storm Lake has some of the answers to the question of how to turn this rig around. It starts with building a community that can sustain itself. That became the entire focus of the newspaper.

It's why we deplored our negligence toward our lake. It's why we called to embrace immigrants with big dreams and ambitions. If they are willing to cross the Rio Grande and the Sonoran Desert to get to Storm Lake, that's the kind of people we want. It's why we called for a new middle school when a bond issue failed twice previously—before *The Times* was founded.

After we explained the need in an endorsement, the third time was a charm. It's why we helped engineer a $40 million resort along the lakeshore.

Because if you can't build something that lasts, if you can't get people in this city of friendly neighbors to pull in the same direction, if you can't find a civic life here, where all can be engaged, then where?

That's what the newspaper is about.


We ran weekly for a couple of years. Things were doing so well another publisher, whose signature was not on our loan documents, suggested that we should go daily. We could knock out the twice-a-week *Pilot Tribune*. Or something like that. So we went daily.

Our ad manager, Marty Gallagher, wrote in big capital letters on a yellow legal pad: DON'T GO DAILY. He showed it to us, then covered it with a blank yellow page. It was a big mistake that put us back on the right road.

To be a daily you had to have a press. To have a press you had to have a big building. So we built a building. Storm Lake's nicest machine shed in gray metal. It was 1993, the year of the first big floods. Des Moines and Cedar Rapids were under water. It never stopped raining. We bought a press. It was coming. We had to get that metal up. It stopped raining for three weeks that summer. The building was put up in that time. We had not seen a monsoon season like that. Now we are getting them, it seems, every decade.

The big Harris V15A (1973 vintage) was on a truck bound for Storm Lake from Missouri. We called the bank to let them know they should cut the check on the loan so we could pay for the press.

Say, about that loan . . .

They had reconsidered.

But the press was rolling down the road.

Sorry.

I ran across the street. I told another banker my story.

"No worries," he said.

Now sign these papers and give me the rights to everything you have and your children might have. Sign away.

To be a real daily you had to print in the wee hours of the morning. John or I were up here many nights and early morning hours searching for a lost ad, a lost page, or a lost printer's devil.

The other paper, meantime, also went daily. Both our circulations were plummeting. In one year we lost $120,000 on revenues of about $500,000. Not good, they would have told you in accounting class if you had showed up.

This town was just not big enough for two daily newspapers. Not enough ads. Not enough news. Not enough readers. Not enough oxygen or working capital.

We were broke.

A stroke of genius born of desperation hit John about two a.m. when the press threw out its drive shaft: We're switching to twice a week. We will work during the day. We will learn our children's names again.

Circulation jumped immediately from a low of 1,600 to 2,400 within weeks. Before long we were up to 3,000, where we have been ever since. Eventually the other paper went to three times a week and has a reported circulation of about 1,400.

After we came up for air and sighed, Marty lifted the blank

yellow page on his legal pad. He told us so. We have hard heads and steep learning curves. And, as John proved by starting the paper, we can be subject to spontaneity. Sometimes it works, sometimes you learn. Often you fail.

With the wind at our back a friend suggested that we could lock things up if we started a free weekly shopping guide. The idea was that we could scoop up the grocers, which would bring every other advertiser on board. We had a press, which by now I was helping to run. If you own the machine, you should know how to run it.

We ran the guide and lost $120,000 that year because we couldn't lock down the grocers. The chain that owned Brand X had deep pockets to cut prices and outlast us. Outlast us they did. We killed that shopper gladly and learned one big lesson from two big mistakes: Don't do it for the money; do it for the reader.

We went daily for the money—to take over the market. We started the shopper for the money first and not so much to offer a valuable service to the community. We ended up crippling ourselves by our own mistakes with more than $500,000 in debt. It took us two decades to pay it off.

I don't pay much attention to the competition anymore. That's like letting somebody else edit our newspaper. When we react we make the wrong choice. When we lead with our own reporting, our own thinking, we are better off every time. I am aware that another newspaper is published in Storm Lake, as I am aware that there are banks on the Bank Corners. I don't dwell on it because I should dwell on our newspaper and nobody else's. If we can't find out the news without reading another paper or listening to the radio or melding our minds to Twitter and Facebook, then we are not reporters.

And we are reporters, above all, who try to play by the rules of balance and verity. That is, honesty.

"They're just editors," said the owner of a chain that used to own Brand X, trying to figure out how we cockroaches were still hanging out in the dirty corner.

At one point Dolores and I had four kids under the age of four. Our two families had six children leaving diapers under our desks with drawers that had uncashed paychecks in them so we could barely cover payroll. We were getting fed with the help of the Women, Infants, and Children's program offered through the federal government. We were lucky to get on the state children's health insurance program. Dolores's parents bought our house for us; were it not for that we would have been living at the county poor farm until they shut it down a few years later. There were times when I calculated that if we went under, I could make it at Tyson to feed the kids and pay off our debts.

We worked eighty hours a week, John and I, while Dolores and Mary tended the home fires and pitched in at the office where they could. Mary also held down a job at the public library. But by concentrating on the newspaper only, just the news, and offering a fair price and decent service to customers, we at least stabilized into keeping our noses just above water. It is a victory every issue, every month, every year. Our main goal was to build this into something that our children wanted to be a part of. But, like most small-town kids, they wanted to get out of Dodge.

We never could. Although we quit losing huge chunks of

money, we remained chained in debt. The only way out was work. School board meeting tonight, city council meeting tomorrow, chamber of commerce ribbon-cutting photo in the morning, unload a truck of paper in the afternoon. We couldn't take a vacation. Ever. John tried to take a vacation after nearly twenty-five years and nearly had a heart attack in South Dakota. No time for doctors. There was always another press run looming. Another deadline. Payroll approaches. Sign on the dotted line and hope to pay it off in the fall, like the farmer borrowing to get a crop in not knowing what corn will fetch in November. Thank God for local banks, even when they do throw you an unexpected curve. As we paid off the debt from our earlier miscues our darkest fears subsided, and our work schedules eased as our cash flow improved.

We all agreed: The newspaper is the family. If it goes down, the family goes down with it.

John's daughter, Bridget, worked for us a year after college as a copy editor and girl Friday. My daughter, Clare, took her chair when Bridget moved off to Chicago, where she became an insurance broker. Clare left after a couple of years for the Cedar Rapids (Iowa) *Gazette*, where she is a night copy editor. One of our twin sons, Kieran, took her job for a year after she left. Then he split for graduate school after putting up with my bark. The other twin, Tom, might be the one who sticks. He has been with us for three years as a general assignment reporter with an economics degree from the University of Northern Iowa. It was not what I might have guessed.

Back when we worked like fools Dolores brought in ham sandwiches for lunch on press days. Mary never complained about what the children never had; neither did she growing up in Pocahontas. Neither ever mastered the concept of a deadline. It was almost divorce court twice a week when Dolores would be late with photo captions and I would be turning blue after red. Dolores also creates stunning illustrations, and Mary handles legal notice billing, a crucial function at any weekly.

Mabel the newshound, our English setter mix, sleeps at Dolores's feet under her desk until a customer comes in. She gets up for a petting. She is a tremendous stress reliever and sales dog.

I feel terrible for days after telling Tom that the story he finished at three a.m. is flabby—that he is better than that, echoing Pat Cullen. He still is one of the best reporters in Iowa and, unfortunately for him, I am his dad and editor. I have a quick temper that blows hot and then cool in seconds with a burst of expletives, although I can nurse a grudge for a lifetime for certain nonfamily members. I am grateful for Tom's and Dolores's forgiveness. Living with John in tight Algona quarters and being with him twenty-four hours a day for four years has taught me how to bite my little brother lip. Plus I remember that he owns 51 percent. We saw what the Wallers went through. You get along fine when you have no money. When some piles up, gentlemen, make it a fair fight with no blows below the belt.

John and I never cared that much about money for ourselves because we never had any, and because Mary and Dolores kept the checkbooks. They kept us solvent.

John once asked Mom what her legacy to him would be.

"An education and a good name," she replied.

Plus *The Times*, her actual legacy. We live for the newspaper, just as Dolores's family lived for the farm; it organized their everyday lives. Like the crow of the rooster at five a.m., debt awakens you to put your shoulder to it on that back forty. The whole family would go out to pull weeds from the soybean fields. The whole family would come in and insert sections into papers as soon as they could see above the stuffing tables. John oversaw it all with patience and cheer even when his gut was upside down. He never killed a story or an editorial, not that I can remember. He would ask plenty of questions. I would get defensive, and he could sense it and back off. When the place was about to explode John would act at just the right moment to snuff it in a way people could accept. He did it under tremendous financial pressure, deadline pressure, and personal pressure. I could feel it. We didn't have to say it.

We worked off the debt. We breathe easier today. John still worries about payroll, because selling anything but beer in a meatpacking town isn't easy, and the beer business is plenty competitive with more than thirty bars in town. He never gives up. Now sixty-seven, John tried retirement for a few months, but that didn't suit him because he has no hobbies other than newspapers. So there he sat in his cubbyhole five feet away from me composing Page One for the July 26, 2017, edition. The leading story was about eleven immigrants found dead in San Antonio in the back of a sweltering trailer owned by a trucking firm in Schaller, ten miles from Storm Lake. Where were they heading? How did that truck get to the Walmart parking lot when they died? Tom chased it down while John wrote heds.

We sat in the cab of a pickup in the middle of black clumps of frozen dirt. It was ten below zero out there on Buffalo Ridge. Don Gallagher, seventy, in white hair and black wing tips, told me to get out and take a picture of Paul Koth, farm drainage man. Say, Art, this is how you sell an ad.

You go out and take photos, freeze your well digger's ass off, and do a story about how Paul Koth has improved farmland. Paul had all the time in the world to visit out there leaning on the pickup. Don had already sold a half page in our *Farm Times* monthly tabloid. He was warm looking out the window. He was going to make damn sure I made the customer happy that day.

Don sold ads part time after selling feed for a lifetime from Strawberry Point over near Dubuque. The eight kids went to a school out on the highway near a cooperative elevator because none of the participating towns in the consolidated district could agree on which town should get the school. So none of them got it, the Iowa stubborn way, where cousins won't speak to one another because they live eight miles apart and one got the better eighty acres from Gramps.

Don and his wife, Anne, decided to move back to her hometown of Storm Lake in 1988 when Don hung it up for Yoder Feeds. (It no longer exists, like most regional feed companies. Don called on independent cattle and hog producers, almost all of whom are history.) Son Tim had enrolled at Buena Vista, where he met brother John on work-study in the Beaver public relations office.

John approached Tim in the fall of 1989 about joining his new newspaper in the spring.

"I'm giving you a chance to do something that is rarely done: to start a newspaper," John told Tim.

That appealed to the young upstart. "Yeah, I liked that, I really wanted to write, and I really liked John. He was easy to work for, a great manner with a sense of humor and adventure.

"I just didn't understand what it would take."

He was the first employee of four. Then I made five in a twenty-by-twenty-foot room. We had tiny little first-generation Macs that chugged and gurgled and took forever. We laid out the front page by printing it in two pieces on a computer printer, then pasting it up on a layout grid on our hands and knees on the floor. We did not have a layout table. We barely had desks. A farmer would walk in and step on the front page, leaving a manure imprint on my byline.

Tim and I would knock off at two a.m. while everyone else finished up. We would be back on the road to Le Mars, Iowa, an hour west, by six a.m., where we printed at the *Daily Sentinel*'s press. We would wait over at The Pantry Café drinking bad coffee with bad breath and bad attitudes while the press crew ramped us up. We would roll the copies on back to Storm Lake, tie bundles for postal routes by hand, and then become the newspaper diaspora by delivering mailbags to every town within thirty miles. We would get home by six p.m. that night. The next day was a complete waste. We all were exhausted. But you have to get going again.

We had nightmares about filling the front page. There was no wire service. Just Tim and me. But Tim said that's what he carries with him from Storm Lake:

"There is a story everywhere. The well can never run dry, you cannot let it run dry. We couldn't allow it."

Jay Miller was our first sports editor. Betty Schmitt was ad compositor. Jeff Myers sold ads and shot photos. John was editor of editors, publisher, ad salesman, and circulation manager. IT manager, too: Computer locks up. "Did you save?" he asks. No. He frowns. "Restart." No sympathy. Rewrite story.

Then Marty Gallagher joined us as an ad salesman. He's Tim's brother and followed him to Buena Vista. And then father Don. And then Tim and Marty's younger brother, Ed. And then their brother Jerry when he was in high school.

At one time or another there were three or four Gallaghers and three or four Cullens packed into that little space, each trying to one-up the other on wit while at its end.

Tim once photographed a wedding ceremony held in a hospital room so the dying mother could witness. He took photos of a wedding between a black man and a Lao woman on the steps of Lakeside Presbyterian Church, the first interracial marriage we had seen in the City Beautiful. Several years later the groom murdered the bride.

We sat in the rain in our newspaper van outside the cop shop about midnight. We waited for my old high school buddy who ran the jail, deputy Gary Launderville, to bring out Paeng Sangaroun, who had been accused of murdering his wife and her father over a divorce discussion. Tim had the camera. I called to Gary to get them to turn around. We got the shot and printed a four-page EXTRA! edition with all the sensational news. Yes, we wanted to sell newspapers, the sin readers lay on us so often. I personally hawked copies in front of the Walmart just like the newsboys from Chicago in the gang wars. Later, Tim was allowed to photograph the exorcism of the family home by two Buddhist monks. Sangaroun was convicted of first-degree murder and sentenced to life in prison, where he died in 2016.

Like Don, the Gallagher boys could sell a manure sandwich to a fed man.

The Gallaghers trailed off over time to different jobs and places. Tim edited a newspaper in Jackson, Minnesota, for a short while but really wanted to get back to just writing. He told the editor of the *Sioux City Journal* that, knowing what he had learned at Storm Lake, he could go to a high school football game in a different town on ten successive Friday nights and find a story from each that had nothing to do with football. The editor created a roving columnist job for Tim and he did just that on Friday nights. Still does it.

"You have to cover the courthouse, the city council, and the school board. The meat and potatoes. I see myself as putting life into the paper," Tim said. It's what Dolores and Mary do now. Tom and I serve the meat and potatoes; Dolores and Mary provide the life with feature stories.

Don continues to work with us on an unpaid basis as political, sports, and occasionally legal consultant.

"Say, boys, you can't do that. You'll get sued! I'm here to tell ya, fellas, YOU'LL GET SUED!"

He's ninety-three. Dolores learned that there were no funds to send Buena Vista County veterans on honor flights to Washington, DC. She told Don. Don started leaning on the bank presidents, widows, little kids with spare change, and raised fifty-two thousand dollars with the help of Dolores and *The Times* to send to DC any vet who wants to see the war memorial of their choice.

We never would have made it without our staff who dedicated themselves to a crazy proposition that remains so, the Gallaghers chief among them.

## CHAPTER 9

# State Slogan: A Place to Grow

*We can stand touchin' noses*
*For a week at a time*
*And never see eye-to-eye.*
*But we'll give you our shirt*
*And a back to go with it*
*If your crops should happen to die.*

—Meredith Willson,
"Iowa Stubborn,"
from *The Music Man*

The Native American word *Ioway* is said to translate into English as "sleepy people." Our land was so rich and our bounty so great that the pioneer white settlers chose to hibernate over that first prairie winter dug into the side of a hill. They started to build a town once the place thawed out. The railroad came along later, en route from Fort Dodge to Sioux City, and charted out Fonda, Newell, Sulphur Springs, Storm Lake, Alta, Aurelia, and Cherokee.

There was enough bounty for us to spread out.

At first, in the 1500s, it was the Ioway who lay mellow among the reeds for 250-plus years. They had come down from Green Bay, Wisconsin.

Then came the Sac and Fox. They liked it here. Room enough for everyone. They even ceded some land, including Storm Lake, to the Dakota, who made sure the Ioway headed south and out of the way.

As Mason City native Meredith Willson knew, Iowans can be contentious. Back when River City was debating pool, conservative Herbert Hoover of West Branch was president. Coming up on the Far Left was Henry Wallace, the crop scientist, editor, and politician. Most of my adult life we elected ultraliberal Tom Harkin and ultraconservative Chuck Grassley to the U.S. Senate. And we kept electing them because Iowans don't necessarily like change.

Trust is an issue with Iowans. We love and trust our neighbors but we don't want them to know how many acres we farm because they might try to rent it from underneath us. People in Primghar do not trust what's going on in Des Moines. People in Des Moines do not trust what's going on in Washington. And neither of them trusts what's going on with the Chicago Board of Trade or with Wall Street.

Ethanol was pretty much born and reared in a big Iowa town called Ames, home to America's first land-grant university devoted to agriculture. We don't trust Texas or Oklahoma oil barons. We trust that our own corn will free us from the shackles of Big Oil and sheikhs. It has, to an extent. And it has helped reduce carbon congestion in smog-choked cities. Yet growing all that corn has environmental consequences we would rather consider some other day, because we have work to do. We believe that if we can raise more corn than Illinois and more hogs than North Carolina the world will be a better place because we succeeded.

We do not care what they think in Kansas because they can grow only wheat.

Seeded by Prussians fleeing conscription from Europe's great wars, our Lutheran friends made work their song in the three northern tiers of Iowa counties. The Methodists held sober court—no drinking, dancing, or Sunday sales—in central and southern Iowa, while the Catholics held their ground along the Mississippi. You could drink all you wanted there. The result was tolerant moderation. Iowa was an early leader in women's rights and against slavery. Iowa gave up more sons per capita to the Civil War than any other state. My farmer father-in-law says it was because Iowans as a class are property owners willing to defend it.

The topsoil was so black and rich that the small towns sited within a day's horse ride from one another would prosper. There was a farm every forty or eighty acres before the turn of the twentieth century, populating the place and creating trade. The same could not be said for the Dakotas or Nebraska, where the land could not support such closely clustered communities. No city dominated Iowa like the Twin Cities tower over Minnesota or Chicago—the hub of the great Midwest—hulks over Illinois. Des Moines does not throw much of a shadow across Iowa, although it expands as rural places contract.

Iowa is the only inland state to have its own grain-shipping infrastructure built by nature in the form of the Missouri and Mississippi rivers. Our good fortune of being at the center of the

U.S. brought the web of railroads, highways, and gravel roads
laid out in right angles, precisely every mile, that make it almost
impossible to get lost in Iowa. That lode of natural resource base
and transport sustained the network of small commercial centers that we see today.

People in Sioux City still know their bread is buttered in Sioux
Center. Wealth and power resided in the four corners of the state
and its small towns because no city was big enough to sit on the
small towns and dictate terms to them. The most powerful political organization in the state has been the Farm Bureau, not the
chambers of commerce. Our sixteenth governor, Francis M.
Drake, hailed from Centerville in southern Iowa, where his bank
was so profitable he was able to found and endow Drake University in Des Moines. Other governors in my lifetime: Terry Branstad is from Lake Mills in northern Iowa. Chet Culver is from
McGregor on the Mississippi. Tom Vilsack is from Mount Pleasant. Harold Hughes was from Ida Grove, not far from Storm Lake.
Leo Hoegh was from Elk Horn and Herschel Loveless from Hed-
rick. Norm Erbe was from Boone. The only governor from Des
Moines was Bob Ray (who later served as president of Drake University). Kim Reynolds, Iowa's latest governor, is from rural
St. Charles (Madison County, with those steamy covered bridges
of pulp and celluloid fame).

Iowa produces more renewable energy per capita than any
other state; half of our electricity now comes from wind turbines. We are first in that, in corn and hogs, and in elderly and
wrestling, and in almost every other category we are thirty-
seventh. We like being thirty-seventh. It keeps us out of the way
of Texas. We used to be first in education. Governor Branstad
decided to catch up to Texas on the way to the bottom by burning the school budget over the past twenty years.

Shenandoah would claim Clarinda's Glenn Miller as its own, and Clarinda would claim the Everly Brothers of Shenandoah. But someone from Clarinda would rather go to Hades than Shenandoah. That sort of explains Iowa.

When you ask someone living in Clive, an upscale suburb of Des Moines, where they are from, they are as likely to say Algona or Emmetsburg as they are their current place of postal receipt.

Despite all those people in Clive hailing from Kossuth or Palo Alto counties, the hometowns they left behind are resilient. Stubborn, if you will. Humboldt is humming. Algona got a facelift following the farm crisis, even though the villages and rural routes around it have drained and withered. Fort Dodge is becoming a hub for new ag product uses—the South Koreans have moved in to break down the corn kernel for all sorts of uses, from foam padding in Ford car seats to sweetener to biodegradable coffee cups—in hopes of reversing steep population losses as beef packing and manufacturing fled and a quarter of its people with them. Storm Lake and Denison are the new lands of opportunity for thousands of immigrants hoping to make it big in a small place. Our new neighbors help us learn tolerance again. Except then we elect the intolerant just to keep ourselves honest.

Iowans have known since Drake served in 1895 that education is the way out from behind the horse. Buena Vista University is heavily recruiting those Latino meatpacking families to fill the dorms along the lake. It closed a $30 million capital campaign drive launched in the depth of the Great Recession. The biggest donors came from Storm Lake (Jim Haahr), Booneville (Don Lamberti), and Holstein (Doug Clausen).

There's still money here. Buena Vista County farmland was selling at or above ten thousand dollars per acre in 2017. A guy with one hundred acres is a millionaire. And there are quite a few of them around the county. That residual wealth keeps Storm Lake stable and buoys the community.

As long as those big small towns—where everyone knows everyone else's business, even how many acres they farm—thrive, the sense of cohesion and comity that makes Iowa special will flourish. By the way, *The Music Man* reminds us that you bring your own food to the potluck. No free lunches here. Unless, of course, the implement dealer is serving free pork burgers. That will draw a bigger crowd than seventy-six trombones on Federal Street in River City.

I was waiting for a phone call that never came.

"Hey, when you coming out?"

Big John Snyder would be on the other end. Matt wants to meet for The Picture at 7:00 p.m. Sunday, then he has to go play football in Manson.

Okay.

I would show up on Sunday. You see no one but maybe an old dog. You go down to The Shed. There they are, shearing each other for fresh butch haircuts and T-shirts with no sleeves.

John would lean against Old Blue and talk about the kids, and later the grandkids, and the corn and the cherry trees and the rain and the drought and, when he had them, hogs and Matt and baseball and broken windows.

He would reach into Old Blue and pull out The Book, which recorded all things of import. Such as:

How tall is the corn against the boy?

For twenty-five years he recorded how tall the corn was and how tall Matt was.

It started way before that, actually, when my wife's family, the Galeses from St. Joe, would pose next to a cornfield on the Fourth of July. They never got in the paper.

John and Matt did. The headline read KNEE-HIGH BY THE FOURTH OF JULY. To an elephant's eye. Or a Snyder's.

We started when Matt was a fireplug taking naps in the shade of the corn end rows. We're sorry to Kayla, Allison, and Patti, but the picture was of these two big boars who look alike wearing matching butch haircuts, matching Ts, and a pair of pliers in their belts. None of us meant to be sexist.

John Snyder and I go way back. John had a birthday party when I was in first or second grade at the ancestral Urban and Deloris Snyder estate just south of tony Sulphur Springs. For whatever reason, I was inside a pen full of pigs when a sow came straight at me. As I approached the fence Carl Lewis had nothing on me.

John laughs about it to this day.

That's how it was back then. You could ride your bikes out to the Snyder farm on gravel from Storm Lake and waste the day chasing pigs or chickens around.

It was probably Tim Gallagher who came up with the idea. He had seen the St. Joe photos and suggested we should publish something like that. Either Gallagher, John Cullen, Tom Wallace, or I—usually I—would stand in the back of Old Blue and shoot a photo as the sun set over Sulphur.

Green fields rolled down from the family home on a knoll just a half mile or so east of Urban's. Big clouds billowed overhead. A pickup would leave a cloud of dust down the gravel in the still air. The only thing you would hear was a pig feeder clank, back when John tended hogs.

And you could think for just a while that the world was good.

Every year our readers could get an annual glimpse of a family farm maintaining amid a swirl of change, and watch the boy grow.

During that year we might chronicle floods and price falls and yields. We explained the anguishing decision John had to make in swine: Get big with contracted production or get out. He got out, and took a job in town plumbing with his old buddy Jerry Seiler. John farms with his brother, Tom, who lives near Schaller. Tom's "hogs" are now expert auto body work.

After John and Tom retire their planter, who knows what will happen?

It is a story written across Iowa. Consolidation. Scale. The family farm is now often a family corporation spanning thousands of acres. The Snyders offered one fleeting look at the family farm we all once knew.

Sure, there were challenges. But there was a sense of balance. That you really did have everything you needed out here. That somehow you could roll with the punches when your family was all around you. But then they all grow up and things change.

You just never know, John says.

The girls are married to farmers, and John feels blessed to have these grandkids just down the road experiencing the same sort of life he had growing up. They should know how lucky they are.

Then Matt up and moved to Minnesota, where he is a diesel mechanic. He and Rachel have a baby and, well, you know, it's tough to arrange things to get the picture and . . . And all good things come to an end.

John and I took a ride on *The Times* float for the Fourth of July parade in 2016. It was called "Knee-High by the Fourth of July." Jon Robinson found us some fine stalks of corn through which we could emerge à la *Field of Dreams*, taken from a stand that shall remain nameless for fear of angering his father.

It was clear that John Snyder has higher popularity ratings in Storm Lake than any politician or newspaper editor. Which isn't saying much, I guess. But it is evidence of a life well lived, and I am grateful to have been allowed to look into it.

And the corn is looking good.

G uns boom over the lake. Geese fly south against the gray top. Pheasants scare out of the corn in the great dustup closing another dry season. The lake is down. Docks are in. Ghouls ring the doorbell and the clocks fall back.

November is that bittersweet month of golden giving way to winter. We prepare to move indoors, shift from football to basketball. We hustle into the holidays. We are busy with school plays and fall fund-raisers. The tons upon tons of iron have almost rolled their last field. Some ground is already turned over, black for winter.

Up pops a photo on Facebook of the final harvest.

Two young boys run down the final rows in the stubble toward Grandpa Jim Benson in the combine filling up a grain cart. Another photo shows three of them jammed into the combine cab with the old farmer, one of them plopped on his lap.

They camped together at the homestead in a trailer. Grandma Terry and Grandpa Jim, now in their late sixties, moved south from Marathon, not far from the mouth of the Raccoon River where it gurgles out of a hill, to Dallas County to be closer to children who drifted toward Des Moines. They spent their whole lives within spitting distance of that farm. Grandpa and his cowpoke cousins rode horses to Rembrandt and beyond in their childhood great adventures. Some of them must have come back to life over the past few days in tall tales from the moors of Buena Vista County.

Farmers retire every year. No big deal, I guess. But this guy was one of the really good ones. When he talks, you should listen. He spent a lot of time sitting by himself in a truck or a tractor listening to WOI-AM from Iowa State University and thinking about what he heard. Some go crazy with their own thoughts. Some just get smarter. Our friend could explode your latest idea with a simple grimace or smile. He explained to us that the way to convince people to do the right thing was to trade with them. You become bound to each other and begin to understand expectations. He thought a lot about Tiananmen Square and Chinese demand for his soy. He figured that you right what is wrong by first selling them soy to feed their pork complex, and the Chinese premier visits a farm in Iowa and understands better. China gets a little, just a little, better on human rights. It used to be the Iowa foreign policy, written unofficially by smart independent property owners like Jim Benson. That's wisdom. He knew the grandchildren of internationalist, scientist, and vice president Henry Wallace. He served on the public boards. He mediated among friends. He helped out people who never asked or maybe never knew. He gave to every local cause in treasure and sweat.

He went as a student down to Ames with dreams of soundboards and TV cameras. He probably could have been an electrical engineer or a macroeconomist. He went into the wild blue yonder with the air force, which landed him at home following that Southeast Asian conflict.

There he stayed at the house where he was born. He was the elder son and there was a bustling enterprise to mind. Despite that big world out there he tended his little world with love and attention to detail. He got his share of diversion from the grand-boys. No doubt he had one eye on his yield monitor. He does not fully appreciate the grace found in disappointment, at least not when it comes to the most important number.

They say the corn is coming in all over the place, from 120 bushels per acre near Nemaha to more than 200 bushels north of Highway 3. Corn is fetching nearly half of what it was five years ago, but these are still the days they will remember as good ones. Buyers in Buena Vista and surrounding counties were bidding premium prices over the market in Chicago. Farmers with cash are storing it and sitting on it as local demand grows with etha-nol, hogs, and poultry.

He will miss that.

He won't miss those dark days at two a.m. when sleet shot horizontal as he loaded out turkeys bound for Storm Lake. He's happy that his children are professionals with clean fingernails building happy households. He also believes, as his children do, that there were lessons to be learned walking beans, cleaning turkey sheds, or handing the old man wrenches.

He will miss those hours of idling around the co-op coffee-maker gleaning wisdom from his neighbors. He will see geese in a bean field and cuss them, even though it won't really be his field. And he probably will ache every spring with the anxiety it brings though there will be no rational reason for it.

Another farmer who made his last round eight falls ago re-calls it. He was working the final six rows. He could see the end coming in fractions of a mile. Then in hundreds of yards. Then in fifteen yards.

"Then I thought, I guess that's it."

The image resides with him.

Relatives have worked the ground since as the retiree watches.

All the corn is in the bin today. The final harvest is complete. The photos are in their place. It's hard to conceive, going into winter, what things will be like come spring. There will be a little hole in the county, I think, that probably does not get filled.

# CHAPTER 10

# A Purple Hybrid

I owa will go Democrat when Hell goes Methodist," U.S. senator Jonathan P. Dolliver of Fort Dodge declared around 1900 after the Democrats lost the governor's race three times in a row. He was a Republican, of course, the son of a Methodist minister, first a Taft conservative and later a progressive ally of President Teddy Roosevelt in pressing for free trade and reduced tariffs ninety years before Bill Clinton.

Flames licked the heels of Methodism increasingly as the century progressed, a few times with a Democratic governor or congressman in a thunderspit. We sent politicians of either stripe, but never a woman until 2014, to Washington to complain about wasteful spending, to keep us out of wars, and to speak for farm concerns. Dolliver set a Senate doorman to weeping as the Agriculture Committee chairman delivered a thunderous defense of butter over oleomargarine.

"I hope that the time will come when the American hog, with a curl of contentment in its tail and a smile of pleasure on his face, may travel untrammeled through the markets of the world," Dolliver orated from the Senate floor on another occasion, arguing against tariffs that favored railroads and commodity traders, that would give rise to a celebratory homecoming in northwest Iowa. We have always thought we could feed the world, and that notion animates our state's politics.

Henry Cantwell Wallace of Johnston, near Des Moines, was a Presbyterian minister who saw helping farmers as his mission from God. He was the founder of *Wallaces' Farmer*, then the must-read weekly in farm country. He was appointed secretary of agriculture by President Warren Harding in 1921.

His son, Henry Agard Wallace (also an editor at *Wallaces' Farmer*), was appointed secretary of agriculture by President Franklin D. Roosevelt in 1933. Henry A. was still a Republican but jumped the fence to work for FDR. Henry A. became vice president in 1941. Passed over for Harry Truman in the second chair for the fourth term, Henry A. tried to organize a new Progressive ticket in 1948 against Truman from his perch as editor of the *New Republic*. Wallace was a dreamer and was derided in Washington as a wild-eyed mystic enamored of a Russian occultist. He also was accused of being a Communist sympathizer despite his condemnation of Stalin and Soviet repression. Like George Washington Carver, who befriended Henry A. as a young boy, Wallace was motivated by seeing how the earth could feed people and their souls. He said he was mystical in the way Carver was: The famed African American plant breeder taught Wallace that God is found in creation and it is there that you find answers. Wallace's shock of country preacher-cut hair and populist evangelism didn't fit the Washington style. He went back to Iowa, eventually settling in Connecticut, to breed flowers and chickens.

The plant-breeding company he founded in Johnston, Pioneer Hi-Bred International (now owned by DowDuPont), came to dominate the seed corn market and Iowa fashion with the ubiquitous green Pioneer seed-corn cap. His Hy-Line chicks of Spencer, Iowa, are still used for most breeding stock of egg-laying flocks in North America.

Henry A. Wallace was the driver behind hybrid corn breeding, the creation of a federal soil conservation service, and the modern federal farm program. He advocated setting aside farm ground to increase prices and save soil during the Dust Bowl years. Wallace was operating in a cultural milieu that saw Grant Wood express a regionalist utopian vision on canvas and articulate it in a little-known but influential book among progressives at the time, *Revolt Against the City*. From his studies at the University of Wisconsin, Iowa native Aldo Leopold gave form and voice to a land ethic that informed Wallace's thinking during the Great Depression and the Dust Bowl.

"When land does well for its owner, and the owner does well by his land; when both end up better by reason of their partnership, we have conservation. When one or the other grows poorer, we do not," Leopold wrote in a seminal series of essays in the book *The River of the Mother of God* in 1938. It was the philosophical forerunner to the acclaimed *A Sand County Almanac* (1949), which is held alongside *On Walden Pond* by Henry David Thoreau in the canon of conservation thought. Jay Norwood "Ding" Darling of the *Des Moines Register* was agitating along the same lines in his Pulitzer Prize–winning cartoons. He went on to become the first chief of the U.S. Fish and Wildlife Service.

You could argue that it was this period that set up what most of the country knows us for: the first-in-the-nation Iowa caucuses, just before the New Hampshire primary. The caucuses would not have been possible in a one-party state like Utah or Rhode Island.

Wallace set the stage for the era of modern politics in Iowa when it started to turn purple. Democrats lived along the two great rivers and in the manufacturing cities. Republicans populated Storm Lake's main street and rural routes. W. C. Jarnagin operated a stridently Republican editorial page from the Storm Lake *Register* and *Pilot Tribune*. It was a different sort of business Republicanism that revolved around working hard, keeping taxes low and liquor to a minimum, and making sure unions didn't get too cocky. But he paid the prevailing union wage in town to the back-shop workers. He had to.

Republicans continued to control the levers in Iowa but Democrats gained ground during the Great Depression and again after World War II as U.S.-fed world trade (including ag exports) expanded. Expectations rose among workers and farmers. They liked electricity coming to their homes, and Social Security. Farms prospered after the war. Unions were doing well in town slaughtering hogs in Storm Lake and building tractors along the Mississippi River.

The Iowa Democratic Party is rooted in the prairie populism that fought the railroads—Abraham Lincoln and his partner C. H. Moore were the lawyers for the railroad, paid in land grants that run right along our lakeshore and which farmers resented—on behalf of the farmers and merchants. They nearly hanged a foreclosing judge during the Great Depression in a small town near Sioux City. In the 1950s they were shooting hogs and throwing them in mass graves during farmer revolts in western Iowa. This bubbling of resistance was kept from boiling over by persuasion, peer pressure, meager crop subsidies, and an occasional show of force. Yet it has always simmered beneath the surface: a resentment for a system engineered—rigged, if you will—from a distance, whether in the commodity trading pits of Chicago or in the marbled conference rooms of Washington, that keeps prosperity and security against the vagaries of the prairie just over that vast horizon.

You could then understand how a recovering-alcoholic truck driver named Harold Hughes came out of Ida County about thirty miles from Storm Lake with the fire of the Holy Ghost blowing him toward the governor's office in 1963. Hughes was a force of nature, big with a black mane and a booming bass voice. It took a born-again lay Methodist minister to launch the community college system, allow liquor to be sold by the drink in bars, and let blue laws that kept businesses closed on Sunday expire—except for auto dealers, which remain closed on Sundays and like it that way. Hughes railed on behalf of union workers and independent truck drivers. He dominated the legislature.

Hughes appointed Storm Lake hell-raising trial lawyer Bones Hamilton to be chairman of the Iowa Conservation Commission. Bones had helped Hughes get sober. Hughes repaid Bones by heeding his call to dredge Storm Lake in the 1960s.

Hughes was elected to the Senate during the height of the Vietnam War, when he abandoned Lyndon Johnson and nominated Eugene McCarthy at the 1968 Democratic National Convention as the peace candidate.

When Hughes got tired of talking to his colleagues or his constituents, he'd call up the dead and talk to them. Henry A. Wallace was one of his favorites. A man who had worked for many Iowa politicians once was asked what his hardest task was. He didn't think twice. "Stopping Hughes from calling old Jim Wallace in Des Moines and saying he had just had a long conversation with Jim's brother." The brother was Henry.

Hughes stepped away after his term in the Senate and dedicated himself to helping men get sober and find a power greater than themselves.

And he made Iowa a distinctly purple state, or maybe he was just there when it settled on that hue.

Hughes paved the way for Tom Harkin and Berkley Bedell in western Iowa. Harkin and Bedell (also a lay Methodist minister) were progressive populists in the tradition of Dolliver, Wallace, and Hughes. They campaigned for Congress against the war machine, Big Oil, and Big Business in the pivotal 1974 Watergate wave election. Democrats were elected in a rarity, and only briefly, from Buena Vista County in the mid-1970s. Hughes had opened a vein, it appeared at the time, but it eventually healed.

Bedell had made a fortune in the fishing tackle business at Spirit Lake. He started tying flies in his garage at age fourteen and grew it into a worldwide company through the years. With the business cruising he followed his calling to campaign. He surprised everyone by beating incumbent representative Wiley Mayne (R–Sioux City) in the collective national nausea over Richard Nixon. Bedell served for twelve years and looked like he could go on forever. But he became ill, with an apparent case of Lyme disease picked up from a deer tick while fishing, and had to step down in 1986 to tend to his health using alternative medicine. He is now ninety-six and still fishing. And he is writing books and preaching the perils of climate change and money in politics to anyone who will listen. I still listen. Remember those VA benefits Mom was fighting for? Berkley Bedell got them for me in 1976 after her eighteen-year quest. The money helped me get through college.

Tom Harkin was the son of an Irish coal miner from Cumming, Iowa, a village near Des Moines. His immigrant mother from Slovenia died when he was ten. Harkin hitchhiked to school in Des Moines from Cumming and worked his way through Iowa State University with ROTC. He ferried disabled fighter jets in the Vietnam War for the navy, and after his hitch took a job with Congressman Neal Smith (D–Des Moines). Smith brought Harkin along on a fact-finding mission in Vietnam in 1969. Harkin got pictures of the South Vietnamese holding prisoners of war in tiger cages. The photos were published in *Life* magazine and added to domestic revulsion against the war. Those photos gave him the foundation to win his congressional seat in 1974.

Harkin used a network of labor, peace activists, Catholic nuns (whom he called his secret weapon), and rabble-rousing farmers to win a U.S. Senate seat in 1984 by upsetting incumbent Roger Jepsen, a Republican whom Harkin was able to paint as an empty pawn of the Pentagon. Harkin ran for president in a primary against Bill Clinton but pulled out after losing New Hampshire. He was the first Iowan since Dolliver to chair the Senate ag committee, which endeared him to rural Iowa and inoculated him electorally. Harkin served for thirty years in the Senate, and retired as junior senator to Senator Chuck Grassley, a Republican.

The progressive surge of Hughes and then Harkin was countervailed in the 1980s by Terry Branstad of Lake Mills in the northern Iowa Upper Des Moines territory. Branstad was a

Reagan conservative who served as lieutenant to the right of affable Governor Bob Ray of Des Moines, a moderate Republican. Branstad succeeded Ray and served as governor for sixteen years through the pain of the farm crisis. Iowans are loath to unseat an incumbent, but Branstad was in a class by himself. He could bound from town parade to town parade in a single morning like a speeding bullet. He worked constantly. He knew every Republican county auditor in the state, and he knew every GOP county chair. Grassley, similarly at one time a pragmatic Republican who chased waste in the Pentagon, brags about holding his town halls in the ninety-nine counties. Branstad did it times three. More important, Branstad built an enduring rural network that would give Democrats fits in trying to win statewide races. He resigned to become ambassador to China in the Trump administration in 2017. By then he set the national record for years as a governor, elected six times and serving twenty-two years over two tenures.

As part of an agricultural trade visit to Iowa in 1985, Branstad struck up a friendship with a young regional technocrat: Xi Jinping, who became president of China in 2012. As vice president, when he was about to ascend to the presidency, Xi returned to the Muscatine farm where he had stayed as a young man. He spoke of his desire to work with Branstad to improve agriculture technology in China, where the major seed companies already had beachheads in labs supervised by Iowa State University seed scientists. It makes one nervous to think of a man who couldn't make it as a lawyer in Lake Mills mediating nuclear tensions, but it is reassuring to know that Xi wanted him there. You can trust Branstad to not let things blow up, I think. He will not screw things up by lying to Xi, at least.

Branstad built a solid gubernatorial platform on farm property rights, lax environmental regulation, tax cuts, and property tax freezes, batting around public employee unions and putting public universities to work for business.

The Branstad policy was business, no matter what. You need a tax credit? We have something for that.

Branstad was a terrible speaker and his policies added up to a steady decline in the very place he was reared: Winnebago County was one of the worst hit during his tenure by any economic or demographic measure. But he is so aw-shucks and dull—and as honest as you will find—that Iowans were perfectly comfortable with him. He told me that he tried smoking cigars once at the University of Iowa but burned a hole in his sweater. The expense of it made him swear off smoking forever. The governor's wife, Chris, hated living in the fishbowl. He left office in 1999 to become president of Des Moines University, an osteopathic medicine school.

D emocrat Tom Vilsack was another nice and self-effacing man, like Ray, who got a lot done, especially for Storm Lake. He was from Mount Pleasant, accordingly, a county seat in southeast Iowa. Vilsack was orphaned as a baby in Pittsburgh and reared in an alcoholic and abusive adoptive household. He found Christie Bell, the daughter of an Iowa country lawyer, in college in New York, and they moved home together, where they both dug in to build Mount Pleasant.

Vilsack was thrust into the spotlight by gun violence. His first elected office was to the city council. He became mayor when a gunman stormed a city council meeting and shot the sitting mayor dead. Vilsack won a seat in the state senate, where his ambitions were too much for the chamber, so he pursued the governor's race when Branstad made his first exit. Vilsack came from fifteen points down to beat Jim Ross Lightfoot, a popular farm radio host and Republican congressman who had everything he needed to win except for Vilsack's doggedness. Vilsack served two terms and flirted with a run for president. Although he supported Hillary Clinton, he was appointed secretary of agriculture by President Obama, and was the only Obama cabinet member to serve a full eight years. He took a job as a dairy lobbyist and is now positioning himself as the senior spokesman on rural affairs for the national Democratic Party.

Governor Chet Culver, a Democrat and son of former senator John Culver, followed Vilsack for a four-year stint but was done in by the Great Recession of 2008 and his own seeming lethargy. Branstad returned in 2010 with a vengeance, beat Culver, brought together the state evangelicals and libertarians, and wrested control of the state senate back from the Democrats in 2016. Iowa went from purple to red again. It is likely to shift back to purple, perhaps aided by Branstad's absence, as power generally has been balanced between the parties since 1965. Iowans typically vote for divided government.

David Yepsen, the dean of midwestern political writers from Des Moines, thinks Iowa is reverting to semipermanent red. The voter registration spread doubled to 50,000 in favor of the Republicans from 2007 to 2017—not insurmountable but clearly going in the wrong direction for the Democrats. Independents outnumber either party statewide, leaning Republican. People without college degrees don't belong to the union anymore and vote Republican. Rural Iowa is overweighted with this bloc because there are so few jobs for people with college degrees in a town of 30,000,

3,000, or 300. The rural vote remains decisive and conservative in Iowa, but the rural vote fades as population recedes every two years. And the Latino vote grows in those rural places like Storm Lake and Denison, where the first children born here are just getting old enough to vote. Latinos accounted for about 14,000 registered voters among a universe of 500,000 voters in the Fourth Congressional District in 2017.

The same windswept land that blew in Harold Hughes brought a polar-opposite populist in the wake around 1990: Steve King was plowing the ground for a Trump revolution while the New Yorker was still divorcing his first wife and telling Howard Stern about it on the radio. King was sitting in the cab of a dirt grader installing terraces for federal ag conservation programs and sketching out a blueprint in his head for a wall that would span the border and keep the Mexicans out of northwest Iowa.

King was calling for a new run at the Crusades as a state senator from Kiron, Iowa, a tiny burg in Sac County just south of Storm Lake, and twenty miles from Hughes's hometown of Ida Grove, before most of us had heard there were some atmospheric problems in Syria. He became an expert on Iraq during one weekend visit.

King was born in Storm Lake, the son of a state police radio dispatcher and a homemaker. The family moved south to Denison, where he graduated from high school. He went off to Northwest Missouri State in Maryville just long enough for the student deferment to get ditched during the Vietnam War. He dropped out and decided to move dirt. All wealth flows from the dirt, he believes. It is his organizing principle. On that point we agree.

He ran for the state senate by launching a primary against

kindly old Republican senator Wayne Bennett of Ida Grove. King was doing Steve Bannon before Bannon ever imagined Donald Trump.

King sued Governor Vilsack over issuing executive orders protecting gay and transgender people from state job discrimination. King made English the official language of Iowa. He started talking about how his mission in life is to move the nation to the right, from his base precisely to the right of nowhere. He has traveled many cosmic miles beyond creating wealth from dirt, and moving dirt.

I got to know him a little bit when he talked friendly about lake restoration. (Dirt work turns him on.) He has these steel-blue eyes that command your attention and a ready smile and a mind dialed in for debate on terms he creates while debating. Sort of like Trump. Then you get off that gaze and all the crazy things he just said—that he doesn't expect to meet gay people in heaven—shake the water out of your ears, and ask yourself, "What did he just say?"

I knew the world was changing when King won the nomination for what was then the Fifth Congressional District at a special Republican nominating convention in 2002. The convention was called after a crowded primary ballot failed to produce a nominee for the new open seat created by redistricting.

King bested a field whose leaders included business moderate Brent Siegrist (former Speaker of the Iowa House) from Council Bluffs, across the river from Omaha, and John Redwine of Sioux City, who married into the omnipresent Bomgaars farm-store chain and appealed to the evangelical delegates. King clearly had worked every country Protestant church along a blacktop road where the red votes are exhorted. A Roman Catholic, King was able to bring in the evangelicals who secure the activist base that gets elected to Republican nominating conventions. Redwine depended on them, but he did not calculate that King was ten degrees to the right of what we thought was the Right.

The Times had endorsed Siegrist in an editorial, the kiss of death. I approached King after he locked up the convention and asked for a happy quote. He said he didn't have time, he needed to speak to his base. He turned and left and I have not spoken to him since. It's his choice. He was elected easily without us. King eschewed the "mainstream media" and took his message directly to the base through whatever channel he could use to lay it out straight his way. Trump perfected the strategy with Twitter.

King vanquished all comers, all of whom were weak. Democrats thought they had a live one with Christie Vilsack, former Iowa First Lady loved dearly by every librarian in the state. She was Iowa nice. She and Tom set up residency in Ames after his governorship so she could mount a bid. She ran against King on the platform of nice. During a debate on Iowa Public Television the topic turned to guns. King pointed those steel-blue eyes into the lens and said something to the effect of prying that blue steel from his cold, dead hands. The camera turned to Vilsack. She was mortified and speechless. King buried her that night.

Iowa lost a congressional district in the 2010 census because it didn't grow as fast as the rest of the country. The nonpartisan Legislative Service Bureau redrew the boundaries to combine the Fourth and Fifth Congressional Districts. The Fourth District now comprises thirty-nine counties in northwest Iowa, where Independents outnumber Republicans and where Democrats trail Republicans, 653,000 to 605,000. A Democrat must win nearly 80 percent of the Independent vote in a high-turnout year to overcome the Republican registration edge. King is king.

U.S. House Speaker John Boehner of Ohio was hanging along-side a stray Texas Democrat when he blew the cover: King was a "horse's ass." Not long after that, Boehner stepped down. He had enough of King. Boehner's best friend in the House, Representative Tom Latham, a north-central Iowa moderate Republican, had just decided not to seek reelection for the abuse the Freedom Caucus had laid on the droopy-faced son of an Ohio bartender.

This time it was over Boehner wanting to strike a "grand bargain" with President Obama on the budget. The thirty-some members of the Freedom Caucus, where King holds sway after so many years as a backbencher, wanted to bring both of them down over it. They prevailed.

But before that it was immigration. King was the first and loudest to call for a wall spanning the U.S.-Mexico border. He said that Mexican youth are drug runners with calves the size of cantaloupes from hauling stash on their backs across the sand. And that most of the great contributions to the world come from Europe and not those continents south of the equator. (The wheel was invented in Bedrock, which is near Stonehenge?) Stuff like that. The Senate produced a comprehensive immigration reform bill on a bipartisan vote, twice, but each time it was suffocated by the Freedom Caucus. By Steve King and Louie Gohmert of Texas, mainly. King says that giving the children of undocumented status a pass amounts to amnesty. Amnesty implies an offense. That children can be considered to be violating the norms of Iowa or America by merely being here and going to school and wanting to get ahead puts logic upside down and mocks the biblical values held high during the ceaseless campaign.

If you are a black woman drinking a cupful of lead in Flint, Michigan, you could think America passed you by and left you for dead. If you live on South Dakota's Rosebud Reservation, you could resent the fact that your land was stolen and your future is locked behind gates. But if you're a white male living in Storm Lake, what gives with the angry routine?

We have been angry here for some time. We were angry out here when William Jennings Bryan was impaled on a cross of gold. King's main plank is to run off all the Mexicans who have invaded the City Beautiful and made it impossible for a WASP to get ahead these days. Donald Trump beat Hillary Clinton three to one among white men, probably by more in the Fourth Congressional District.

King has been our congressman for sixteen years. That's a long time to stew over disenfranchisement—just like the Flint lady, who has been on the outside looking in forever. From the cornfields of the Great Plains to the mines of Appalachia to the suburbs of Ohio, the farmers and miners and insurance salesmen have been told on AM radio that they got screwed since Rush took over the clear channels in 1988.

When they elected a black dude president, it proved Rush right. We were going down the tubes, and the leading white guy from Appalachia, Mitch McConnell, declared that the black dude shall not succeed. He blocked everything Obama tried. He even blocked him from nominating his final Supreme Court justice, with the help of a sputtering old white farmer from Iowa in the person of Chuck Grassley.

What actually happened in Storm Lake?

From 2005 to 2015, per capita personal income in Buena Vista

County increased 33 percent, from thirty thousand to forty thousand dollars a year. That beat the rate of inflation.

During that time period, every angry man got himself a cell phone, then a smartphone with which he could share angry memes about that Crooked Hillary and show pictures of Barack Hussein Obama in a turban. The angry and forgotten man's wife is driving a huge SUV and texting on her smartphone to the girls that she will pick them up after cross-country practice because they are too tired to run home.

He is living in a house with a view of the lake. But he complains that his taxes are killing him, despite the fact that the Storm Lake school board had cut the property tax levy three years out of the last four. If his retired farmer dad dies with an estate of just $4 million, the angry son will be excused an inheritance tax. If his old man had $12 million jointly with the wife, though, the angry son would have been ripped off with a tax of $1.2 million on the estate.

The retired farmer would remember when the hospital was a vet station better fit for a calf. He would remember the Farmall with no cab. He would remember how his dad worked 120 acres with horses, seven days a week. He would remember walking beans and slopping hogs and milking cows. Life is so much worse today for the angry white son. And his son is in dental school with a cosigned debt that is absolutely crushing.

Something is wrong with me. I am fairly happy with the American Dream.

Growing up we did not have air-conditioning in the house. You would sweat yourself to sleep. We have air-conditioning in the garage nowadays. We are glad that our daughter is driving on radial tires. All our kids got through college, some with more

debt than others. It was considered a huge deal that our dad went
to community college in 1930.

John and I live in about the same relative universe as our parents: not rich, but not that much to worry about. As Mom used
to say: "I never knocked myself out." I figure we live like kings
compared to where all our neighbors came from: El Salvador,
Honduras, and Guatemala. They mow their lawns and corral
their pets and wave when I drive past. They have deprived me of
nothing.

I have never seen so many huge, shiny pickups as I do today.
They can cost upward of fifty thousand dollars. They get ten
miles per gallon. When gas prices go back up to three dollars per
gallon, the white man will get angrier. He also gets angry when
he has to wait in line at the Storm Lake Marina to get his boat in.
Up at Okoboji on the lakes lined by million-dollar cottages, all
those angry men can barely fit on the lake. If the Mexicans were
crowding them off the lake or at the beachfront restaurant you
could sympathize. But they haven't let them or the blacks in yet.

People in Spencer and Okoboji look down on Storm Lake.
They talk about the Mexicans here whom they do not know.
Spencer, just a forty-five-minute drive north up Highway 71, decided twenty years ago that the community did not want to re-
open a closed meatpacking plant because, citizens said at a public
hearing, they didn't want to become like Storm Lake. But the jobs
in Spencer are disappearing, its population declining. After Spencer beat Storm Lake on a recent Friday night in football, the visiting students lipped off at the hometowners as a bunch of
"beaners." What was that about? Spencer won the rivalry match.
The students went on to post their nastiness on social media and
rubbed old wounds, later apologizing. They pick up this stuff

from all the noise around them. We published an editorial that said Storm Lake money spends green in Spencer, so lay off. That piece generated more support and chatter from local school parents than any we published in the past year. These Anglos want their children learning alongside Samoans and people from Myanmar and, yes, Latinos. They have tremendous pride in their inclusive school district. They see the benefits in their lives, and in Storm Lake they vote that way. Storm Lake voted for Harkin, Vilsack, and Obama and against King every time. Storm Lake is a dot of political blue. Buena Vista County negates the Storm Lake vote because the rural vote is so red—a microcosm of Iowa or Wisconsin in the 2016 election.

I understand the anger and frustration of Appalachia. The coal mines will be gone. Something similar happened in rural Iowa during the 1980s. Everyone drained out of agriculture and rural communities. Populations plummeted. Dislocation was real. Young people went back to school and got different degrees. Fathers told their sons to forget about farming, that it was a game for the integrators and those who already have capital. The sons got engineering degrees at Iowa State. They got jobs at the Chicago Board of Trade. They bought farms back home and manage them from afar. They invested in new technologies like renewable energy. They were replaced in rural America by immigrants who got their first step onto the ladder, just like our great-great-grandparents up near Emmetsburg. They are building new critical masses out here that hold the potential for revitalizing wayward places. Storm Lake has seldom looked healthier for the white guy who owns property.

The formula to revitalize rural America through education

and federal/state investment could work—it is working in Storm Lake—if our politics didn't have the attention span of our president or any other typical politician. Like stock market investors demanding dividends in the next quarterly report with no long-term view of the future of the company, our political class is tuned to the next poll, whose curiosities distract us from the real goal: You get an education, you get a better job. You innovate. That is the American way. It was the Iowa way.

It's harder to get an education when the legislature continues to cut the budget in a relentless attack on public universities in particular and higher education in general. Legislative appropriations for state universities have dropped by a third since 2001, subtracting inflation. Tuition is rising every year at Iowa Central Community College in Storm Lake and its local property tax rate is rising because the state legislature is starving higher education. At the same time, the state's leadership is telling us to get better in math and science because advanced manufacturing demands it. We are not getting that much better in math and science, and certainly not in English. Iowa used to be number one in school tests like the ACT (in part because many of the national tests are written in Iowa City). Now we're in the top ten. We are falling behind. K–12 public schools are living on 1 percent raises in appropriations from the state or no raise at all most years. Our student debt loads are among the highest in America. Buena Vista University trimmed its sails in 2016 by eliminating the religion and philosophy major; every private college in Iowa is going through similar sacrificial rituals.

With an education you can figure out new uses for corn, new crops that don't erode soil, a new way to skin a hog or make medicine and food enhancements out of plants. White guys are doing that right now in Storm Lake and are paid pretty well to do it. Brown men and women, too. Iowa slowly is reinventing itself as a state.

White men who hit the books, work hard, and thank God they were born in Storm Lake, and not born female and black in Flint or brown in Guadalajara, will get over that anger thing in due time. They have to. But the adjustment is hard to watch.

There are about twenty-five hundred of them in Buena Vista County, white guys over age fifty who were reared to think we all could feed from a silver spoon. That's just about the Trump margin over Clinton. That guy still has his voice. That guy is very clear that food stamps are for losers and moochers, not him. And that gays should just zip it, and that blacks in Ferguson need to calm down, and quit trying to tell his cousin who stole the farm how to farm it, and you know, he really doesn't like Muslims because they seem to be trying to kill him. Even though he has a gun and knows how to use it.

He sees his grievance in The Donald's scowl.

G od bless Steve King," said the hero of the Klan culture, which is essentially as American as Louisiana, David Duke.

Duke was reacting to King's assertion in 2015 that we are diluting our national identity and culture by welcoming immigrants. King said before that occasion that white people in rural places need to have more babies to preserve that culture. He is "pro-life."

From King's Sac County perspective, it makes sense. Rural schools now carry names like OA-BCIG (Odebolt-Arthur/Battle Creek–Ida Grove). Not enough babies. Enrollment at Laurens-Marathon in Buena Vista County is down 40 percent over the past fifteen years. Down 24 percent at Galva-Holstein, which is now Ridge View along with Schaller-Crestland. Some of these schools have only enough players to put eight boys on a football field.

Those few babies born in these small rural counties grow up, grow beards, and can't wait to get out of northwest Iowa for the big city, where they can get a job to maintain a culture that they shook off their boots. Not a lot of jobs in Kiron, Iowa (population 273).

Civilization is under siege, then, in places like Storm Lake, where we are having the wrong kinds of babies. They are babies born to people who weren't babies born here themselves. Natal nabobs of cultural deconstruction and dissimilation. They are coming out the windows of the Storm Lake schools. Babies everywhere. And they want to stay here. The son of a dad who works his own store during the day and the night shift at Tyson. That's not the culture King has in mind. There are just a couple of blondies in the Storm Lake second grade of 180. Who will carry us forward?

King says it's about culture, not race. If you were born here ignorant, you are of our culture. If you grew up hearing Lee Greenwood sing "God Bless the U.S.A.," then your children will appreciate Lee Greenwood, the logic would go. If you move here smart, you should just keep on moving and don't drop a baby while squatting on my land. The land we took from the original civilizers, as it were, the Ioway and Sac and Fox and Dakota. King is a modern apologist for the tradition of Henry Lott.

Am I that different from him? I walked into the bar and grill off the courthouse square in Rockwell City, about forty miles east of Storm Lake, on a recent noonday. The main thing the town has going for it is a minimum-security prison. And a

Subway on the highway. The small-town cafés can't compete with the pizza at the convenience stores anymore, or the Subway.

I rolled through the door and got the hairy eyeball from a guy my age in a crew cut and T-shirt. I wore a white shirt, blazer, and Wranglers. I looked down at him seated at the table with three other workingmen. He thinks people have been looking down at him since junior high school. I smiled, nodded my head, and said, "Hi." He did not smile and said nothing. The Iowa convention is to greet everyone you see, either with a hello or with the famous index-finger wave from the steering wheel to every vehicle you meet.

Why do people vote for Steve King and Donald Trump?

He wants to flip the bird, not the index finger, to the power centers in Washington and New York and Chicago. California, too. Actually, so do I. He knows it won't do any good but people will get the message. We're sick and tired of it. Those people who flew the coop are making out like bandits shuffling paper in Des Moines and the rest of us are shoveling manure from a hog confinement pit. People who don't speak English in front of him at the supermarket checkout were using food stamps, and that honks him off. Despite his school taxes going down, he thinks they are going up because of immigrants. Or at least they could be lower were it not for them. Nobody gives him a break. Young black men could be going to college for free but they riot in the streets. Nobody gave him a full ride.

I've heard him or his country cousin say all of this in venues just like Rockwell City. This man I am culturally profiling in the local grill makes just too much to get a subsidy on Obamacare, and his premiums are higher than they used to be. Try to remind him how his life has improved. He might remind you how manufacturing left Iowa for Mexico—and still Mexicans are moving in around him or at least close enough, and getting food stamps and not paying any taxes. That's what people are told, and that's what they repeat. When you see your position erode relative to everyone else, you want to blame those people who are coming in and changing everything. Repeat it often enough, and have it affirmed repeatedly on every media channel available to you by your own congressman, and you begin to believe your own story.

I could attempt to understand him. Or I could just eat my cheeseburger and smile at the tremendously friendly waitress. It was faster, cheaper, and better than a fast-food burger place. I told her so, and she so appreciated it. She was a friend of my peer with whom I locked eyes. They laugh together. Can he be as intolerant as I thought he was when we first met?

Digestion made me start to think about how I look at my peer the same way he imagines me or the brown man who lives next door to me, and whom Steve King and Donald Trump want to deport. The diner and I suppose we have nothing to say to each other—not even hello. But if we did get over that hump of just looking at each other and thinking we don't like each other, that guy might say he wants to deport my neighbor, a Dreamer. But I don't think he really wants to. He sees his destiny slipping away and can't do much about it. Just like in school, when the bully lays it on you then you look for someone weaker to lay it on. You always have to have someone to fight. The Latina can't fight back. Well, he really doesn't want to deport that nice college girl when it comes down to it. But you do need a secure border. Whatever happened to the rule of law? And King may be out there, but he speaks his mind. He is not afraid of The System or The Man. That's freedom in its purest expression.

My peer at the table wishes he could speak his own mind, probably to his banker and his boss and his lawyer and the county treasurer where he pays his property taxes. But that newspaper editor would never run his letter, and if the paper did run it they would want to put his name on it. He has enough trouble. King appears to offer him a way out by challenging all the forces of change that bring nothing but more isolation to a man in Rockwell City. I can see it and feel it among my friends. I spring from the same ground and drink from the same well and sing the same fight song, yet we tread in and out of parallel realities. The premature death rate among white men with a high school diploma or less is rising while the same rate among blacks and Latinos is declining. The researchers from the University of Wisconsin say that the self-perception of being stigmatized as rednecks by so-called elites drives them to internalize the stigma and causes their own self-destruction. By suicide, by opiate, by meth, by tobacco, and by liver disease, the data about rural mortality say. For sure the liver disease around here. And the suicides. And for sure the smoking, even though they won't allow it at the corner bar anymore.

Thirty years ago an old boy would have asked, "Hey, where ya from? I see ya got BV County license plates."

"Storm Lake."

"The walleyes hittin'? You got a half inch of rain last night so they might not be settled down."

We don't ask each other anymore. It's hard to have a prejudice against someone you know. If you could break the ice, they might ask you today: "Storm Lake. How you dealing with all those Mexicans? Pretty bad, huh?"

"No, it's really pretty good," I say, when I do get that chance to look eye to eye and not down. They are surprised and they start to think about it. King doesn't need to talk that way, and generally my friends agree. If you can just visit you can change hearts and minds. Most, anyway. Or at least get them to think about the brown guy, like I am trying, at least, to think about my peer in the bar and grill. It is more difficult all the time to have those conversations when our shields are up, when we are cocooned among "friends" on Facebook, conditioned by the constant ideological, cultural, and class battle in which Iowa is set.

The constructive nature of Iowa politics and civic life began to corrode around 1990, and politics now often works against solutions in communities like Storm Lake.

It started with the Iowa caucuses and the dirty money.

Jimmy Carter put the first-in-the-nation caucuses on the map as a peanut farmer from Georgia who was just folks to just-folks Iowa. After George McGovern's historic defeat in 1972, the Democratic Party anointed Iowa with its caucuses and New Hampshire with its primary to lead the nominating process out of the smoke-filled back rooms of 1968 and Chicago. The Republican Party joined in for practical purposes. Each was a small state where a newcomer could shout his or her name. Each had a reputation for scrutiny and clean government. Anybody could vault to the fore of American politics by campaigning several times in Storm Lake, the lesson went. You could do it on the cheap. Brush up on the farm bill and the notch-baby problem with Social Security and you could go far in Iowa.

Because it was first, and because it was purple, Iowa came to be among the most important patches of political turf in the land. It's a filter for the nomination process and something of a bellwether for which directions general elections might blow because it is so Middle America.

Brother John shot photos of Senator Howard Baker shaving

at a mom-and-pop motel in Algona as Baker rose to greet a handful of voters one winter morning. I was shaving one Saturday morning in the Algona newspaper office when Senator Paul Simon walked in wearing his bow tie. The former muckraking weekly newspaper owner from southern Illinois said he liked to visit weekly editors when he was out by himself. We talked for two hours about the farm crisis and how to shore up failing family farms. He drove off by himself to the next small town. Lamar Alexander played ragtime piano behind the white picket fences of Chuck and Carla Offenburger's house across College Street from the Beaver football field in Storm Lake. I rode for a half hour in a van with John Glenn while he waxed on about seeing Earth from space. You could have coffee with Ethel Kennedy and talk about what a great guy Sargent Shriver was. That's how it was. Political columnist Mark Shields once said that it was good and proper that Iowa played the role of winnowing the first field of presidential candidates: It had the lowest abortion rate and the highest literacy rate in America. Voters at those house parties questioning Pat Robertson, after he landed here in a helicopter, had studied the life of Medicare and Social Security, they could talk world trade and energy dynamics, and they understood how the Defense Department spends money.

The rise of money in politics changed all that. It started with the Koch brothers, oil refiners, and fertilizer kings from Wichita, Kansas; the American Legislative Exchange Council (ALEC), co-founded by then–Reagan acolyte legislator Terry Branstad in 1975; and several other conservative foundations coming together to coordinate capture of the state's politics through showers of money. Through the years every Republican legislator in Iowa joined ALEC, which was joined at the hip with the conservative Club for Growth, run by Grover Norquist and funded by the

Kochs. No Republican runs outside that system. Their aim was to turn purple states like Iowa and Wisconsin red. It worked as they took over statehouses and redrew legislative districts across the country to keep blue votes corralled. The agenda is all about controlling the courts, undermining public employee unions, and eschewing any regulations. And, it almost goes without saying, cutting taxes.

The money and propaganda wave crashed in earnest with the first George W. Bush campaign, against Al Gore, and dived into the gutter to slander John Kerry with the Swift Boat TV ads. The effort reached its zenith with the 2010 Citizens United ruling that allows untold millions to flow in, and the takeover of Congress by the so-called Tea Party (created by Charles Koch) that same year. The groundwork was laid first by Branstad in Iowa. Scott Walker replicated the Branstad model in Wisconsin when he took down the public worker unions and survived a recall election thanks to Koch funding.

Candidates quit coming to Storm Lake. Neither Hillary Clinton nor Donald Trump nor their veep proxies visited Storm Lake, home to a college and a sizable bloc of immigrants eligible to vote. They would do only airport campaigning. They raised funds for TV advertising from the super PACs.

Presidential candidates mine focus groups to seize on issues they can use to greatest effect, whether it is corn-based ethanol incentives or immigrants, and shape their messages to rip someone down. The attack ads start two years out from a presidential election and crest into constant vitriol over the broadcast and cable channels, any that can be bought at any time.

It's not that the rural Iowa vote is unimportant. Quite to the contrary. The flood of money makes operating by remote easier. The candidate can spend flesh time in Des Moines but can cover

Storm Lake with any medium. That leaves him or her more time to spend on the phone with the big donors. Broadcast conglomerates prize Iowa TV stations when they come up for sale because the flow of political ad revenue to Iowa dwarfs anything seen in a neighboring state. On top of it—and now perhaps subsuming TV—digital media is layered with Facebook and Google and Twitter and YouTube for a panoply of misinformation, grave male voices of doom, and, of course, propaganda we now call "fake news" with no gatekeeper to filter the white noise.

Barack Obama attempted to undermine the network until it worked for him. He visited Storm Lake twice during the 2008 cycle. The first time he posed in Circle Park just south of the university with the young and colorful of the town, a couple of hundred in the frame. He marveled at how lovely the lake was, and that its restoration spoke to the generation photographed. He spoke about health care for everyone. I was able to corner him between the pine trees and ask: Will health care really be for everyone, and how will you pay for it? Well, people could opt out if they wanted to, he told me, and he would pay for it by assessing businesses. I wanted to know why and how businesses would pay for it. The senator saw national TV correspondent John Harwood out of the corner of his eye and pressed off on my second question and into the eye of the lens. The process was changed and under control. The message was hope and change, not complicated stuff like payroll taxes.

The Iowa Republican Party launched a fund-raiser in 1979 called the Iowa straw poll that turned into an open bid of money for voters. The straw poll started as a tailgate among activists in the Iowa State University football stadium parking lot. It swelled into a circus where candidates with the most funds could rent buses and haul people to the parking lot, where the hauled-in voters would cast their preferences over corn dogs. It was supposed to show organizational strength, but what it really showed was that money could buy votes. That's how candidates like Mike Huckabee won, when his main pitch in 2008 was that he could play the bass guitar with a cover band from a flatbed trailer outside Jack Trice Stadium. Michele Bachmann of Minnesota, Steve King's closest friend in the House, won in 2012. By 2016, candidates started buying and trading players. A Republican state legislator–cum–conservative kingmaker, Kent Sorenson, went to prison in 2016 for taking payola to jump from one campaign to another.

Sam Clovis, a political science professor at Morningside College in Sioux City, latched on to the Trump campaign in Iowa when Rick Perry ran out of cash and couldn't pay him. Clovis became Trump's campaign cochairman in the state and ended up on his foreign policy advisory team—the one that might have told the Russian foreign ministry that they sure would like some dirt on Hillary if the Russians could dig some up. Clovis became a friend, or at least a cooperative acquaintance, of special counsel Robert Mueller in the summer of 2017 as the former FBI director inquired about those Russian back channels.

One of the main benefits of kicking off the presidential campaign in Iowa was the state's hallowed reputation for being an honest broker offering a level playing field. We proved that we have a price like anybody else. Iowa's reputation of being squeaky clean has a big stain on it from the mud of dirty money. It pours so heavily the temptation is too great not to drink it. At least Branstad killed the straw poll in 2015 for its depravity.

Nobody will admit it but the Democrats secretly like having Steve King around as a fund-raising machine for them. Every time he talks the Democrats raise money to spend on more competitive districts in, say, Ohio. King gets endless free TV exposure, plus he gets in on all that money that flows through Republican presidential candidates, whom he takes pheasant hunting, if he wants or needs the money. This year, he shot pheasants from a hunting preserve near Akron, Iowa, along the Missouri River with Donald Trump Jr. Trump is a good shot, King said. None of the money raised off King makes it back through the Democratic Congressional Campaign Committee to organize voters in rural Iowa. The DCCC looks at the party registration numbers and writes it off as a lost cause.

Mainly, the money flowing into Iowa is funneled to fuel the noise machine that made corn-based ethanol a litmus test for GOP candidates in particular. Iowa's political class is fixated on protecting the fuel oxygenate because the corn economy is addicted to alcohol. Fealty to ethanol buys rural votes. Governor Branstad was able to control most of that cash flow to keep his agribusiness-driven political machine finely tuned. It sets the tone in the state. The premise is that what's good for the fertilizer industry, what's good for DuPont Pioneer and Monsanto, what's good for the consolidated pork industry, what's good for insurance (Des Moines is a leading insurance center), is good for Iowa. Sort of Calvin Coolidge/Herbert Hoover redux. The message we don't hear as much is how that fealty to ethanol might be undoing rural communities or polluting our lakes and streams from corn cultivation.

The caucuses turned Iowa from a state that sought middling solutions to a people set on in pitched battle. Most Iowans never met a Mexican or thought about wielding a knife eight hours a day in a chilled room over a pork carcass. Yet they started believing that immigrants were threatening the way of life where no Mexicans or black folk live, thirty miles from Storm Lake. Rather than invite the poor to live in their communities like Ida Grove or Sac City, they bus them in thirty miles from Storm Lake to work in their village factories and return them home when day is done. The noise machine makes us think that way, that brown people are dangerous or somehow corrosive to our community. If their labor is cheap enough, it is good enough, but they need not live in the town they are bused into. Let Storm Lake house them and school them.

The noise machine, spewing and seeking money, justifies the demand for law and order, and rationalizes arming every man, woman, and adolescent. Rural areas grow redder and urban areas bluer, the prisons grow even more overcrowded, and the money drives the message and turnout. The money even creates news as fact finders are marginalized by fantasies planted in social media and through email networks as fact: They will take away your freedom to farm, plus your guns. Immigrants will infest your town with drugs. The propaganda is meant to distract from the reality that contemporary corporate agriculture shall grow unimpeded.

Stoking fear helps strengthen the underlying message: Don't mess with Big Ag. It is our lifeline. Even though you are living paycheck to paycheck, you wouldn't have a paycheck were it not for agri-industry. It gets people to think that they must put up with water pollution, thyroid cancer, and a deteriorating Main Street or they surely will starve to death instead. It makes the immigrant lie low and not raise any dust, even though the ones peddling the message with a wink know they need Mexican labor as much as anyone.

The Iowa caucuses are so important because they winnow the field of candidates, along with New Hampshire and, increasingly, South Carolina, as a key test of the African American vote. They say there are three tickets out of Iowa. New Hampshire often knocks the field down to two. During the last cycle Iowa didn't winnow the Republican field much at all—other than to knock out Governor Scott Walker, a clone of Terry Branstad from Wisconsin, who rode a Harley across the Mississippi into Iowa, where Walker was born, but strangely found no traction. He had blown up public employee unions in the state next door and survived recall without a sweat but Iowans wanted someone decidedly more radical, giving the top two caucus tickets to Ted Cruz (King's closest ally in the field) and Trump.

Iowa is also one of a dozen or so battleground states in the general presidential election. As Iowa goes, so goes Ohio. And as Ohio goes, so goes the U.S. No Democrat wins without Iowa. No Republican wins without Ohio.

We are a battleground because we are essentially purple, centrally located, with a simple TV market layout and an electorate that is constantly tuned in to national politics because of the caucuses. Often lost on Democrats, but not on the Republican data miners, is that they must expand their base in Iowa beyond the Mississippi River's vacated manufacturing centers—Dubuque, Davenport, Clinton, Burlington, and Fort Madison, the old union strongholds where labor no longer holds sway—and in Des Moines. Despite the challenges of hanging on to the vote in manufacturing-heavy eastern Iowa, a Democrat must make a serious reach into rural Iowa to win. Not one Democratic state senator lives west of Interstate 35, which divides the state in half east to west.

Tom Harkin understood rural communities and felt at ease speaking with farmers. Bruce Braley, his hand-picked successor, eviscerated himself by contemplating in public the horror of a farmer (Chuck Grassley) heading the Senate Judiciary Committee. That is how you lose the rural vote, even if Braley was right. Joni Ernst of Red Oak in southwest Iowa, who recalled wearing bread bags over her shoes in the winter on the school bus and talked about castrating pigs, emasculated Braley and took over Harkin's seat. Terry Branstad knew that eighty rural counties out of ninety-nine always were his firewall against defeat. Ernst was a quick student. She became the first woman from Iowa to be elected to the Senate.

John Kerry was up by four points in Iowa on election night—until the west side of the state phoned in about the time thunderstorms roll in from Nebraska. Good morning, President-elect George W. Bush, a new best friend to ethanol. Kerry never fought back against the Koch brothers' Swift Boat ads that called him, essentially, a coward in Vietnam—when in fact Kerry was an injured war hero. It worked on Iowa "patriots." Those TV ads and lack of turnout infrastructure in rural Iowa beat him.

Barack Obama appealed to our sense of hope, which Iowans share each spring, that this fall will be better than last. We always plant in that spirit. Iowans vaulted him to the fore in the caucuses and twice in general elections. You could hardly argue that Iowa's politics are that confused by race. They are not. What they are: populist. Obama had a decidedly populist theme: that the people can overcome by bringing midwestern values of honesty, hard work, and fair play to Washington. The son of a

Kansan who adopted Illinois, Obama understood Plains language, and it resonated in rural reaches like Storm Lake.

The past few falls hadn't been better than the previous few
leading up to 2016. The rural economy still stinks, as it has but
for the 1970s. Corn prices dropped in half from 2009 to 2017, for
starters. Blue-collar voters doubted again that subtlety or new
computer advances could bring union jobs back to Newton, once
home to Maytag and the United Steel Workers. No matter how
smooth and cerebral and patient Obama was, it didn't add up to
much for Newton (where the Maytag plant now makes wind
turbine blades with a small fraction of the workers who made
washing machines). The continued and rapid decline of manufacturing, the erosion of household income, and the decay of
those communities set a dusky stage for the act to follow.


Mike Gronstal of Council Bluffs knew he was in trouble in
the fall of 2016. He had been a Democratic state senator
for thirty-two years, the last twenty as majority leader. He had a
tough challenge in Dan Dawson, a law enforcement professional.
The gun lobby was after Gronstal hard. He also was taking a
wave of heat for trying to get driver's licenses for Dreamers. His
district was weighted by registration eight percentage points in
favor of a generic Republican, but Gronstal was as hard a cam-
paigner as he was a brilliant legislative strategist. Money was
raining on his race. When he became majority leader he had to
raise $290,000 to win. The last cycle he had to raise $2.5 million. And that was a mere fraction of the spending that came
mainly from dark Republican money that simply was not there
twenty years ago. Gronstal said he could not guess how much
was spent to defeat him in 2016 on a district that surrounds a

town of sixty thousand people. Two years before, longtime incumbent senator Daryl Beall (D–Fort Dodge) was ousted in a race where more than $5 million was spent in total, most of it against the incumbent and much of it from the gun lobby. Fort Dodge has a population of twenty-five thousand.

It was another chilly October night of door knocking for Gronstal on the rolling streets of the Bluffs, a tough river gambling and meatpacking town in the shadow of burgeoning Omaha. He went to one door after another hearing the same refrain. "These were identified as Democratic voters, and they were so disgusted by the presidential campaign that they would not be pulled out of their living rooms," Gronstal said. "I told them, 'Okay, but I am on the ballot.' It didn't matter. They completely overlooked the down-ballot races. They weren't even thinking about it."

Door knockers were hearing it across the state in Burlington, another hard-hit Mississippi River town where United Auto Workers member Senator Tom Courtney, a Democrat, was knocked off. He didn't have a college degree. He worked at the Case-IH tractor plant alongside the Trump voters. He knew the language of white disenfranchisement if anyone did. How did Courtney go down?

"It was death by a thousand paper cuts," Ron Parker, chief of staff for the Senate Democratic caucus, told me.

Bill Clinton's North American Free Trade Agreement was a big paper cut. Since 1990 Iowa manufacturing has reeled. Even Ertl toys near Dubuque moved production of those cute little toy tractors south of the border. It was happening all over. Anxiety has been palpable in rural Iowa and its small towns for thirty years. Now it is building in the larger towns like Burlington and Council Bluffs and Fort Dodge. A host of issues were in play. The Iowa Supreme Court ruled that gays cannot be discriminated against as a class, allowing them to marry. Three justices lost their seats in a 2010 retention election driven by out-of-state money. It was still a matter of debate in the pews and the pool halls in 2016. Rural Iowans were convinced by the Farm Bureau that Obama was out to control their farms through a proposed EPA rule called Waters of the United States (WOTUS is the code word). People were riled up about it. A strong property rights sentiment is embedded here, and that was a significant if overlooked theme in the last cycle. People could not tell you what the rule actually meant but they knew they didn't like it because the Farm Bureau and the cattlemen were against it. Regulations, guns, immigration, health-care premium increases, and on and on. And Obama really didn't deliver for them when they were stuck in a nowheresville job grinding metal for sixteen dollars an hour.

Hillary Clinton wondered what happened and wrote a book about it. A few paragraphs would have sufficed. Yes, it was misogyny. I heard that with my own ears before the election. And, yes, there was FBI director James Comey and the on-again, off-again email probes. Clearly, the Russians meddled in swing states. But there is also this: She didn't show up and ask for our vote, the first rule of politics.

The Clintons never much liked Iowa because Tom Harkin upstaged Bill Clinton as the favorite son in the Iowa caucuses in 1992. The Clinton camp said Iowa was too liberal. They might have been right. Iowa Democrats thought the Third Way too conservative when Bill Clinton ended welfare as we knew it. In the 2008 caucus, Iowa snatched away Hillary's Beltway pre-ordained victory and handed it to Barack Obama. She never overcame her disaffection from the state, and in 2016 there was this strong populist Bernie Sanders insurgency that gained its foothold in the college towns. He was offering something other than an anti-Trump. He was calling for single-payer health care and free college. But if Bernie could only tie Hillary in Iowa, one could imagine him running into the same problems in Council Bluffs during the general election: Trump would have been calling him a Commie from Vermont who honeymooned in Russia.

Clinton's attitude about Iowa could be felt in the fall of 2016 by her absence and the complete diffidence of her surrogates about campaigning in rural areas. Tom Vilsack never campaigned for her in Storm Lake. Neither did Tom Harkin, who had just retired and begged off politics. We implored Tim Kaine to come and speak Spanish to us; we never received so much as a courtesy reply from his Iowa-bred chief handler. They thought they had us. Ann Selzer of Des Moines, who maintains the gold standard of political polling in America by getting it right, knew better. She called Trump by seven in the *Des Moines Sunday Register*, and by Tuesday he won Iowa by ten. Mike Gronstal knew Sunday morning when he opened the paper that the show was over. He woke up Wednesday morning leader of nothing and getting after a list of household fix-its he had ignored for the past three decades.

Hillary Clinton did not ooze empathy or passion in public. She counted on identity politics (women, blacks, gays) to defend her against identity politics (deport illegals, restore law and order in Ferguson, defame gays, grab women wherever you want if you can get away with it). Resources were shifted away from white working-class states like Iowa and Wisconsin and toward more diverse states like Virginia and North Carolina. She lost. Would "Lunch Bucket Joe" Biden have whupped Trump in Iowa? Probably. Would he have lost Wisconsin, Michigan, and Pennsylvania? Probably not. He would have shown up, as he

did repeatedly through three decades in Iowa. But he didn't run.
He was grieving his son's death. Nobody wanted to get in front
of that Clinton steamroller but Bernie Sanders, who had nothing
to lose, and Martin O'Malley, who played a nice guitar.

Trump didn't show up much either. He didn't have to. He
knew he had us locked down from his huge rallies. Terry Branstad's son Eric was leading the Iowa Trump campaign. During
the caucus phase, Branstad the Younger was the chief spokesman for the corn ethanol lobby.

Iowa is not lost to the morass of Trumpism or narcissism or
nativism. Urban areas that tend to support Democrats are growing, and so are the ranks of the college educated in those urban
centers. That is where the population is headed. Those shells of
river towns will become interesting political artifacts but not necessarily routes to any determined destiny. Democrats say the pen-
dulum is swinging back. The all-Republican statehouse is in
classic overreach—gutting Medicaid and collective bargaining,
building unconstitutional budget deficits that upset even the gov-
erning Republicans, putting state universities at the foot of business, and causing property tax increases by defunding K-12
schools and community colleges. One-party rule has not been especially well received here either in the state or federal iteration.
The Republicans controlling Iowa may be too successful at wreck-
ing things, while the Republicans in Washington can't even get
their shoes tied over repealing the Affordable Care Act (ACA)
without assistance from somebody's parents.

Steve King, meanwhile, remains his own political phenome-
non. Iowa could give the mojo to Deval Patrick or Elizabeth
Warren or Kirsten Gillibrand, all of whom have admirers here.

Tim Kaine sends me emails regularly, just to stay in touch, as do Ted Cruz and John Kasich. Since the sexual harassment spree of revelations, friends of Warren and Amy Klobuchar of Minnesota are reaching out to me. No word from Kamala Harris . . . say, a fund-raising pitch from her hit my in-box the first week of January 2018.

No matter who ends up on top, King remains the voice of a hardscrabble western part of the state that forever thinks it has been forgotten and neglected and flown over. Big waves can drown anyone, but King's nose is so long he can breathe through a tsunami. As long as the national Democratic Party thinks it can write off western Iowa and allow King free rein it will have a hard time maintaining a structure in the state.

In 2018 King will face a challenge from J. D. Scholten of Sioux City, a former semipro pitcher in his thirties and now a bachelor paralegal. He is campaigning hard among rural activists. Scholten is rolling down the blacktops in a Winnebago motor home built in Forest City, inside the district. King probably will win, but everyone had the same doubts before Berkley Bedell beat Nixon defender Wiley Mayne in 1974. Iowans like honest. They think King is honest, that he tells hard truths, which are actually half-baked fantasies. But the more King chums around with a liar like Trump, the more suspicious they may become in devout Dutch Reformed enclaves like Sioux Center. Latinos have just begun working in their dairy barns and small meat-processing plants. They don't dislike them as much. A state senator from up in that ultraconservative northwest Iowa neighborhood, David Johnson, dropped out of the Republican Party in 2017 and went Independent, because he was so appalled by Trump and, finally, by King as their outrageous remarks just became too much. Johnson decided not to run in 2018 as three young Republicans lined up to succeed him; of course, a King aide won the primary. All congressional seats are presumed safe, because the power of incumbency is so overwhelming in tradition-bound Iowa. Yet an Iowa Poll conducted by pollster Selzer at the end of 2017 showed a big swing against Republican incumbents. Representative Rod Blum (R-Dubuque), in the First District, was down eighteen points. King led a generic Democrat by just five points, an eye-opener to the downcast. Congressional polls are read as proxies by Republican legislators who know their grip on the statehouse is greasy.

All eyes are on the 2018 governor's race. A prudent bet is that the GOP will maintain control of the legislature in the midterm. Democrats have a chance of taking back the Iowa House. The real energy is in the governor's race, which is essentially for an open seat with the departure of Branstad for China. He left his successor, Lieutenant Governor Kim Reynolds, with a huge budget mess wrought from years of tax cuts, corporate giveaways, and a disastrous Medicaid privatization plan that has made everyone angry—patients, doctors, hospitals, and insurance companies. Republicans are sniping among themselves absent Branstad's glue. Reynolds faced a primary challenge from Cedar Rapids mayor Ron Corbett, a former Speaker of the House, which would have been significant coming from Iowa's "second city." Corbett had to drop out when he failed to produce enough signatures on his nomination papers.

A half dozen Democratic contenders were lined up to run for the nomination. Fred Hubell, sixty-seven, comes from one of the wealthiest families in the state, a founding family of Des Moines that owned the Equitable of Iowa insurance company and the Younkers department store chain. He is ready to open his wallet. He spent $7 million on the 2018 primary, a record in Iowa.

Nate Boulton, half Hubbell's age, is a handsome trial lawyer from Des Moines who came in with strong union support. Labor thought he might topple Hubbell, who spent his career in corporate suites. But Boulton was brought down a couple weeks before the June primary by allegations of groping two women years apart. He blamed it on misunderstanding, apologized, and exited into the shadows.

Hubbell won with 55 percent of the primary vote. The morning after, Reynolds already was painting him as a plutocrat while she was the poor girl from just down the country lane, even though she will have all the money Hubbell could dream of to create a caricature of him.

Reynolds is vulnerable from being mucked up in Branstad budget hubris that is causing real pain at the local level—turning Medicaid management over to private companies caused the closing of thirteen nursing homes in rural towns in 2016 because of short and late reimbursements. In Storm Lake, North Lake Manor closed down abruptly, upsetting families. It is a potent, and potentially explosive, political issue in a geriatric state.

This is the best shot in a state worn out from too much Branstad and shocked by too much Trump. The governor's race will be a key test of whether Iowa is indeed reverting to perma-red. Candidates are hearing that voters in those swing river towns already regret their Trump support, and they don't like to see bargaining rights stripped from public employees. They don't like more tuition increases and more property tax increases. Few are getting rich quite yet and patience is wearing thin. Iowa always comes back to its senses, just before it's about to ride off the cliff into Kansas.

Whoever controls Terrace Hill, the governor's mansion, has a fair influence over how well a Democrat will perform in an Iowa presidential election. Remember Tom Vilsack and Barack Obama. That governor will have even more influence in how a Democratic presidential nominating field shapes up. Iowa Democrats are lost without good old Tom Harkin and Tom Vilsack. They need a state leader like one of them to rally to the presidential ticket. It's easier to raise money, to recruit candidates down-ballot who generate support up-ballot. As Branstad proved, the governor can be everywhere, flying the flag for the ticket. Democrats will have a hard time in 2020 if they can't take back Terrace Hill (donated to the state by the Hubbell family) in 2018. Governor Reynolds embraces Trump and King. If the Democrats lose this governor's race, it could be a sign that the voters really did flip the switch off in 2016.

The lesson, which the Democrats from DC and Des Moines have a hard time grasping: Show up, ask for their vote, and don't forget about rural Iowa. That's where the state races are won, and where the national race ultimately is won. Tom Harkin, Barack Obama, and Tom Vilsack are recent enough reminders that Iowa has not necessarily turned red, or that 2016 predicts a thing about 2018 or 2020 or any other year. I predict this: Rural Iowa will make the difference in 2020, along with those rusty Mississippi River towns yearning for a revival message—not necessarily the message that tears down. At least, that's how it always worked in the past. It worked for Obama. Iowa has not fundamentally changed since then.

We can make Latinos into bogeymen because everybody knows they will climb any fence or ford any current to make a living where they can. We can keep those people in limbo (and many of them at slave wages) because they can't or don't vote. They can't rise up and stake their claim in America out of fear. Even the people with legal papers are afraid. There is nobody to speak for them but this little newspaper—no union, no

Organizing for America, no Democratic Party out here. When somebody tries, they get frustrated.

A Latina from Storm Lake, Sara Huddleston, in 2016 ran against incumbent state representative Gary Worthan (R–Storm Lake), a Farm Bureau and Steve King boy all the way. Not one Democratic politician bothered to help her. The state party and the traditional Democratic institutional donors wouldn't give her a dime. Huddleston and her husband, Matt, knocked on every door in Buena Vista and Sac counties. Worthan told us that he would not talk to us because he could not get "a fair shake" from us—despite the fact that we had run every one of his weekly legislative columns verbatim, which he generally used to complain about the minority Democrats getting in his way. Every committee appointment of his we duly noted in the paper. Now the strategy of running against the news media had seeped down to the local level. Tom Cullen was perfectly willing to report what Worthan wanted to say, but Worthan used his ridicule of our straight news reporting to pick up votes from a hard-core King base that believes we are patently dishonest.

Huddleston, a twelve-year veteran of the Storm Lake City Council, won her adopted hometown but lost everyplace else. More than fifteen hundred Latinos are registered to vote in Buena Vista County (out of a total county universe of eleven thousand voters) and another thousand more would be if anyone outside this town gave a damn or told them that they matter. They knew Sara Huddleston never had a chance against that wall. So did we. I advised her not to run. I told her that nobody in Des Moines would support her. All the statehouse people who told her to run could not be found when it counted. I warned her and she understood. Huddleston said she wanted to run as hard as she could to lose and pave the way. She wanted to inspire more Latinos to get involved in civic life. Of course, we endorsed her, which shows how much sway the manipulative mainstream media actually have.

We trifle with public employees and try mightily to decertify their unions by legislative fiat. (If public employees make less, private sector workers can feel better about making just enough to pay the rent.) We can argue about whether Mexicans should get food stamps. Those are side issues to divert attention from the main dogma: You do not tread on ethanol, corn, hogs, or Roundup. Not in the current context. Rural people today know that things are changing around them just as the indigenous people knew when Fort Dodge was first an outpost on the western edge of what we know as civilization.

The people in Des Moines who were reared in that rural county seat know how farming has industrialized. They know that the Raccoon River, which feeds their drinking water supply, and which emanates in Buena Vista County, is a stream toxic from the agriculture that fed them. These people one or two generations removed from the farm know what is behind the message, according to Selzer's polling—they favor enhanced water quality, gay rights, deportation waivers for Dreamers, and stronger K-12 schools. But they vote the opposite way when the bullhorn is wedged in their ears. Politics almost always lags behind the people, especially when the people have resigned themselves as chattel, for the time being, in the world market and swirl of pitches funded by the Koch brothers and the National Rifle Association. We are collateral damage, as the waterworks farm boy called it. When they figure it out they vote. Our job is to help people figure it out by reporting the facts on who is running this state.

# CHAPTER 11

# The Young Men from Jalisco

It took us a while to get to know our new neighbors from Latin America. We acquaint ourselves through eating. The basic Iowa social gathering is a potluck supper where you bring your own covered dish and table service. We sit and visit over tater-tot casserole. Back when Latinos were starting to arrive, a bunch of good-hearted people in town set up a community get-to-know-you potluck and invited all the cultures to bring a dish.

Where the immigrants come from, it is considered rude to invite someone to supper and tell them to bring their own food—much less knives, forks, and chopsticks. So the Latinos and Asians never showed up—no enchiladas or pad Thai, just scalloped potatoes and ham for us white folk. We decided we needed to learn a little bit more about where our friends were coming from so we could better understand them. A few of us from Storm Lake decided to travel to a *pueblito* in Mexico that was our twin city—Ayotlan, a farm and meatpacking county in Jalisco—in October

2005. We tried to help our readers understand why the young men came to Storm Lake.

## FINDING THE CITY BEAUTIFUL IN SANTA RITA

*Ayotlan, Jalisco, Mexico, October 22, 2005*

The sun set Sunday over the mountains surrounding Santa Rita, a pretty little town of 4,500 people.

I threw my bag in one of a half-dozen rooms at the Mi Pueblito Hotel, and walked outside for a smoke overlooking the town square. A man and his son stood on the corner next door at a soda fountain.

"Buenas noches," I said.

"Good evening," the young man replied.

"Oh, your English is good," I told him.

"It's okay. I lived in Storm Lake for 10 years," he said.

So it was that I met José Liceas and his son, Brian, 10, the first people I encountered in Storm Lake's sister city 2,500 miles from home.

I was not so far from home after all. José bid me welcome, mi nuevo amigo. But no friends are new, I was reminded, all are old.

Four Storm Lakers made the trek to West Central Mexico in the state of Jalisco: City Councilwoman Sara Monroy-Huddleston, Public Safety Director Mark Prosser, Code Enforcement Officer Scott Olesen and I. We flew out of Omaha Sunday, Oct. 9, not knowing what to expect. My idea of Mexico was formed by the Clint Eastwood spaghetti Westerns: the rotund banditos with belts of bullets strapped around their shoulders and a few teeth, dirty spans of desert dotted with adobe taverns.

Imagine my corn-fed anxiety as we waited outside the Guadalajara airport for our hosts from Ayotlan County. Up walked Sergio Quezada, a handsome man of 30 in a sharp black suit and open-neck white pressed shirt, accompanied by three lovely señoritas: Johanna Soto, Aricelli Tabarez and Aricelli Perez. Johanna, a native of Phoenix, spoke perfect English. Relief washed over me.

We piled in the blue state-owned van and traversed winding roads southeast from Guadalajara, a city the size of Chicago, for a 90-minute journey into the isolated heart of rural Mexico.

First sights: green corn, Pioneer Hi-Bred (from Iowa) seed signs, teal-colored agave (ah-gah-bey) for tequila, John Deere tractors (from Iowa), Holstein cows, bicyclists and horses on the highway, adobe businesses and dwellings in brilliant purple, yellow, red and blue whizzing past.

We made a pit stop. I tried to buy a bottle of water. Sergio will not hear of it. This is on him. Everything is.

José worked at Tyson Fresh Meats for 10 years, so he could afford to return to Santa Rita five years ago and work in the El Mexicano meat processing plant. He is why we went—to find Iowa in a different nation.

It was everywhere we looked.

In the classroom: How many of you have friends or family in Iowa?

The hands went up, the faces beamed.

In the pool hall: the proprietor, Ruben Mendoza, has an uncle, Javier Torres, in Storm Lake and other family in Denison. (Turns out Raul Andrade of Storm Lake, who loads turkeys at the local plant, also is Torres's nephew.)

In the county government building: Ayotlan County Councilwoman Norma Arambula of Santa Rita thanked Storm Lake for taking care of her town's children so far away. She has heard the stories of the good, big and warm hearts in Iowa.

The Storm Lake delegation was invited by Ayotlan County to establish a sister city relationship through the states of Jalisco and Iowa. The relationship is a piece of paper formalizing what has existed de facto for the better part of a decade. They come from Santa Rita to Storm Lake, they work, they dream of going home someday to this pretty little place full of warm hearts and sad faces.

Why do they come?

The answer is obvious. Meatpacking in Santa Rita pays $40 to $100 per week. They can make up to 10 times as much at Tyson in Storm Lake. Field work pays $40 per week or less. Garment workers in Ayotlan city (county seat, pop. 15,000–18,000, about 10 minutes from Santa Rita) make up to $100 per week. Women string beads in the small town of La Rivera on the front stoop of their humble casas in the evening for rosaries sent everywhere. It is the largest rosary manufacturing center in the world outside of Rome. All done by hand.

"I make enough for my family to eat," said Police Lt. Rudy Vasquez, a smiling cop who played guitar for children on the town square at Santa Rita. "But to buy shoes, we have to think long and hard and plan.

"You live here, it's like a family. You wanna have a soda with me, that's fine. This is my land."

Simple poverty, simple suffering, simple joy, simple life.

The old woman sold sugarcane on the street in Ayotlan. It was stacked all around her. She tried to hide behind the cane from the camera, but eventually emerged smiling. I asked for sugarcane. She chopped it with her worn machete and put the squares into a plastic bag with tough, brown hands. I held out my smooth, white palm full of pesos and told her to take what she needs.

"Oh, no. You are my guest," she says.

I chewed it. The cane was subtly sweet. It would be riper next month, and sweeter. I could not chew it all, so it was discarded with my guilt into the trash can before I entered the community health center, immaculate white and bright in the sheer mountain sun. The clinic is free for basic care, federally funded. Women patients mop the floor to earn their keep.

Dr. Gloria Irma showed the maternity ward. One bed. Clean. Eight hours after birth, the mother and baby go home.

Across the hall is a rehydration room for the young and old suffering from diarrhea. A boy waited. Ayotlan has chlorine in the water, but not Santa Rita. You drink bottled water, if you can afford it. You use soap, if you can afford it.

Back in Santa Rita, Dr. Miguel Hernandez welcomed Huddleston to his casa with hugs. He invited us inside for fresh orange juice. Droplets from heaven, this. In a room next door, an old woman lay dying with her son at her side. Dr. Hernandez has a hospital, by Santa Rita standards, attached to his house. Six beds held the seriously ill and dying. The son greeted us with a somber "buenos dias." Dr. Miguel closed the door.

After meeting José on the street at Santa Rita, the van took us with police escort—one cop drove, the other stood in the back of the pickup with an M-16 on a turret—back down the winding road to Ayotlan. A marsh is on the left. Local legend has it that six crocodiles are in the marsh. Nobody knows for sure. Horses drank there anyhow, oblivious.

The van pulled up to the town square, with the county building and St. Augustine Church. Inside the church, people laid wreaths at side altars with pictures of the young who have left for Storm Lake. They said a prayer to Santo Toribio, patron of immigrants.

Outside, a thousand people gathered on the square. A band played the Jalisco state song. A fiesta was in full swing.

"It is all for you," Johanna Soto tells us.

We were floored. Mayor David Soto, 61, welcomed us. We greeted legions of people in suits and ties.

Faces were a blur. "Hola. Muchas gracias. Buenas noches."

The mayor climbed the gazebo. The band stopped. He grabbed the microphone and told the crowd that we are friends of Ayotlan from Storm Lake. The crowd erupted in applause. They offered tequila sangria in stone cups. We paraded around the square shaking hands and kissing. It was dark under yellow lights. Surreal.

We were whisked off to a castle on a hill overlooking Ayotlan, the first of nightly banquets that start at 10 or 11 p.m. and end whenever. The owner has a beef packing plant. "Salud!" (Cheers!) they shouted as the tequila glasses clinked. A mariachi band played. Pumpkin soup was served for the first course. More "Salud!" The next course came.

Prosser was asked to speak.

"Your people have enlivened and brightened our community," he told the gathering of county officials and businessmen, the oligarchy. "They've made it grow and made it young. Your brothers and sisters, nieces and nephews, who live in Storm Lake are wonderful people and have made our community a better place to live."

Mayor Soto was as dissatisfied with the Mexican political system as Americans say that they are.

"The parties are not convinced that the problem is themselves," Mayor Soto said through his son, David. "They need to follow democracy for the people, not just for them."

I asked Mayor Soto what he wanted from Storm Lake. Investment? Donations?

"We want your friendship, to feel like friends. We need to get close so that in the future you can pass your culture to us," he said.

His wife, Elva, told Scott Olesen that what the mayor is after is democracy, liberty and the rule of law. That's what Mexico wants from Estados Unidos.

But, the peasantry has been under the thumb of a single, dominating power for the better part of 1,500 years. The Aztecs invaded in 620 AD and made their human sacrifices on the steps. Ruins remain in Ayotlan. Five hundred years ago, the Spanish Conquistadors came and vanquished the Aztecs, ruling hand-in-hand with the Catholic Church. Santa Rita was established formally as a community in 1574. One party takes over for decades, the people tire of it and elect the other party and nothing changes.

Mexico has a revolution every 100 years or so: 1810, 1910 . . .

Poverty permeated like the morning dew on the wrought iron benches in Santa Rita's town square. The unemployment rate in Ayotlan County was estimated at 30%, but it was probably greater considering under-employment. The illiteracy rate was 50%, but was probably greater considering functional illiteracy.

The roosters crowed at 5 a.m. Women and children swept the sidewalks and the streets in front of every house. The houses are clean, almost all have TVs and telephones. Water is heated by the sun on tanks atop the casas. The church bells ring the Angelus at 6 a.m., 6:30 a.m. and 7 a.m., when Mass starts. Twenty women and five men sang a capella inside. Girls and boys polished in uniform walked past the church on their way to school, offering smiles and greetings to a stranger.

They will go to school maybe through the elementary level. If they can afford bus fare of $50 to $60 per month to Ayotlan, their education might continue. At the high school in Ayotlan, a town of 15,000 has 240 students enrolled—in Storm Lake, the same size town with fewer young people, the high school is three times that large. Three students shared a computer.

The principal made $2.95 per hour. He also worked as a psychologist and homeopathic physician (natural medicines). The assistant principal worked for free. Teachers are paid for the morning, and volunteer in the afternoon. The school is funded through the University of Guadalajara. The city donated the building. The state and federal governments do not fund schools directly.

The people know what the schools are like in Storm Lake. To be enrolled in Iowa is a privilege. Dr. Hernandez, in a visit to The City Beautiful, urged his compadres not to blow the opportunity. He wants them to come back to Santa Rita and build their hometown. Hernandez and others lament the fact that when some children come back home from Iowa, they bring crass materialism with them. The same gang signs in Storm Lake were in Ayotlan County. That culture they can do

without. The gang culture did not sprout in Mexico—
it was imported from California.

Storm Lake already is building Santa Rita. A third
to half the income earned by Latino workers in Storm
Lake goes back to families in Santa Rita. The money
builds houses and streets, buys cars with Buena Vista
County plates parked around the cobblestone streets.
The money from Iowa buys much: a great meal in
Ayotlan costs $2. A big house $5,000. Despite the
exodus, Ayotlan County is growing at about 2% every
three years.

The mayor is something of the county godfather.
(In fact, he is the literal godfather of Guillermo Man-
riquez of Storm Lake.) People lined up outside his office all day, waiting for the chance to ask for a couple
of bucks to buy the day's propane, or help a friend in
need. The mayor also straightens out property disputes where no documents exist.

The people eat. The campesinos (peasant farmers)
grow enough corn on five or six acres to feed themselves. None is left to sell. The cows give milk, the
roosters meat. It is not the poverty that was Cabrini
Green in Chicago, or that exposed in New Orleans,
or the utter desperation of Sudan. It is quiet.

Most people are resigned to their caste. Almost everyone I met had worked in the United States. The
mayor's top aide, Ayotlan County General Secretary
Moises Delgado, washed dishes for a year in Los Angeles before returning to Guadalajara for law school. The
young see the U.S. as their only way out of poverty.

The schoolchildren dream of attending Buena Vista University. Others just give up.

Why did Soto persist in Mexico?

"I had no other option," he told me. "I had to work hard."

But why does not everyone do what he did?

"My father is an enigma," David, Jr., said.

An update from 2017: Mayor Soto died a few years back. Drug cartels dominate Jalisco. There have been cartel executions in the Ayotlan square. Not sure about Lt. Rudy. Our Storm Lake police chief tells me not to go back. My friend Moises moved on to Puerta Vallarta's government in the Jalisco resort town. That's where they nailed the drug kingpin El Chapo. Meth factories compete for floor space with tequila distilleries. Since I visited, more than 100 journalists have been murdered in Mexico, with a dozen killed in 2017, ranking it alongside Syria as the most dangerous place in the world to report the news. The final victim of 2017 was Gumaro Perez, a reporter for a weekly in Veracruz, who at age 35 was shot dead at his son's school Christmas party. That's why they flee for Storm Lake still.

Pork processing in Storm Lake grew like a boar gorging on pecans. Hog confinement buildings seeded by Wall Street investment cropped up in a network so dense all around Storm Lake over the past thirty years that the Iowa Department of Natural Resources actually lost count of them. When our friend

Dan Smith worked his final day at Hygrade they were killing 7,000 hogs a day. Production doubled to 14,000 hogs a day at the IBP plant in the 1980s. Today, they kill 17,000. There were only so many Asians to do one of the hardest jobs in America. The obvious route was to rural Mexico to attract fresh hands.

The company put out the word around 1990 with billboards along the border with Mexico that there were jobs available in Storm Lake. The young Latinos started coming. From San Antonio, East L.A., El Paso, and then deeper into Mexico. Down into Jalisco they heard about Storm Lake and Denison and Sioux City.

Many were being driven to *el norte* in increasing numbers by the North American Free Trade Agreement passed in 1992. Corn from Iowa flooded into Jalisco. In Chiapas, it caused a campesino revolt that was quickly quashed. More quietly, a changing climate was hampering agricultural productivity and cutting corn yields as Jalisco and Chiapas warmed. The campesinos were driven out and up Interstate 35. Climate has always dictated migration and continues to do so.

Life in rural Mexico was never easy. The peasants always looked for something better. In previous generations they migrated through Iowa seasonally, working the sugar beet farms near Mason City in north-central Iowa or the melon farms near Muscatine on the eastern side. When the farm boys disappeared, they briefly showed up around Storm Lake to pull weeds from soybean fields. Roundup Ready beans killed that.

This immigration was different. It was young men coming to work permanently, with or without papers.

They would get in bar fights. They didn't speak English. They crowded into trailer houses. There was violence—a Latino teenager stabbed an adult Peruvian forty-nine times; he had just moved here in his midforties to work at the pack. It was not the first murder, even among the immigrants, but people had a different reaction to this new wave of people. Unlike the Laotian war refugees, we had no perceived moral obligation to them.

What is NAFTA about, other than greater corn exports? Nobody really knew. Iowans didn't see how our exports were obliterating Mexican peasant farmers. Iowans didn't necessarily make the connection between the campesinos leaving the farm suffocating in our imported corn and coming to Iowa to get a job cutting meat.

Then the Maytag plant closed in Newton. The Amana appliance factory left its namesake near the Amish colonies around Iowa City. Electrolux left Webster City. That's what NAFTA started to mean to rural Iowa in the 1990s, still reeling from the gut punch of the farm crisis a decade earlier. First the farms drained out, then the light manufacturing jobs on which many rural towns depended for off-farm income.

There were still jobs, just not as good. IBP was going the color of the rainbow in search of labor near the minimum wage. Many earnest workers couldn't last at those harrying line speeds to make it long enough to get health-care benefits. Patients lined up at the hospital emergency rooms. Clinics were getting stuck with no-pays.

The white guys weren't ascending like they did in the Hygrade days. They were correct to appreciate that something had changed—that the white working-class male might not be better off than his father was. He had been replaced rapidly in the regional economy by brown people who many thought were not assimilating. Spanish was spoken everywhere; signage in three languages was popping up. It was uncomfortable, unsettling.

Police chief Mark Prosser was hired by the mayor in 1990 through a revolving door to the office that saw three chiefs bail town in just a few years. He had led a multijurisdictional homicide task force around East St. Louis, Illinois. Prosser wanted to get away from bodies in bags every day. He was, you could say, an immigrant to Storm Lake seeking something, just like all the others.

Change was washing over Storm Lake. As employment at IBP ramped up, so did petty crimes, including a lot committed by people with foreign names. People didn't quite hear Prosser say that Mexicans and Asians committed crimes in the same ratios that Anglos did. They objected to him sending out press releases about crime. It was getting into the Des Moines paper and the Sioux City TV stations. They wanted to run him out of town. Some of the big shots at the college were on his case. They said it was harder to recruit students.

The subtler message: Don't let people know that Storm Lake is a meatpacking town where people of color now work.

Their obvious concerns were borne out in 1996 when there was a big raid run by the U.S. Border Patrol and the Immigration and Naturalization Service (now ICE, for Immigration and Customs Enforcement) on the IBP plant. They penned up several Asians along with Mexicans out in the tractor-trailer parking lot in the sun. These were our freedom fighters in Laos and Cambodia wearing plastic bracelet handcuffs like hogs awaiting slaughter.

Prosser was disgusted. He said he would never work with the Border Patrol again. He expressed Storm Lake's outrage over their treatment to anyone who would listen. People backed off the chief because they sensed he had a moral foundation and that he couldn't be cowed. They started listening.

By now Storm Lake appeared on the national radar. National anti-immigrant groups were using our town as a foil in a distorted national debate over crime and community disintegration. One of them ran a TV ad about Storm Lake with chained factory gates—the picture was actually from Flint, Michigan. They said Storm Lake was the most awful place.

Everyone was offended: the mayor, the bankers, the bosses and the meat cutters, the car dealers. Storm Lake was getting a black eye from fake news.

People who didn't live in Storm Lake liked Steve King's American exceptionalist message. He had an uncanny way of getting his zany views of history and European (read: white) culture on national television. While we were trying to defend Storm Lake, he was on the steps of Congress, talking up the garbage that was dragging us down.

But Storm Lake wasn't having it. The community was alarmed by the beating it was taking. A diversity task force formed by the chamber of commerce prodded everyone to step up their game. Schools added scores of aides to help English-language learners. The police refused to arrest undocumented immigrants just for being here, which got them some guff. The churches started to advocate for the vulnerable, the children of immigrants who were brought here through no fault of their own. Iowa Central Community College filled night classrooms full of adults yearning to learn English. A charter school was formed that allows students to get a high school diploma and a community college degree in a five-year program popular with immigrants. It hooks them into wanting to pursue further education or skill enhancement. Line workers learn to become machinists and earn more money than they ever could have dreamed about in Guatemala. They love Storm Lake and want to hang around. So do their children, who now are matriculating in college. It is organic growth that happens rarely in rural America.

*The Times* led the discussion by promoting the idea that immigrants are our future, just as the Germans, Swedes, and Irish who broke the prairie were. Every chance we could we found success stories among immigrants to change the tone of the conversation. Yes, there were and are problems with a small community absorbing a score of new cultures—from Mexico to Myanmar. But what was the alternative? If the meatpacking companies could not find labor here, they could always ship the corn to Mexico and raise the hogs there under weaker environmental standards, and worse working conditions, using NAFTA.

And working conditions did improve in meatpacking here through the years in an attempt to reduce costly turnover and workers' compensation costs. Tyson cleaned up its look when it bought IBP, promoted from within (putting people of color in $50,000 per year management jobs), and raised minimum production wages to cover what we expect as a basic living in Iowa, $15.50 per hour to start in 2017. Nothing fancy, but nobody starves.

Those young men kept going back to Jalisco to find a mate. They would return here and start families. They didn't get in as many bar fights. The kids started going to school at Buena Vista University. They want to stay.

Ofelia Valdez, thirty-two, has everything: a baby boy, a loving husband, their own home in Lakeside, a college degree, and a good job. Why is she crying?

"I got lucky because I fell in love," she said as she broke into tears.

Others aren't so lucky.

Her uncle was shot to death for reasons unknown to her, maybe just gangbangers driving by, in Durango, Mexico. Her aunt was hit by a bullet in the shoulder and wishes she could be here. So many others are trapped in the shadows working nights in Storm Lake, Denison, Marshalltown, and Columbus Junction—all over Iowa. They live in fear that the *federales* could show up at any moment.

Ofelia has been there—still is there, in a way. "So many people I know live the way I used to: in the shadows. I don't want to ever forget. Their stories make me think I had it easy," she said.

She had it tough enough. Her aunt came to Storm Lake to work in the turkey plant. They had family here already. Ofelia came to Storm Lake at age fifteen to help her aunt raise her two daughters. Ofelia could learn English and get out of Durango—maybe even get an education. The aunt had found freedom from the terror and poverty she knew in Durango.

Ofelia lived with the three others in the Alta trailer court five miles from Storm Lake, home to so many undocumented Latinos, which the city council thought about condemning. The conditions are dilapidated. Ofelia watched the girls while her aunt worked. Down in Durango you were fortunate to get through eighth grade. Ofelia got the opportunity to enroll at Alta High School. She ate it up.

They enrolled her as a freshman. She could not converse in English. They had her in the arithmetic class but she found the advanced algebra book and showed the teachers she could work those problems. They bumped her up to higher classes as her English quickly came around.

"My biggest desire since I was a little girl was to go to school and learn," she said.

Her own mother had a second-grade education.

"I started acing all my classes. They named me to the National Honor Society and had this ritual and I had no idea what it was."

She graduated from high school with a 3.98 grade point average.

Her aunt was shelling out thousands of dollars per year to her lawyer trying to get permanent residency. Finally the lawyer told her to give it up and move back to Mexico. Ofelia raised her two cousins in that trailer and saw them through high school after their mom got deported. Ofelia worked three jobs.

Ofelia earned an associate's degree at Iowa Central Community College and took a year off to save money to attend Buena Vista University. She could not ask for financial aid because she was undocumented. So she worked seventy hours a week to pay for her education. She received her bachelor's degree in business management in 2008.

Ofelia got a job in human resources at Faith, Hope & Charity, a group home for severely disabled children. She still laid low, always in fear of being deported. President Obama offered her some hope with his program called Deferred Action for Childhood Arrivals (DACA) through executive order, because Congress had refused to take up comprehensive immigration reform.

She realized the risk of signing up: It puts a stamp on your forehead saying "Come and get me" when the executive order expires. Her cousins signed up as well. One of the girls she helped rear earned a degree from BVU and made off for San Antonio. The other got her licensed practical nurse certificate through Iowa Central and works as a nurse in Storm Lake, where there is a critical shortage—especially for Spanish speakers.

Ofelia, meantime, had met Ben Rumbo. He works at Tyson

and moonlights as a fitness trainer. She took up jogging and Ben. They dated for five years and married just over a year ago. The baby was born four months ago. That makes her safe from deportation no matter what anyone does about DACA or the Dream Act, which would give the children of undocumented immigrants safe harbor. It passed the Senate but never the House, where our own Steve King led the charge against it.

Even with her DACA papers she could not return to Mexico. When her sister died in April 2014 Ofelia got special permission to travel from Storm Lake to Mexico for the funeral. But when she got back she was detained in Chicago for four hours while authorities determined whether to let her back in. She was terrified.

The government also sent her a notice that her DACA certification would not be renewed on grounds of "abandonment"—that she had left the U.S. for her sister's funeral. She was engaged to Ben. They got married and she applied for permanent residency by virtue of marriage to a native-born U.S. citizen. That almost got tanked, too. She told Ben he should start thinking about what he would do in Mexico. By now, she had become human resources director at Pro Cooperative, a regional farm-supply operation with more than 150 employees. She still had no papers or any idea of her future.

The baby was due in thirty days.

"I couldn't plan for the baby. I couldn't even buy a crib because what was the point if we were going to get deported?"

They had to prove that they had been dating for five years. She had to provide old Facebook postings to show that she was in love. She obviously was pregnant. She wears a lovely diamond ring. She submitted letters of support from twenty-one friends in town, including Chief Prosser, who got to know her well through her deep involvement at St. Mary's Church. She welled up thinking about the love she felt mixed with the fear.

"For two months I was afraid to check the mail," she said, dreading a deportation order.

Ofelia returned home from the hospital three days after Benjamin Rumbo III was born. In the stack of mail that piled up she found a letter from the government. It was her permanent residency documentation. Finally. It was mailed the day the baby was born.

"The baby came with a blessing," she said.

She has to go back in two years to prove that she is happily married and not somebody trying to plant an anchor baby, as our congressman likes to talk about. After that, her permanent residency is good for ten years until review. She can earn her citizenship in three years, which she has every intention of doing. Ofelia wants to get her mother here, and her cattle-buyer father (fifty-seven years old), and then her siblings. President Trump is angling to end that practice, which he calls chain migration. He claims it supports terrorism.

Ofelia remains cautious about her own status. She is wary until she becomes a citizen. She worries about all her friends and what might happen to them. "I sense things are going to get worse." She is building a family, home, and career. She will not give up on the people living in the shadows or under the terror of violence in Latin America. But she has to take care. She is keeping her powder dry.

Ofelia stood up for Dreamers across the country and became an emblem of them in January 2016. Senator Ted Cruz of Texas was running for president and was having a bro fest with King at King's Pointe Resort (the congressman had nothing to do with the resort or its naming). King is so tough that Chuck Norris wears Steve King pajamas, Cruz claimed. He opened it up for questions from the crowd.

A Latina voice came from the back. What would the senator do about the Dreamers in our midst? She was dark and pretty and confident. It was Ofelia.

"You were a product of a decision that brought you here illegally," Cruz told Valdez. "You were violating the laws and the Constitution . . . and there are tragedies when people break the laws, but I can tell you the laws of every country on Earth. If I emigrate to England or Germany or China or Mexico, they will deport me. There's no reason why U.S. law should have less perspective than every other country on Earth."

Cruz said he would deport the likes of her, and that doing so would be his first order of business.

That story went around the world—this young woman standing up in the shadows of a Republican, white crowd. She met weekly with about thirty Dreamers who shared their anxieties in sort of a support group. She spoke for them. She became something of a heroine for Dreamers everywhere, not that she sought it. She was not looking for a bus ticket out.

"You listen to their stories and you want to give everything you have to them. They want to be police officers or social workers or teachers. They want to be someone. They want to be here," she said.

Cruz looked so presidential, so constitutional, so in command, depending on your glasses. One conservative blog called him "masterful" in his response.

Some claim Ofelia was a plant by the Democrats. King knew better, because she had confronted him before. Ofelia denies being paid by anyone. She said it was a spur-of-the-moment thing, to speak out about all the sadness of her peers. Ofelia keeps speaking out, and she is the perfect voice: humble, relaxed, always ever so polite, cheery, perfectly composed.

In June 2016, the U.S. Supreme Court ruled in favor of governors who sued the Obama administration, arguing that it did not have the authority to create the DACA program. Trump said he would leave the Dreamers alone. Then he said he wouldn't. Steve King howls about amnesty. So does Senator Grassley, Republican chairman of the Senate Judiciary Committee. Latinos worry. This limbo has grown mold over two decades.

"I remember two years ago, when people were talking about working, buying homes, coming out of the shadows," Valdez said at the time of the Supreme Court ruling and Trump's seesaw over the status of Dreamers through the first year of his presidency. "Now we're sad more than anything."

Amid all this the sanctuary city claim arises, mainly from outside media that continue to press the question. School superintendent Carl Turner said he will not deny service to any student, and he does not ask about immigration papers. Chief Prosser serves on a law enforcement task force through the National Immigration Forum, a center-right group, to argue for comprehensive reform. He has met with House Speaker Paul Ryan, whom Prosser thinks sympathizes but is paralyzed by the base, led by King.

Bringing immigrants out of the shadows builds trust in the community. They are not afraid of the Storm Lake police. They cooperate. But since Trump's election, Prosser has noticed that they are going underground. Ofelia confirms it. We can't talk to them because they aren't really here. The churches offer quiet support. You could call it a sanctuary. But officials insist it is not. It is just a community of people trying to support one another. Latinos feel it. They know who their friends are. They stay put and nervous but they trust Storm Lake.

The Iowa Supreme Court ruled in 2016 that police shall not arrest undocumented immigrants for working under false documents. A conflict has been set up between state and federal authorities over whether police may round up immigrants. Prosser continues to follow the state court direction pending further orders from above.

Prosser has become a national spokesman on policing diverse rural communities. He speaks to police and school groups about how to work with an undocumented and wary population. Prosser has the support of the city council. The school district, with more than 130 teacher aides helping immigrants, is a model for the Midwest in English immersion with support. Buena Vista University holds big Latino festivals hoping to attract families and loyalty. They know who their future Beavers are. The new college president, Josh Merchant, wants to focus on delivering education to immigrants in rural settings. Buena Vista already operates a network of satellite campuses at community colleges around the state, offering bachelor's degrees in high-demand areas like teaching and business. BVU is offering full-ride scholarships to first-generation collegians from the county.

Leading the Fourth of July Star Spangled Spectacular Big Parade is the Parade of Nations—people dress and group according to ethnic heritage and fly the flag of the Czech Republic, or El Salvador, or wherever they are from. The Sudanese and Lao women are especially striking in their colorful full-length dresses and often elaborate headgear. Mexican horses dance along Lakeshore

Drive. You feast on pupusas, egg rolls, and pork burgers—you name it, we eat it here, and a complete meal costs four dollars.

No place has worked harder to make it work. Because of all that, Ofelia never wants to leave.

After they were married her husband suggested that she drop the name Valdez. When you Google "Ofelia Valdez," all the hits come up as "undocumented immigrant" or "Dreamer." Wouldn't it be better to create that new identity in a new life?

"Undocumented is my identity. This is who I am. I am not going to sit and watch this happen. So much needs to be done. We are not there yet. We need to build a foundation among us, the Dreamers, the younger people. The future? We're building a foundation now. And it's going to look bright."

No wall could keep Ofelia Rumbo Valdez from pursuing her dream. She won't fully catch it until the dreams of those who have been deferred are made real and permanent. Courage overcomes fear in time.

# CHAPTER 12

# Saving a Prairie Pothole

The primary reason anyone—Ofelia Valdez or Inkpaduta before her—stayed here was not for the mosquitoes or the blizzards or even the tall grass but for the lake. What is Storm Lake without it? Sure enough, we were losing the prairie pothole to our industrious enterprise of agriculture.

It was getting so shallow in the early 1990s that docks couldn't reach the water. Boats couldn't get in, but soil did. Hundreds of tons would wash in after a three-inch rain. Corn stalks swam with the crappies, the few left when their spawning beds were suffocated from light by muddy-brown turbidity.

The easiest way to drain the sloughs around the lake so the land could be exposed for farming was to dig a drainage ditch, which they named Powell Creek, leading southeast into Little Storm Lake, a marsh complex connected to big Storm Lake on its western edge. As the mud roiled in, the sixteen-feet-deep little lake decreased to a depth of three feet in a wet year. It developed a hard cake of mud so the next big rain would roll the farm ground right into the big lake. Borings showed the big lake bottom was twenty-six feet deep, but the mud was piled seventeen feet deep atop the blue clay.

The Storm Lake soil conservationist for the Natural Resources Conservation Service (NRCS), Jeff Kestel, could see in the early 1990s what was happening. He drafted a grant proposal that came across Senator Tom Harkin's desk. Harkin saw to it that the first watershed protection program in northwest Iowa was started through USDA funding. He was chairman of the Senate Agriculture Committee and a senior member of the Senate Appropriations Committee.

Kestel and his helpers and successors were able to convince landowners holding about 80 percent of the acreage in the lake's watershed to use some sort of conservation practice on their land to protect the lake—terraces, buffer strips along Powell Creek, infield bioreactors to filter water, silt-catching basins, and the like. For the first time, we were attempting to re-create some of the protection that the hand of nature drew with the glaciers. Farmers liked it. Landowners liked it. The Ballou family, who owned Security Trust & Savings Bank in Storm Lake, quit farming and grazing their land near Powell Creek and put it into a wildlife reserve. Everyone started pitching in. The ball was picking up circumference. We were saving our lake.

*The Times* heaped praise on Harkin for singling out Storm Lake. Local Republicans asked why we were fawning so much over the only Democrat they could never beat. Harkin remembered us. He started talking about dredging a century's worth of silt from the lake and seeing if we could revive the Clean Water Act funding from the 1970s that was abandoned in the Reagan

Revolution. He couldn't. But we started talking about using state and other sources of federal funding.

"This was the poor man's paradise when I was a kid," Harkin told me. The senator grew up near Des Moines. They couldn't afford much for a vacation. When they did, they went to Lake Darling near Des Moines for a day or Storm Lake for a weekend. The Cobblestone Ballroom swung on the east shore with the sounds of Glenn Miller and Lawrence Welk, and an amusement park called Casino Beach on the west shore housed working-class visitors in tiny fishing shacks.

Water quality steadily deteriorated. Clear water turned brown and green. They quit coming to Casino Beach, and to the Bible camp next door. The lake got so shallow you could nearly walk across it. The visitors quit visiting, but Storm Lake didn't seem to care. We had our own thing going. It was our lake to enjoy, even if it was slowly being choked by farmland. A few fishermen would float by on a Saturday morning, a half dozen boats might pull skiers on a Sunday afternoon.

There was a little zoo and amusement park behind the Cobblestone Ballroom, owned by Junior Lawrence. Next door Junior's brother operated Shorty's Boathouse and Marina, where you could rent a rowboat or get a twelve-pack of beer if you left the money outside at just the right time, Sunday or not.

We had our prosperous farmers, our happy meatpackers, and our little university. It was a salesman's town, dead center in the northwest quarter of the state. A pleasant place with wide, shady streets where a boy could play unsupervised along the lake all day until the streetlights came on. Where you could still catch sixty bullheads in an hour, but that was about it. Where the town's most obviously insane person could ride his bike down the middle of Lake Avenue and holler and wave at the shoppers passing by with vulgar epithets.

It was a free and easy place. Of course, it was nothing without the lake.

Governor Nelson Kraschel knew it in 1938. He was a Democrat from rural Harlan, south of Storm Lake, near Omaha. Kraschel succeeded Democratic governor Clyde Herring, who started Storm Lake's first dredging project to remove decades of silt from the lake. The spoil was used to fill in wetlands along the east side of the lake abutting the Cobblestone. The dredging was enormously popular, and Kraschel promised to develop a state park where the dredge spoil was laid. The park was outlined in state deeds, but it was never developed after Kraschel lost the next election to Republican George Wilson.

Harold Walter Siebens never forgot about the lake. He grew up here hanging around his grandfather's mercantile store downtown, and by the lake. The family went off to St. Louis, where he was kicked out of military school, and he took over his father's sporting goods business and moved back to Storm Lake. When he took a hunting vacation to Alaska he discovered he could make a fortune in Canadian oil wildcatting. He never came back. But he always wanted to do something for the lake. His buddy Harry Schaller, the banker, told him there was nothing going with the lake at the moment. So Siebens wondered what he could do for the town. Schaller suggested the college, even though Siebens didn't put that much stock in book learning—he was suspicious of BVC's advertised "liberal arts" education because he feared it could create leftists. He was assured that BVC was not a socialist outpost. Siebens saw education as a shortcut to making money, so therein it had value. In 1979 he sold Dome Petroleum for $350 million and laid $18 million on Buena Vista College. It saved the college, which historically trained teachers who couldn't give that much back. Later on, an anonymous donor dropped $500,000 into the lake-dredging account. We know who it was. There is a little bronze statue of the fishing boy just south of the BVU football field. Brother John wrote Siebens's obituary for the *New York Times* while a public relations Beaver.

All the talk about lake dredging, with some nudging from Harkin, led the Iowa Department of Natural Resources to announce a limited dredging of Storm Lake's west side in 1992. It would give game fish like walleyes a hole to hide in from winter fish kills in shallow years.

Storm Lake, led by *The Times,* asked for more. We wanted a complete dredging of the lake. IDNR said that was impractical.

State senator Mary Lou Freeman (R–Storm Lake) invited IDNR director Jeff Vonk to take a bus tour around the lake to see for himself how things could be done. Everyone was afraid of IDNR and resentful, because the agency treated us like an ugly duckling. Nobody wanted to sit next to Vonk on the bus. So I did.

I asked him when the state would dredge the entire lake.

He responded: "When will you folks show some initiative and get everyone behind it?"

Touché. We had met an honest broker. And I made a friend.

We went fishing. We went hunting. I introduced him to farmers to talk about how agriculture and the environment could work in harmony. Previously, Vonk worked as a federal soil conservationist, so he understood how to talk to a farmer without threatening him. We were getting somewhere.

I watched him drink with my Republican friend Gary Lalone,

who made a minor fortune selling prefaded tight blue jeans to teenagers. Lalone pumped gas to work his way through Buena Vista College. He joined a publicly traded clothing company, Buckle, on the ground floor with stores across the Great Plains and Upper Midwest. He made millions as vice president of sales, jetting across the country to refit a store in the shank of the evening. He had enough of eleven p.m. steaks and hotels, and quit for his home on the lakeshore, where three young children were grateful.

Lalone was bored and took over the meandering lake-dredging committee, full of good intentions and short on gumption. He put the same energy into the Save the Lake campaign as he did peddling denim with holes in it.

Lalone led an effort to raise $1.4 million privately from local donors in about six months. Storm Lake had never seen the like. City administrator John Call pledged the city crew to run a dredge over two shifts during the ice-free season. Buena Vista County agreed to purchase the dredge, the city of Lakeside (adjacent to Storm Lake and created to protect the Cobblestone Ballroom's clandestine activities from the vice hawks) threw in its local-option sales tax funds, and Harkin came through with a supplemental federal funding.

Diane Hamilton, grand dame of local Democrats and the daughter-in-law of lake champion Bones Hamilton, was hosting lake fund-raisers and writing big checks to keep politicians interested. Vonk agreed to put roughly $1 million per year of state funds into lake restoration.

We had Republican state legislators, Republican county supervisors, Democratic governor Vilsack, Harkin, farmers, fishermen, bankers, lawyers, meat cutters, and teachers all rowing in the same direction. *The Storm Lake Times* provided the rudder.

The dredge pulled 700,000 cubic yards of mud from the lake every year and dumped it in huge berms designed to hold up to 9 million cubic yards of spoil. We have filled two of them. And there's still a dozen feet of mud on the bottom of the lake.

Vonk took our story wherever he went: A small town pulled together and brought everyone along to prod the state into action. You can change the world when you get the people lined up—that was his message.

Vonk had been talking up the idea of destination parks around the state that would merge natural and recreational amenities. It appeared to be a natural next step from lake restoration. A bipartisan effort between Governor Vilsack and Republican legislative leaders created the Vision Iowa Program to create community attractions because Iowa has no mountains or ocean. It used funds from gambling revenues and a tobacco lawsuit settlement to issue bonds designed to revitalize communities.

Governor Vilsack had appointed Michael Gartner, my mentor from our days in Ames and Algona, as chairman of the Vision Iowa Board. The stars were aligned, and we were in the middle of them.

I called Gartner and said: "We need ten million dollars from the Vision Iowa Board to build a waterpark resort along the lakeshore where some horseshoe pits and a flower garden were."

He said: "Will eight million dollars do?"

I said: "Yes." The result was a $40 million hotel resort with indoor and outdoor waterparks fueled by sales taxes, state investment, and profit from the city-owned enterprise. Finally, the City Beautiful is attracting tourists who were driven away during the Great Depression. Motel stays are up all over. Great restaurants thrive representing all the cultures that flourish here, from Thai to Mexican to cheeseburger. The north lakeshore is festive in the summer as throngs line the ladders up the water-park slides.

Old townies still grouse that it is too expensive. That fifty-year-old swimming pool and fountain were plenty good for twenty-five cents.

S torm Lake continued to pump mud from the lake until it shut down on September 1, 2017. Lalone was getting tired of it. So was the city. And so was IDNR, which would like to devote some of those millions to more than one hundred other impaired lakes in Iowa. We are relieved to report that 7 million cubic yards of mud have been removed to two distant spoil sites through trenched pipes from the lake across the fields. It cannot be sustained long enough to get it all sucked out.

We dredged Storm Lake in the 1930s. We dredged it again in the 1960s and created Frank Starr Park by infilling a patch on the west side of the lake with the dredge spoil. In so doing, we smothered a lot of weeds and reeds that are important to fish diversity and overall aquatic health. Cleaning up a mess sometimes cannot restore you to the original, but it was the best we could do some fifty years ago.

This was the best we could do by our generation. Iowa devotes a paltry $9 million per year to lake protection and restoration. Storm Lake is the reason that fund was created. We argued for it and got it. Before that, it was nothing for our lakes. We take baby steps toward progress, but we need to take strides.

We nearly killed this lake and we have an obligation to save it.

Because so many lakes await funds that might slow their death spiral, one could say that we were fortunate to get ours. That's the zero-sum game it has become. But when they are closing state parks and eliminating the state geologist (who studies drinking water aquifers), Storm Lake is expected to count its lucky stars. We accept it and move on.

I suppose that the lake will be dredged in another forty or fifty years, unless we stop the mudflows. We have slowed them, but nature seems to have a way to lay asunder our best-engineered plans. But at least now you can see a couple of feet deep in the lake water, not a couple of inches, as it was when I was a kid wading for carp in the shallows. It is one of the top walleye fishing lakes in the Midwest because of a multifaceted partnership among levels of government, and all classes of people, to save the lake. When the wind blows over the water now, it creates whitecaps that are, for the first time in my life, white. I walk along the lake and see clear water and am awed.

# CHAPTER 13

# A Challenge to Industrial Agriculture

We count on farmers to voluntarily protect our lake and rivers from pollution. As it stands, the lake is better off because a cash-strong family farm operation controls more acres near it. The large family farm corporation is a leader in conservation—it can afford to conserve. You want to root for the cash-strapped farmer who would have liked to rent that ground. But who is the better steward, and who can be more resilient in the face of enormous challenges ahead? The way it is set up, we depend on noblesse oblige.

A 155-acre farm near the Storm Lake airport, not far from the lake, sold in 2016 for $12,000 per acre to a Nebraska family with marital ties to a family that works thousands of acres around Storm Lake. That land would have fetched $1,600 per acre in 1990. The sale occurred amid a stream of four consecutive losing years for Iowa farmers. The older farmers still can bid a premium for land because they're sitting on cash from when prices were high ten years ago. The ones locked out of the land auctions are the 20 percent of younger farmers who are under tremendous financial stress, according to Iowa State University research. Banks are not making loans on that steep a price. They get nervous at $10,000. It goes to show that land is flowing every year into stronger hands that can pay cash.

The wrench of efficiency turns and squeezes and turns. Every year, farms grow larger and people fewer.

Everything about agriculture boils down to yield and price. How much corn will the land yield? What is the price of corn this morning? Those are two of the daily topics of conversation in rural Iowa, along with the weather and who died to leave a farm that might come up for auction. Crop yields and commodity prices, plus weather and soil type, are big factors that determine how much land is worth. Farmland value is the foundation of the state's wealth, as we learned during the implosion of the farm crisis.

Commodity markets are volatile. A drought in Brazil can send soybean prices wild in a week. Mind-boggling corn yield increases through genetic engineering—30 percent over the past fifteen years—combined with low energy prices caused corn prices to drop in half since 2009. The one thing the farmer believes he can control is yield—he cannot control the weather or the markets in Chicago's grain-trading pits, but he always shoots for the moon on yield when he makes his final seed and chemical purchases during the girls' state basketball tournament in March.

The farmer who paid cash for his land, or has little debt against it, can make money almost any year if he doesn't have a banker on the payroll. Those are the older, larger operators. They can afford to leave alone that grass strip next to Powell Creek that wends to the lake through their farm. They can put in a bioswale to filter field runoff to the river, expecting no real reward except in heaven. But the farmer who rents land and is losing needs to plant through the river to make it, or so he thinks.

When my neighbor across the street, Steve Drey, was still a plowboy in 1980, he thought 125 bushels per acre were okay and 150 bushels of corn were a bin buster. If you can't hit 200 bushels per acre with your corn yield now, you had better figure out a new occupation in town. Every few years even I could make money at farming during price bubbles such as we saw during the 2008 ethanol boom in consumption. But prices always fall back as growers here and in Brazil rip up more fallow acres to ride those price crests. We always overproduce. It is the chronic problem of the Iowa farmer. Even the most efficient corn grower has to tumble the dice just right to scoop up a profit in the average year. Every year he thinks he will roll sevens.

There is no margin for error. You fertilize or perish. So you fertilize. You put fertilizer on every available acre, because rent is rent. You buy crop insurance to set yourself a bottom. You drain that flat ground or you perish. You lay tile, and you plant up to the riverbank. We are applying five times more fertilizer than we were fifty years ago. We're losing more than a third of that nitrogen fertilizer we apply by its leaching out to the drainage tiles. (Nitrogen also happens to be as problematic a greenhouse gas as carbon dioxide in terms of climate change. Chemical agriculture is compounding global warming.)

Nature left us only so much glacial till. Competition to control that rich land is intense. As bigger farms competed for fewer available acres, cash rents paid by farmers to landlords tripled around 2008. The cost of buying land shot up tenfold from 1992 to 2012. Land prices have stabilized for now thanks primarily to crop insurance, which provides a baseline to farm income when prices or yields tank. To protect the land's market value, owners lay corrugated plastic drainage tiles forty feet apart now. They were eighty feet apart a decade ago. The tile installers have stayed busy right along.

"You got everything you need out here, if you can only see it," my father-in-law reminds me every year. You do if that is how you want to play it. But who does anymore?

The ones farming 1,200 to 2,000 or 5,000 acres today were reared on farms of 500 acres or fewer with cattle and hogs. All of them were. Most raised chickens. Some had dairy cows. Not today. They are now asset managers. They manage grain inventories, interest rates, custom harvest and chemical applications, cash flows, and machinery maintenance. They don't have time to chase calves in March around an 80-acre pasture. They did before the farm crisis. Farms were smaller then, and internally diversified.

When the kids from Early, twelve miles south, got off the school bus you knew they were here. That smell of livestock would gently waft momentarily. You can't get the aroma off you when you have been around hogs just before the bus arrives. Back then it smelled like money.

None of those kids was rich. But they had everything they needed. They knew how to work.

But this land became too valuable for grazing and diversity. You grow corn and soybeans, that's all there is to it. You are a specialist. You pack more corn plants into an acre. You substitute chemical herbicides for human labor of pulling weeds; you don't need those farm kids to walk beans anymore. A thirty-five-year-old farmer has heard of people pulling weeds by hand, but he has never done it. He might yet, as the weeds are figuring out the herbicides and growing resistant to the omnipresent Roundup patented by Monsanto. The life cycle of silver bullets like Roundup lasts twenty to thirty years, until the chemist has to roll out a new silver bullet.

"You know, I think we were all better off when we were growing 125-bushel corn on 320-acre farms," said my neighbor Steve, one of those Early farm boys who had to move to town and take a job as a parts man at the tractor store. He figures on working until he is eighty because he wasn't sharp enough to get a government job and quit at fifty-eight.

His brother Dean farms the family place. One of Steve's classmates who used to be a big strapper has shrunk into the appearance of a man broken by farm chemicals chasing bumper corn yields. His shoulders are hunched over. He has to sit down. He has farmer's lung from too much sniffing around anhydrous ammonia, herbicide, and hog houses. He had to quit farming, our friend. He had to rent out the land to a cousin farming a thousand acres or more.

This great flat land from Storm Lake to Clear Lake was set up to be the tall corn paradise. Drainage systems were installed long ago, and improved upon year after year. They became ever more efficient at removing water from the land and delivering it to the river. And that became even more important after about 1980, as rainfall started to increase and become more extreme. You could get a five-inch rain and think, "That was something," when that amounted to a five-hundred-year flood fifty years ago.

It was climate change in the making, although we did not recognize it as such. It just seemed wetter. And wilder.

Installing drainage tiles is cheap enough insurance to a yield, because the soil here is so gummy—that black, thick glacial till—that my father-in-law, Ernie Gales, has never been droughted out in seventy years. Drowned out, but never droughted out. For the low areas Ernie could use drainage tiles. The water seeps through the soil because "corn doesn't like wet feet" and into the tile lines buried below. The tile lines deliver the fertilizer-rich water to drainage ditches, which feed into rivers and lakes.

In the spring and the fall, when the crop uptake is slow and the fertilizer load rich, the nutrients leach to the drainage tiles and into the rivers. The problem is made worse by the few farmers who plow into the drainage ditches, into the riverbanks, and even plant crops on state-owned lake banks. Those violations of boundaries that never go punished allow incalculable amounts of soil to flow through to the Gulf of Mexico, where the Mississippi steadily builds its mouth with Iowa and Illinois corn ground.

We knew from the earliest days of *The Storm Lake Times* that our area was the hottest spot for nutrient loads into the Raccoon River. We reported on it for twenty-five years. At first the agrichemical complex blamed the municipal sewer plants in Storm Lake and Sac City twenty miles downstream. We were able to prove, using outflow monitoring by the Iowa Department of Natural Resources, that sewage treatment systems were not the problem—the effluent after treatment was perfectly clean. Sitting along Buffalo Ridge not far from the Raccoon are what were once referred to as the world's largest anhydrous ammonia tanks to give nitrogen to the land, the river, and the corn. Two of them sit side by side. "You go down to the Dolly Parton tanks and take a left on the blacktop to get to Nemaha," the old boys will tell you. They know what is inside those tanks and where it goes and how, and where it ends up. Anhydrous ammonia is the mother's milk of corn.

Agri-industry had to own up to the aftereffects of consolidation of farm activities. But that didn't come easily.

M y pressman friend Jim Robinson worked to fish. He thinks about fishing when it is too hot to fish. It is never too cold to fish. Jim sits on a bucket when it's ten below with his back to the twenty-five-miles-per-hour wind out of the west and vents his anger at the dark depths. He also is a photographer. He says he doesn't like most people that much—they screw everything up by starting religions and wars—so he shoots pictures of lakes.

Jim and I set out around northwest Iowa to survey all the prairie pothole lakes dotted throughout the Upper Des Moines region. Most were filling in quickly from soil erosion that has picked up its pace since 1980 because of climate change—more turbulent storms that wash over even the flat ground and spill it down the waterways to the gulf. We photographed soybean stubble on the banks of Pickerel Lake near the headwaters of the Raccoon River. We photographed lakes being converted to filtering devices for the corn-soybean flotsam. We started asking questions of agronomists and farmers, but interviews got canceled. Phone calls were not returned. They knew what we were up to. I could not nail down what was happening without further assistance, which I was not getting. We had no story.

But I had the photos. I took them to the annual meeting of the Iowa Environmental Council in 2013. I showed them how we were filling up and destroying what God designed as lakes. The state, despite all its agricultural bounty, said it could not afford to put them back as lakes or stop their infilling. We must adopt them to our contemporary use as filtering cesspools and sediment dumps. It's called a shallow lake management strategy, developed in Minnesota, where farm fields filled in potholes.

The chief executive officer of the Des Moines Water Works, Bill Stowe, sat next to me at the conference table.

"We're going to sue your county and a few others," Stowe told me.

He explained that northern Iowa counties were polluting the Raccoon River so badly that he could barely clean it up fast enough to satisfy thirsty capital denizens. The waterworks would have to pour about $100 million into a new nitrate-removal facility—and DMWW already operated the largest such system in the world. It uses salt to remove nitrate from the water. The resulting salty sludge is too toxic to apply to soil, so it is dumped back into the Raccoon River downstream from Des Moines, where someone in New Orleans can deal with it. Which they don't, as it happens. That sludge from Des Moines, plus all the nitrate and phosphorous flowing through from elsewhere in the Midwest, ends up in the Gulf of Mexico, creating a dead zone of oxygen deprivation that suffocates aquatic life. The hypoxia (oxygen-deprived) zone is the size of the state of New Jersey and growing. We are destroying the fishing industry so we can grow more corn.

So we published a story with a huge, studhorse bold headline in two decks across the front page, screaming that we would be sued over agriculture. Nobody paid it heed. Nobody thought that Bill Stowe, that guy with the curly long gray hair who was built like a lumberjack and dressed like one, would actually sue. They all read him as a bluffer.

Then, in 2015, he sued.

People started to pay attention. The news flew around the wires. Governor Terry Branstad said that urban Iowa had just declared war on rural Iowa. The Iowa Farm Bureau condemned Stowe and the waterworks and ran ads demonizing him. A state senator from Hull in extreme (in more ways than one) northwest Iowa called on all rural patriots to boycott the shopping malls in Des Moines. Well, resistance does have its limits.

Storm Lake became ground zero in the battle for the right to fertilize and raise crops on a petrochemical base without restraint.

DMWW sued the drainage districts as the agents of the pollution because they own and operate the pipes. Drainage districts are creations of state law, governed by the county board of supervisors, with the sole authority to install systems to get rid of surface water "in the interest of public health." They were not empowered under state law to regulate how those systems operate, other than to keep them clear of obstruction. If farmers petition for a drainage improvement in sufficient number, the county supervisors have no choice but to follow that command and improve it. And they did expand the system by about a third since 1980.

The waterworks lawsuit was actually a direct result of climate change impacts already appreciated for thirty-five years.

The waterworks argued that under the 1972 Clean Water Act drainage districts should be regulated as "point sources" of pollution, as municipal sewer pipes are. Agriculture always has been considered a nonpoint polluter exempt from the Clean Water Act permit prescriptions. Obviously, you cannot sue every land tiller for the sins of one. Hence nonpoint, disparate pollution, which is hard to define because there is no particular point source. Stowe thought he found the point in the drainage tile. The counties, of course, disagreed. And because this was a pollution lawsuit, the defendant counties—Buena Vista, Calhoun, and Sac, all contiguous—had no insurance. They had no way to cover their defense costs.

My general assignment reporter son, Tom, asked the Buena Vista County supervisors: How do you intend to pay your attorneys? Through property taxes? Assessments on the farmers in the drainage district? We knew there would be blockbuster bills coming.

"We don't know," they told us at first.

We asked again a few weeks later to give them time to find out.

"Our friends will take care of us."

Which friends?

"Can't say for sure."

That's a plan? Shouldn't they talk about a settlement with that hippie lumberjack? After all, everyone has been admitting for a couple of years now that Big Ag's hands are not clean on this deal. Even Governor Branstad would acknowledge it under duress.

Thus began our two-year editorial campaign to get answers to questions nobody wanted to answer. Not, at least, for us.

## THEY DON'T KNOW
### AN EDITORIAL
*July 1, 2016*

You have to wonder if Buena Vista County supervisors ever have a twinge of regret or shame when they cash a paycheck. Because, to hear them tell it, they don't know who is paying for their awfully expensive defense of a lawsuit filed by the Des Moines Water Works. About $1 million in invoices were paid to Des Moines and Washington, DC, law firms until March, and the supervisors claim not to know who gave them the money. That's stunning. The Agribusiness Association of Iowa organized a fund that paid those bills, but it reportedly refuses to tell the counties who the donors were. The supervisors believe that they cannot look a gift horse in the mouth to see who planted the bit.

We have just learned that the supervisors, not AAI [Agribusiness Association of Iowa], severed their relationship in April because we wanted to know who those donors were. Monsanto and Koch Fertilizer executives met with AAI when the fund was formed. Who else chipped in? AAI won't say. Des Moines lawyer Doug Gross, who designed the secret fund, won't respond to our questions. The supervisors are too timid to ask in an effective way. They appear to believe that this is a moot point since the relationship was severed over transparency issues. We believe it is a continuing offense against the Iowa Public Records Law and precedent set by the Iowa Supreme Court. The supervisors are fully aware of our opinion—they paid lawyers hundreds of dollars an hour to read our editorials on the matter as if they were court briefs, using funds raised from secret donors.

Yet they do not answer the basic question, claiming ignorance.

We recently asked how much the Belin Law Firm has billed since the relationship was severed with AAI and Doug Gross. Supervisors told us they didn't know. We asked who is paying the bills. Supervisors said they didn't know. This is the company line. Eventually, BV County Drainage Attorney Gary Armstrong informed us that Belin has piled up about $300,000 in legal fees since March that remain unpaid until funds appear. This is at least a $100,000 liability to Buena Vista County, as it presumably will share that tab with Calhoun and Sac counties—but we actually do not know, so secret the public officials are.

We have asked, repeatedly over months, how the county will cover its legal bills. The supervisors say they aren't sure. They say they hope their "friends" still step forward. What sort of friend would leave you hanging with $300,000 in unpaid bills because they covet their anonymity?

Any CEO would be fired with that sort of response.

Of course it all beggars credulity. They don't know who is paying their bills? They don't know how they will be paid? They don't know what the status is of negotiations with AAI to resume their funding scheme?

They should know.

Down to the penny and the period.

Either the supervisors are ignorant or coy. Neither serves the public interest.

The supervisors are paid just shy of $30,000 a year. They are paid to know the basics of who is paying for what in county government. It's not that hard.

The supervisors will say, when they choose to speak, that this is all in the hands of competent lawyers so none of us needs to worry. Including the supervisors. They can fight on with this lawsuit without having any clue what they are doing, or who is actually pulling the strings, while encumbering the county potentially with huge unpaid legal bills or, worse, hundreds of millions of dollars in liabilities from a federal district court judge's ruling next year.

That's what is at stake here.

Millions upon millions in BV County taxpayer liability.

It offends the supervisors that we have suggested the county should pursue settlement talks with the Des Moines Water Works to avoid a mega-judgment. Agri-industry and the state's political leaders acknowledge that we have a big problem with stray nutrients finding their way to the rivers, and ultimately the dying Gulf of Mexico. So let's get about solving that problem through a settlement endorsed by the state's political leadership who can make something happen.

The people who paid the bills for Buena Vista County do not believe in settling. The Kochs and Monsanto have too much at stake to leave it to the people of Iowa to decide how to manage agriculture and a clean environment in a sustainable way that allows farmers to prosper.

The supervisors can blithely tag along for the war, savoring their victory at the top of the hill, so long as they have no skin in the fight. They don't have to pay attention to who is paying the bills, setting the terms for the debate, whispering in the lawyers' ears about what to do and how to do it.

They can just shrug and say, "Beats me."

And then cash that paycheck. You could call that malfeasance.

That editorial was among our dozens of salvos in what became a two-year argument for transparency in how the lawsuit was administered.

Buena Vista County has its own drainage attorney who serves the board of supervisors: Gary Armstrong of the Mack Law Firm in Storm Lake. He bills by the hour. It also has a county attorney: Dave Patton, a Republican, who is paid an annual salary. Gary Armstrong argued that drainage districts had almost no legal authority. Patton felt the same way. But the supervisors wanted to bring in some big guns, from Des Moines and Washington, DC.

That's the way agribusiness wanted to control the litigation. They were falling all over the supervisors trying to shape the lawsuit defense. The ag supply chain was at risk.

Mess with one link and you break the whole chain. Restrict acreage and you lose sales of seed and chemicals, and you cause the price of ethanol in relation to oil to increase. Storm Lake has been surrounded by corn distilleries that gobble up a third of the crop annually. The rest is fed to hogs that are booked on contract so producer profits narrow when corn prices rise. Farmers and landowners are woven into that supply chain in a ritual of efficiency: fertilize; spray herbicides and pesticides; plant corn genetically designed to resist drought or rootworms; spray Roundup over beans that are resistant to it and, increasingly, weeds that have adapted to resist it. Feed crops to hogs in Iowa that are contracted in advance with the packing company and cattle in massive feedlots in the southern Great Plains. Ship some of the corn and raw pork to Mexico for further processing, and then ship the high-end finished product to Japan, while competing with Brazil. Ship Mexicans to Storm Lake to slaughter the hogs after the Anglos drain out, and ship our soil down to the gulf. It is the cycle of agribusiness.

What was at stake was not so much a way of life but a way of doing business more sacred than the life of the community, which is: We know we are dying from pollution but we accept it as a cost of doing business. We live with fouled water because that's how the markets organize our lives. The cigarettes will kill me but I choose them. The atrazine on that corn ground will kill you, too, and I suppose we all choose it because it looks like that's where the money is these days. You go with the money if you want to run with the big dogs.

The Farm Bureau wanted in. The Iowa Drainage District Association wanted in. The Iowa Corn Growers and the Iowa Soybean Association wanted in. And the Agribusiness Association of Iowa, advised by Governor Branstad's former chief of staff, Doug Gross, an attorney in Des Moines, wanted in. AAI solicited Monsanto and Koch Fertilizer during meetings in the summer of 2015 in Des Moines to lead the fund-raising drive for the defense of agriculture. But they refused to acknowledge it to us. We were the mosquito on the elephant's behind.

The supervisors were furious with *The Times* for questioning their judgment, and for calling on the counties and the waterworks to seek a mediated settlement. During phone calls with Stowe and county attorney Patton, I encouraged them to at least talk to each other—stepping beyond the bounds of journalistic neutrality. Stowe and Patton agreed to meet in Fort Dodge on a

Sunday afternoon and see where it would lead. Patton told the supervisors, and they ordered him to cancel the meeting.

"If Art Cullen says something, we'll do the opposite," said board of supervisors chairman Dale Arends (R-Newell), a Farm Bureau man through and through.

The county attorney knew where he was not welcome. He let the board run off with the starched shirts charging $450 per hour. They would meet behind closed doors every Tuesday without him. The public was kept in the dark.

We asked the Iowa Freedom of Information Council to help. Executive director Randy Evans, that former state editor at the *Des Moines Register* to whom I had submitted my anonymous news briefs as a young outstate stringer, wrote letters of warning to the counties that they violated Iowa law by hiding the donor list and their terms of engagement with the outside law firms. We waited for a response. Evans emailed on April 4, 2016, to tell us that he was driving up to Storm Lake from Des Moines with about three hundred pages of attorney billing records he had received from the three counties. It was a Monday. He would be there by eleven a.m. We had to have the story done the next morning.

Randy rolled in and sorted through the heavily redacted records with son Tom. Anything of substance was blacked out. Such as: What terms did the counties agree to in return for getting the secret money? And: Who gave the money? But it told us how much the counties racked up in billings: $1.4 million.

And it confirmed that the slush fund existed.

Over the spring and summer of 2016 it became clear that the counties agreed with our legal position: that if the county accepts funds from an outside source it must be in a public record. But the counties were in a pickle: They agreed to keep the donors secret. If they demanded the public records from the Agribusiness Association of Iowa they would violate their own illegal agreement and could stand in additional jeopardy.

So they divorced themselves from the illegal fund in late April 2016. We continued to demand to know who the donors were, covering the bills that had been paid to date. They would not tell us. We called. We emailed. Nobody from AAI would talk to us. They wouldn't even say "No comment."

We heard that the AAI was having its annual golf outing at Lake Okoboji sixty miles north. Out of a sense of magnanimity and fairness, I insisted that the Aggies should have their say in full. We dispatched Tom, who found a drinker at the bar loose enough late in the afternoon to direct the reporter to the fourteenth hole, where he would find the gang.

Tom tromped out. A golf cart sped off. Those stuck on the green told Tom to go to the clubhouse, where they finally would speak to him.

"No comment," they said at the nineteenth hole.

We finally got the no-comment comment, but we still didn't have all the names. We considered taking the issue to the Iowa Public Information Board, a state commission that can mete out fines to elected officials who violate open-records laws. We had the substance for a complaint, the director agreed, but we had lapsed beyond the sixty-day statute of limitations. Although it was a dispute spanning more than two years, the law states that a complaint must be filed within sixty days of the initial offense. It took us sixty days to figure out there was an offense. Clearly, the board didn't want to touch this case.

The next step was district court. It is inestimably more expensive than the information board, where we could plead our case without hired guns. As usual, we had no money. The Freedom of Information Council could give us three thousand dollars. That would barely get us to the courthouse door.

This thing could go on awhile. We would have to sue the county supervisors to identify the donors, who in turn would be forced to sue AAI, with its boundless legal defense fund, to fight the disclosure. It could have ended up at the Iowa Supreme Court. Even the most generous of lawyers could not wait for that payday of limited financial return.

We learned through our own reporting and outside the court documents who the big donors were: the seed and chemical companies, along with the Farm Bureau and the Iowa Corn Growers Association. We reported it. But only the court documents would tell us who all the donors were and how much they spent. We never did get that information, only the satisfaction of knowing that the county had to back out of the illegal secret fund.

In the fall of 2016 the Iowa Supreme Court ruled that drainage districts are immune from money damages. That knocked out half the waterworks' claim. The other half rested in federal court: Are drainage districts subject to the Clean Water Act?

Federal district court judge Leonard Strand dismissed that claim later in March 2017 on a motion for summary judgment filed by the counties. They argued that they lacked the statutory authority to respond substantially to the waterworks' claim. The judge agreed.

Case closed. We got dirty money out of the federal court system. The counties got a victory over the Des Moines Water Works.

But that doesn't mean the debate has ended. Far from it.

———————

We reported in the spring of 2017 that pollution levels in Iowa rivers are more dangerous than we first supposed. Nitrate in water can lead to thyroid problems, not just blue baby syndrome, which we had long heard about—oxygen deprivation in babies fed nitrate-polluted water. Phosphorous leads to algae blooms that at least can cause skin irritation and at worst can cause neurological disorders by creating cyanotoxins—poison from blue-green algae, to which residents of Toledo, Ohio, were exposed in their drinking water in 2014. The culprit that parched five hundred thousand Toledo residents for an entire summer: ag runoff from Ohio fields.

Republicans in the Iowa legislature, meanwhile, still feeling threatened by the likes of *The Storm Lake Times*, which can't even afford to hire a lawyer, decided they had to deal with the problem once and for all. They had won in court but now used their Farm Bureau Republican grip on the statehouse to sanitize our institutions of anticorporate virus.

They tried to pass a bill that would have dissolved the Des Moines Water Works, created by charter, and turned over its administration to the city of Des Moines, which didn't want it. That bill, introduced by a legislator who lived two hundred miles from Des Moines, died over suburban objections and lack of capital city enthusiasm. They were trying to snuff Bill Stowe's dissident voice.

The legislature zeroed out funding for the Aldo Leopold Center for Sustainable Agriculture at Iowa State University, which extols alternatives to the corn-soy-chemical production complex. By cutting $300,000 in state funding, the center in Ames would lose $3 million in matching grants for research that could

help farmers improve water quality and profits. It was the nation's leading sustainable research institute. The center survives,
barely, on interest generated by a $5 million private endowment.
So the agri-industry crowd virtually silenced another dissident
voice. The dean of the agriculture college at Iowa State should
have flung herself on the railroad tracks to stop that freight
train, but she didn't. The dean, Wendy Wintersteen, six months
later was appointed president of Iowa State, just six days after
the four job finalists visited campus. She had served on the Agribusiness Association of Iowa board that fought so hard for secrecy. She raised a lot of money from Monsanto and the Kochs
for the College of Agriculture to supplant reduced state appropriations. Wintersteen said she did what she could, but that she
was not bigger than the legislature.

The Raccoon River remains lousy with nitrate and the waterworks hawks it for signs of algae bursts. They can warn their
consumers, if the toxins get too high, to buy bottled water. We
continue to report on those warnings.

We knew we did what we could as a little newspaper with
little clout. But we wanted the case to get a full hearing. It's an
important question nagging the Chesapeake Bay, infected by
runoff; Lake Erie, where Toledo residents sometimes can't drink
the water because of ag-chemical-induced poison; the prairie
potholes of northern Iowa and southern Minnesota; the Mississippi River complex; and the Gulf of Mexico. It involves the un-
derpinnings of the entire Midwest economy. Iowa needed to
hear the arguments, and it needed a considered judgment. We
didn't get one.

Corporate agriculture got a green light to charge full speed
ahead. Yet it was not satisfied as it tried to root out any sustainable heresy against the Corn Creed.

The story was not finished. The lawsuit did intensify the conversation about ag pollution in Iowa. They couldn't run away from it anymore. Legislators continue to talk about throwing state money at the ag-chemical complex to show that they are doing something. *The Times* revealed who pulls the marionette strings in this state. We also began to realize that the far bigger story is climate change.

# CHAPTER 14

# We Can't Go On Like This

It's dry around the Fourth of July. The corn is high but the rain won't come except for one of those million-dollar quarter-inch thunder bursts that just keep it going another week. When the corn tassels it is ready to pollinate. You want rain and cool nights. These are the most critical two weeks of the year, when weather and crop genetics determine how many kernels will pop up on the ear. Too hot and dry and you can lose a big chunk of your yield—the difference between a profit and a loss with low prices. West of Storm Lake on those sandy hills that spill to the Missouri River the leaves are rolling up, an ominous sign that the plant is under enormous stress. There isn't enough soil to hold what little water the clouds allow.

When it did rain in spring it came in buckets. The warmer, wetter nights roll out violent thunderstorms that wash our soils—with few buffers to stop them—down the river to choke the Louisiana bayou and suffocate the Gulf of Mexico with our phosphorous and nitrate and herbicide detritus. What soil is left is not sufficient to feed the plant. Our corn is getting poorer and starchier, although through mechanical, biological, and chemical engineering we manage to ratchet up yields. Over time, the farmer, although he might not quite see it, is losing value for his crops and land, once the full and honest accounting is made relative to what the chemical complex took from him. Hog feeders will have a harder time getting the critter to gain weight for market. Ultimately, we all will pay more for food that is of less nutritional value because we are flushing the nation's greatest soil resource base to the depths of the gulf. And as forecasts predict our region will dry out in a half century or sooner, we are drawing water reserves at alarming rates for livestock and ethanol consumption. We all have a sense of what is going on around here but are just beginning to recognize it for what it is: climate change.

At the same time, we are awash in corn. We plowed up ground to meet the ethanol gold rush of ten years past along with South America, and now we are left to sit on record stocks of corn. In the fall we dump it in huge piles on the ground that look like pyramids next to grain elevators. Because of all that corn flooding the market, prices are rotten. Farm operating loans are starting to creep up, a danger sign.

Farmers like to trade in pickups every year for the tax write-off. Sales are slower the past couple of years—crop prices are flat, machinery sales are down, moods change, and bankers watch more closely—so the iron isn't moving off the lot like it should. The truck salesman won't be buying a new sofa, and the furniture store is feeling it. State tax revenues are down three years in a row, and schools are pinched with no growth in their budgets. The city manager might not get a raise, funds are so tight. Plus it's been so darn dry right in the smack of summer, which scares us or at least causes a rivulet through furrowed brows. Everyone, not just the farmers, wonders what this season has in store with the strange weather of recent years. Too wet and then too dry. It did not use to be like this. What to make of it?

Scientists are watching, too. What they see should alarm Storm Lake.

Climate change already is hurting crop production in North America, according to the top scientists in the field. Gene Takle of Iowa State University and Jerry Hatfield of the USDA were lead coauthors on the 2014 National Climate Assessment chapter on agriculture. Takle says that rising nighttime temperatures and humidity are damping corn yields right now.

Today's child who wants to farm in Nebraska could be dealing with daytime temperatures up to ten degrees warmer than the historical seasonal highs—more akin to Death Valley than to Scottsbluff in the Cornhusker panhandle.

Takle, director of ISU's Climate Science Program, conducted a study on climate change twenty-two years ago. "It showed there would be a general warming, more in the winter than summer; that's happening. More at night than during the day; that's happening. Three percent more precipitation; that's happening— actually, it's been a little more than that," Takle told the ISU College of Agriculture magazine in 2015. "It also showed there would be a shift toward more precipitation in the spring and early summer and less in the fall and winter. We now have 13% more precipitation in the spring and early summer and 22% less in fall and winter than 50 years ago."

Critical thresholds are being exceeded, Takle said. Chronic

drought has set in over the southern Plains. In western Kansas farmers long used to growing corn to feed cattle are unable to raise it even under full, continued irrigation. They cannot pump enough water to keep up with the increasing evapotranspiration demand of the plant. The soil cannot hold enough water even with irrigation to service the plant.

For now some regions are parched, like the Plains and the West. Yet other regions, like Iowa and the Upper Midwest, are for the moment getting warmer and wetter. Which makes for strange near-term opportunity.

"Iowa agriculture should be in a great position, because we have the best land," Iowa State University economist Neil Harl explained to me. "The Corn Belt will be moving north. You will be growing corn in Buena Vista County, but someone in southern Missouri will have a difficult time of it."

Our land is threatened. We will grow corn, but not like we are now—not high-quality corn—because of degraded soil. Protein content already is declining. The corn is getting starchier. That may be good for distilling ethanol but not for feeding turkeys. Genetic engineering in seed labs is generating new drought-resistant varieties that can prop up the gross yield per acre but cannot necessarily maintain the actual value of the kernel for its myriad food and industrial uses without healthy soil. It could have deleterious human effects from higher starch content. Lower value in the kernel suggests higher costs at the checkout counter for chicken, and lower prices for the farmer at the elevator. Ultimately, that must be reflected in the land price at auction when the farmer dies. Less soil, less value. Land appraisers are starting to take it into account. And that suggests a steady decline in Iowa's—and the entire Midwest's—wealth and stability.

The University of Minnesota reports that Iowa corn yields could decline 20 to 50 percent by 2075. Other credible institutional studies tend to corroborate that. The Iowa State scientists do not argue, but they tend not to make predictions about what corn yields actually will do in fifty or seventy-five years. They do not know what genetics might hold. Seed scientists around Des Moines are talking about developing genetics that would double our current corn yields—what is not known is the environmental toll it will take, or if the corn will be junk food, good only for turning into sugar. Such reports seem fantastic, but it was only in 2009 that researchers mapped the corn genome.

We know that growing corn will be more challenging. And it will be more difficult to sustain our current livestock production levels in western Iowa, where soils blow lighter, roll more, and are more sensitive to erosion from erratic weather.

Scientists say northwest Iowa should trend wetter with more extreme rains for the next twenty years. That will be bad enough, because that's what is spurring our river and lake pollution. After that, experts at NASA's Goddard Institute for Space Studies report, western Iowa has up to an 80 percent chance of multidecade droughts—lasting twenty to fifty years—and we are getting a foretaste now with gushes of rain followed by long spans without a drop.

The southwest and central Plains, including the western third of Iowa, are in for deep dry spells in coming years. The NASA research, led by climate scientist Benjamin Cook, used soil moisture studies based on tree-ring analysis to come to the conclusion that we will experience droughts in North America not seen since medieval times. Their research makes us stop and look anew at the challenges agriculture will face in this century—right here in Storm Lake, Iowa.

We assume that because of richer glacial soils and plentiful rainfall we will always be in the buckle of the Corn Belt. The NASA charts show our soil becoming seriously moisture deficient in fifty years. Western Iowa might not be ideally suited to water-intensive livestock production and processing. It appears that northern Minnesota would be better, except that it doesn't have the soil that Iowa has had.

The lake is a first indicator. Our worst droughts in the 1950s put the lake down a full five feet below the outlet dam. Considering that the average depth of the lake was seven feet, that did not leave much room for walleyes, catfish, and perch. NASA's research indicates that the 1950s will look like child's play compared to the year 2090.

Takle would not go so far as to say we are entering a period like the medieval warming. But he would not count it out. Much depends on where the Bermuda airflow from the Gulf of Mexico rests from west to east over the Upper Midwest. The gulf is warming and creating more humidity in Iowa. The high ice clouds out of the Rockies come rolling over Nebraska and explode over Storm Lake about eleven-thirty p.m. Often they come in early spring when ground is bare and vulnerable.

Water vapor is the greatest of the greenhouse gases. It traps heat. Absolute humidity is swelling 5 percent per decade. It makes us warmer. That leads to drought, which seems counterintuitive to a layperson but makes perfect sense when a Ph.D. explains it.

"The western United States will experience long droughts. The East, and the Northeast in particular, will have a huge increase in extreme rains. Storm Lake sits squat in the middle of that," Takle told me. "Drought could well spill into western Iowa, maybe even for decades as it did during the 1930s. My hunch is you will not see massive droughts like the medieval warming. You will be on the high side for precipitation in the next twenty years. You're going to see more extremes. There are some flavors of the Dust Bowl among the variables."

Among the variables: What used to be a one-hundred-year record flood in the Cedar River Valley in eastern Iowa now happens every twenty-five years, Takle found. The Iowa Department of Transportation is using his work to design bridges around Cedar Rapids that take into account increased flooding and river torrents that we did not experience forty-five years ago. The Linn County Courthouse and jail in Cedar Rapids sit in the middle of the Cedar River on an island. Inmate evacuations are not rare anymore. How long can that courthouse stand amid our engineering?

The greatest threat to Iowa, from Storm Lake to Des Moines, is not Islam or Mexicans hopping off a freight train if they don't die trying. The greatest threat to Iowa—and, ultimately, a stable food supply in the United States—is its continued loss of soil. Rick Cruse, an agronomist at Iowa State, notes that wheat production already is falling every year in China because of soil deterioration. Extreme weather events wrought by warming make the task of keeping Iowa soil in place even harder.

Economist Harl recalls that in 1937 his family raised 40 bushels of corn per acre. In 2011 his southern Iowa farm produced 220 bushels of corn per acre. That corn sucked up a lot of fertilizer suspended in a lot of water. That pace cannot be sustained unless there is something to hold the water in place.

And there isn't. Cruse will show you aerial photos of the Des Moines lobe—the corn capital of the world—where the precious topsoil depth has shrunk from fourteen inches to nothing in the span of a century. It starts on the knobs and spreads to the flat ground as the wind whips water across the bare black slate where you don't see a tree for miles.

Soil erosion rates have amplified since the 1980s because of more extreme weather combined with less land in pastures and buffers and intensified row-crop production that packs much higher plant populations per acre.

Soil can hold water during drought, but if there is less soil in place, resiliency weakens. Cruse, who runs the Iowa Daily Erosion Project, tells us that our Iowa and Illinois prime cropland is floating downriver.

Cruse has been taking his analysis around the state trying to get people to listen: Climate change is upon us. The only way we can continue to reach optimum corn production in an increasingly hungry world is to maintain the soil base that the Good Lord left us when the plow arrived after 1850. We can't do that the way we are farming—all out on virtually every acre.

Buena Vista County's flat land is losing soil four times faster than nature can regenerate it. Iowa can regrow up to a half ton of soil per acre per year. Federal authorities say five tons per acre lost annually is "acceptable." Such acceptable losses are common after a two-inch rain. We are losing soil way faster than we can grow it.

Cruse notes that corn potential is derived from genetics, management, and water transpiration. You can get the best genetics and get plant populations as high as possible, but you can reach that crop's potential only with adequate water. Topsoil, rich in organic matter, stores water for the corn plant. For every inch of topsoil you lose, corn production capacity is lost with it.

In the next twenty years world population is set to grow by up to 3 billion people, who will depend on less tillable land to feed them. We will need all the production capacity we can get. We lost 41 million acres of farmland to development from 1982 to 2017. Irrigated land provides 40 percent of the world's food, and we are pumping our aquifers down. Given those daunting facts, it would seem an abomination to just dump that precious soil—which could feed a hungry world—into the river so it can choke the Louisiana bayou.

"Iowa had the world's best soil. Louisiana has it now," Cruse mused of our displaced treasure.

Demand for food and for better diets is increasing. Crop prices are on an average trend line up and will continue that trajectory, Cruse thinks, despite the downturn of recent years. The only incentive is for producers to produce in search of higher yields at higher prices, with a safety net called crop insurance that protects their adventurism. That will cause more water pollution and more soil loss, unless the federal government steps in and requires conservation practices. Discomfort causes change, says Iowa State economist Dave Swenson. Well-settled farmers are more comfortable than ever because of the safety nets and the genetic breakthroughs that defend against drought and pestilence, planted in an oil base that can be purchased.

The cost is not obvious, but it lurks below the surface.

Cruse said he has no doubt that crops are losing yield potential that genetics and technology cannot fully replace. Corn quality has been declining as measured by protein content from Iowa fields. Cruse points to the connection between soil health and human obesity—Latinos who live on a diet high in corn are trapped in a diabetes crisis, according to local health officials. Cruse relates that to higher starch and lower protein content in the corn kernel. Traces of that starchier corn kernel are in almost every processed food and drink on the grocery shelves.

The increase in ethanol consumption brought on by the Renewable Fuels Standard—which made a lot of farmers rich over a three-year span—may mask the long-term implications of how it is destroying our land and eroding rural communities.

"We were living on a sugar high," Swenson said of the spike in crop and land prices leading up to 2009 fueled by ethanol.

It gave us a rush to rip up more grass and get in on that seven-dollars-per-bushel corn for a fleeting time. But the damage was done, the soil gone. And now corn has crashed back to three dollars per bushel, prompting farmers to go after even more acres to get maximum revenue. The rule of modern agriculture: Spread your fixed costs over more acres.

"We're moving down a one-way street," Cruse said.

That black gold swirls in our lakes and rivers and eventually to the Gulf of Mexico. Those prairie potholes are the canaries in the coal mine. Lose the lakes and you won't be growing corn for long. Not in Iowa, anyway. And we are losing them.

Water is the new oil, it is commonly said nowadays. It is vital, it is becoming scarce, and we are consuming it faster than nature can replenish our supply. Iowa is moving water so fast off the land, growing so much corn and feeding so many livestock, that we are sucking our underground aquifers dry.

The Ogallala Aquifer, which provides most of the water for

crops and cattle in Oklahoma, Texas, Kansas, and Nebraska, is expected to be exhausted within the next twenty years. Pockets in western Kansas have already run dry. The great aquifer cannot replenish itself as fast as it is being drawn down. And even with irrigation, corn quality, if not total yields, has been tracking down.

The rains come, all right, often in torrents. Cedar Rapids and Des Moines and St. Louis are flooding because of them. Drainage systems in northern Iowa designed to move water off the land as quickly as possible amplify the gushes toward the downstream cities. We are draining water away so rapidly to accommodate our crop regimen that it doesn't have time to stand in sloughs and leach back into our underground aquifers as it once did.

The principal water source for the eastern two-thirds of the state has been drawn down twenty feet since 1977. Because it is buried so deep, the Jordan, a huge underground lake, cannot recharge as fast as we pump. It takes 5 gallons a day to water a hog. It takes 3 gallons of water, on average, to make a gallon of ethanol from corn. The average-size ethanol distillery in Iowa consumes 330,000 gallons of water a day, or 120 million gallons per year. The livestock and ethanol industries will eventually lick the Jordan aquifer's last drop.

Northwest Iowa is a place of relative water bounty for the geological moment. The sixteen-county corner of the state draws most of its water from the Dakota aquifer, specifically the Lower Dakota. It generally follows the Missouri River—the Anthon channel underground halfway between Storm Lake and Sioux City is considered the pre–Ice Age Big Muddy.

It is thought the Dakota will be an ample water resource well into the future—except in Buena Vista County. Storm Lake is the leading meat processing center of the Midwest. Sioux

City—five times the size of Storm Lake—consumes up to 4.6 million gallons of water per day. Storm Lake sucks up 3.3 million gallons per day thanks to food processing. Meatpacking involves constant washing of product, plant, and equipment. A graveyard shift sprays water and cleans every night at the Tyson plants. Per capita, no place else has near the thirst of Storm Lake.

"The Lower Dakota aquifer has tremendous development capacity," says a 2008 report from the U.S. Geological Survey conducted for the Iowa Department of Natural Resources. Summertime usage was estimated at 31.6 million gallons per day, well below the development potential for the aquifer.

Storm Lake, however, is producing water at or near the sustainability threshold of the Lower Dakota aquifer, the report cautions.

The aquifer's pockets near the Missouri River have a much higher recharge rate than around Storm Lake. "Approximately 900,000 gallons per day is coming from storage [at Storm Lake], which indicates the aquifer is under stress," the USGS report states. "There is some uncertainty in how much higher future pumping rates can be increased in the Storm Lake zone."

I'm not trying to cry wolf. We are not about to run parched. But we have to be careful. We never before had to concern ourselves with where our water was coming from or how much it might cost to ration its use. Now we do. The waterworks lawsuit is a perfect illustration.

Assuming no additional demand, Storm Lake's Dakota water supply is safe. With a recharge rate of up to half an inch per year here, Storm Lake's current activities can be sustained. That is quite an assumption, considering that virtually every ag activity, from germinating a seed to washing a butcher knife, requires plentiful water. Of the world's fresh water drawn annually, agriculture drinks 70 percent of it.

But under a scenario of "medium" future use—a 25 percent increase in pumping from 2008 to 2028—"a significant drawdown" is shown under the USGS model. It gets apocalyptic if we pump even more.

The report has not been updated in ten years because of insufficient funding.

So what do all these numbers really add up to? The reality that our ag activities are bound to expand over the next fifty years and our water supply isn't expanding at the same rate.

NASA modeling shows that the Great Lakes region of the Upper Midwest is the best-situated spot in the world for water availability now and in the future. Storm Lake sits on the divide between the Great Plains and the Upper Midwest. As the water dries up on the Plains, and perhaps around Storm Lake, livestock should move to the Upper Midwest for a readily available feed and water supply.

Western Iowa is on the dry edge of that wet belt. To sustain itself, Storm Lake needs to avoid industrial growth that consumes yet more water and learn how to manage it better. As water becomes more expensive, food processors and ethanol makers are scurrying for ways to reduce usage and reclaim water. The price of water here already is rising 3 percent a year, twice the rate of inflation.

There's a big linked irony in all this. As water availability drops in the western Great Plains and the climate warms, Iowa's importance as an agricultural state will only grow. It would appear that Storm Lake is fully mature in this regard. We need to find other places to expand the economy that do not involve more water consumption—or rethink the way we use our land, restoring its storage capacity so it can let the water soak in again.

Water wars may flare sooner—within the next twenty years—than later. It will involve rural-urban conflict. Already the Great Lakes states are claiming and defending their sovereignty over the waters that flow out of their boundaries. Legal challenges are mounting. There will be interstate and intrastate battles. Will Fort Dodge be considered a crucial watering spot based on state-engineered economic development policies, or will it be allowed to fend for itself against Storm Lake in a coming competition for water?

These are serious questions that are not being taken that seriously. When I have asked meat industry officials about it, they acted as if they were not aware. Few noted the U.S. Geological Survey report on the Dakota aquifer other than our newspaper. Nobody in the legislature is talking about it.

Water and soil are inexorably linked in the cycle of life. Soil responds to what you plant in it. Before corn and soybeans took over every spare plot of land, Iowa farmers planted small-grain cover crops like rye, grazed marginal lands near water, and left buffers by streams to soak up nutrients straying from farm fields during fall and spring flushes. The cover crops left the landscape with the cattle. Pastures and buffers were plowed up as farmers specialized in row crops over integrated crop-livestock rotations.

"We didn't have a problem until we changed cropping systems. It really becomes about water management," said Jerry Hatfield, director of the USDA's National Lab for Agriculture and the Environment in Ames.

Nitrogen enters the water-soil profile in various ways: You can apply it with a commercial preparation, you can plant species like soybeans that fix nitrogen to the soil, and nature does its own thing with microbial nitrification that breaks down organic matter and creates nitrogen. Humans and nature conspire to create excess nitrogen loadings into surface water when there are no crops to take up water during high-flow events in spring and fall.

Now, because the land that once had grass cover in winter is exposed and black with nothing to suck up all that leftover nitrogen, high nitrate levels are hitting in the middle of winter rather than in just spring.

The DMWW highlighted this in its lawsuit. The solution is adding diversity to the cropping systems in the Upper Raccoon River Watershed surrounding Storm Lake, said Hatfield, who has studied Raccoon nutrient loadings for more than twenty-five years, longer than anyone else.

The issue gains urgency with climate change leading to more extreme weather in the spring and fall—like an eleven-inch spring rain in BV County west of Storm Lake that led to soil losses of twenty tons per acre in two days. Much of it rushed to the lake down Powell Creek because nothing could stop the mud. Rain is good if you can retain it.

Iowa is in the midst of a voluntary nutrient reduction effort started in 2013 that is supposed to help lessen the nitrate and phosphorous—the crop "nutrients"—load on the Mississippi River. Farmers are not required to plant buffers next to water; they are politely asked to do so with the offer of a cost-sharing grant. In the first year of the effort, 100,000 acres of Iowa land were signed up for some sort of conservation practice supplemented by state watershed grants. By the third year the voluntary sign-up had increased to 600,000 acres on an Iowa ag land base of 12 million acres. It isn't much, but it's something. The rate of growth is promising.

Some farmers around Storm Lake tried planting winter radishes as a cover crop. The vast majority see radishes or rye with no market as an expense, not an investment in the soil; but they would if they still had herds of cattle. That's where grazing comes in: Cattle can feed off winter crops like rye, which hold moisture and nutrients in place, plus build soil tilth through better microbial activity. Hatfield mentions that there are many cover crops that make excellent biofuels feedstock, such as switchgrass or sweet sorghum. He says we Iowans need to cultivate "more imagination." Yet planting cover crops to retain nutrients infield, where they belong, and not in the river, and building soil health are viewed as expenses not worth the bother. Livestock grazing on cover crops, a system that works, involves labor and risk that most farmers shed a generation ago. It is a hard and slow sell, but the message is starting to take root down on the farm. For forty years the chemical and seed companies, bankers, land-grant ag schools, and neighbors all pushed that sixty-three-year-old farmer into the corner where he finds himself trapped. It takes time and will to work out of it.

Iowa is not alone. Minnesota is having many of the same problems, as is every state in the Corn Belt. The Minnesota Pollution Control Agency reported in 2015 that just 53 of 181 stream sections supported aquatic life in five counties covering the Missouri River Basin. No lakes in southwest Minnesota met standards for aquatic recreation. Researchers studied the Big Sioux,

Little Sioux, and Rock river basins just north of the Iowa border. They found problems with high sediment loads, high nitrate levels, caving stream banks, and little in the way of riparian plantings. In short, it's much like northwest Iowa, where lakes are filling with mud and nutrients.

Forty years of water-quality funding have not helped that much in the Minnesota experience.

Economics presumes rational decision making. Farmers prove every year that if corn prices go down, they do not switch to another land use. They simply seek to plant more corn on more acres to make up for low prices, hoping yield will win the year for them. That is, on its face, irrational. But when you have no hedge like cattle, because the supply chain doesn't want grazing in Iowa, and alternative crops are laughed at by the banker, the farmer is forced to find a break-even point by spreading his costs over more acres and seeking higher yields through more fertilizer. When prices go up, he does the same thing. This is not perfect competition that they teach in business school; it is a broken model controlled by a corporate chemical oligarchy that distorts decision making and thus markets. The same oligarchy in the name of free markets manages the political and judicial processes to keep the broken model in place.

Then there is the central physical force of Iowa: inertia. It cannot be discounted. We are just comfortable enough to go along to get along.

And when you plant switchgrass or sweet sorghum instead of corn, that friendly neighbor of yours just might ask your landlady, who is eighty-five, why she would allow you to do something so risky. You will never know that he called her. He would like to farm that ground with corn (because his banker is telling him to get more efficient) and make more money for her. Those dynamics are real and they are real obstacles.

Storm Lake's watershed has had full-time coordinators through the years trying to work with landowners on better soil and water management. About 80 percent of the watershed has some sort of conservation treatment. But the coordinators never were able to convert the worst violators who ripped out buffers along Powell Creek, which feeds Storm Lake. And this was one of the most targeted, intense, and comprehensive watershed improvement efforts in America.

The city of Storm Lake has spent upward of $20 million in federal emergency funds on storm-water remediation to protect the lake and the Raccoon River in the past five years. Streets are made permeable. Rain gardens are planted at the ends of streets. It's designed to nip the problem upstream and protect Des Moines from floods that have shut down life in central Iowa at times. But agriculture has not been as eager to trot despite the millions of carrots under their noses.

It doesn't cost billions more to let rivers run clean. It takes a conscience. Or a USDA requirement that to get government crop insurance you must set aside 10 percent of your land to grass, as we did before Nixon agriculture secretary Earl Butz urged farmers to plant fencerow to fencerow to feed the world. The world remains starving, and planting through the fencerow is producing more headaches than food. We are beginning to learn that rethinking our approach reaps great rewards. Dr. Matt Helmers, a distinguished ag engineer from ISU, found that returning as little as 10 percent of a rolling farm field to native prairie grass can reduce nitrogen and phosphorous loss from a field by up to 90 percent per year.

Other research has suggested that planting relatively narrow buffer strips near stream banks can reduce pollution loads in the water by two-thirds.

Iowa has committed around a dollar per acre of farm ground, in state and federal funds, to get ag nutrients under control. The plan is voluntary. That's a dollar's investment on land valued at ten thousand dollars per acre. It's peanuts to protect a resource that is so vital to the state's economy.

Approximately 80 percent of soil pollution of water comes from about 20 percent of the acres. The hardheads who control the minority of acres that are polluting will not come to church no matter how much money you offer. They think they can make more money growing corn-on-corn for ethanol year after year next to the Raccoon River than you can sitting on your duff watching perennial big bluestem grow in a twenty-foot strip with a generous conservation subsidy. The owners of the 20 percent will never plant a blade of grass unless the banker or the USDA orders them to. This was our essential argument during the waterworks litigation. The carrots—billions of dollars in conservation funding over the past thirty years, indeed since the Dust Bowl—have not worked by themselves. Sometimes you need a spur for the stubborn mule.

We are tweaking at the edges a few acres at a time. Patches here and there won't work. Behavior glaciers creep slowly.

Farmers aren't just polluting their own water and losing their own soil. The load feeding blue-green algae infesting Lake Erie is attributed mainly to agricultural production. There was much hue and cry in 2014 surrounding the putrid pollution of the Great Lake. The politicians talked. The state held conferences. Congressmen lobbied the EPA and USDA for help. Nothing happened. The algae returned in the fall of 2017 and crept from Toledo to Canada across Erie. Nothing has changed appreciably after years of talk and throwing money here and there.

Cities have their own miseries, waterwise. Toledo is saddled with an antiquated water system that can't deal with the new biological pressures thrown at it. The Des Moines Water Works is faced with installing a new nitrate removal system because its current system is more than twenty-five years old and worn out from the load we are shipping down the Raccoon River from Storm Lake.

What Hatfield suggests—a few hooves here, some sweet sorghum there, combined with small grains, corn, and soybeans—is not onerous or that complicated. He is basically suggesting that we look into our recent past for solutions that could be immediate and don't cost that much. Adding cattle actually helps farmers build profits while restoring the landscape.

There's a significant hitch few people talk about: As agriculture has industrialized and chemicalized and specialized, we lost our diverse base of knowledge. Farmers today grow corn but do not husband animals. It is hard to bring cattle back to a restored Iowa landscape if we have lost the art of raising them. The hog house operator near Storm Lake may have nothing to do with growing anything, even the contracted hogs in his care and custody. He deals with instructions from a computer in Virginia that dictate his daily decisions. The cattle class is gone and the cattle with it. They don't know how to pull a calf from a heifer on pasture like Granddad did.

Political support for whole-system changes has not taken hold. For the moment, the reverse is true: Political systems are propping up the existing narrowed supply system against the interests, ultimately, of rural communities.

Dennis Keeney, the retired and founding director of the Leopold Center at ISU, tells me that Iowa needs to retire at least a third of its corn acreage to reverse surface-water pollution. That's about how much ethanol consumes. It is apostasy in Iowa for the moment, but religious beliefs change over time. Iowans are using less fuel, and electric cars are coming on fast. I drive one. The pooh-poohers perk up when I tell them my car averages eighty miles per gallon. That's where the automakers are driving. General Motors says it will convert its entire fleet to electric over the next twenty years. Swenson foresees falling ethanol demand as that conversion occurs. The Iowa Renewable Fuels Association, birthed by the Iowa Corn Growers, is sponsoring a conference looking into it. They are thinking about it.

People are talking. Farmers are paying attention. They listen when economist Swenson questions the value of ethanol for the environmental toll it takes. They listen when Takle describes climate change. And they hear Cruse evangelize the gospel of soil conservation. It helps that Iowa's own Academy of Science study group has been warning for a decade about the dangers of climate change seeded in a carbon economy. The signatories to the annual statement include all the leading scientists from Iowa's colleges and universities. It helps when Rick Lampe of Buena Vista University, himself a local farm boy from Albert City, agrees that human activity is impacting carbon dioxide levels, humidity, and thus climate change.

But the action must come from Congress, which continues to insist on cutting the conservation programs that actually have been proven effective for the land and appreciated by farmers. We have wasted a lot of conservation money, but we also have done a lot of good with it at the margins and especially with the Conservation Reserve Program. The most recent speciousness is an argument that conservation programs hold back acres that would otherwise go to beginning young farmers. Which beginning young farmers are those? The ones whose fathers already control a couple of thousand acres? They will say anything in Washington these days.

Jon Robinson, thirty-six, works next to me. He is our general manager and ad compositor. He has been with us since he quit playing baseball at the juco in Mason City. He has a wife, Amanda, who is a registered nurse at Buena Vista Regional Medical Center, two blond daughters, and a newborn son.

He could farm but passed.

"I just don't understand," his late grandpa Wayne said at Jon and Amanda's wedding.

Jon grew up throwing rocks on the shed roof. As they rolled off he slammed them with an aluminum baseball bat just like Ken Griffey Jr., still his hero. He never walked bean fields pulling cocklebur and buttonweeds; he rode in a bean buggy spraying herbicide. Jon shoveled out grain bins and drove trucks and tractors while Grandpa Wayne, at age ninety, was driving a combine all over the field and into the side of a building.

Jon has a good eye for design, likes computers, and maybe didn't want to be stuck on the farm—except he lives there now and would trade it for nothing. Maybe he wanted to strike out on his own. He bought a bar for a few years until the state banned slot machines and smoking. He watched his tap and cash register dry up on Lake Avenue at Smokey's Bar. Smokey Robinson. You know.

His dad, Rich, seventy, was reared on a farm near Nemaha with rolling hills and a little creek, Skunk Run, that bubbles up out of the ground as an artesian well and runs about four miles east to the Raccoon River.

"I could make some money if I bottled that stuff," Rich says.

What would you call it? Skunk Run Water?

Rich sticks to farming. He made some money doing that. And there's a good story behind it.

Rich's grandfather, George Robinson, lost his 80-acre farm during the Great Depression when the Nemaha bank went on a permanent banker's holiday along with George's mortgage. An old bachelor farmer, Roy Stenhouse, bought the parcel out of foreclosure and let George continue to live on the acreage and farm the land. George's son, Wayne, came of age and was a hired man on another farm. Roy Stenhouse watched him. He liked Wayne. In 1955 Roy approached Wayne about buying his 240-acre farm. Wayne told him he didn't have the money. He was a product of the Depression.

"Roy almost had to beg him to buy it," Rich recalls, laughing. He assured Wayne that he could buy on contract with low interest and easy terms, no down payment. He was, essentially, offering Wayne a whole new start after the Depression. They don't grow bachelors like that anymore.

As soon as Wayne bought it, corn tripled in price to three dollars per bushel and he was able to pay the farm off free and clear in ten years, never missing a beat. He never bought another acre of ground. And Wayne never told his father, George, that he bought that land. He said he was just renting or crop sharing.

"It would have worried George to death," Rich said.

So it remained a secret.

They had feeder cattle. It was a big day when Wayne would drive over to the sale barn at Alta and the Canadians came in with their cattle. Wayne would return and announce to Rich a load of feeders was coming, and then the truck would unload. They had thirty sows and farrowed hogs on pasture.

It was good, flat ground. They would grow oats, then alfalfa, then run hogs, and in the fourth year they would plant corn on the ground the hogs fertilized the year before. It was a complete cycle. Years later soil fertility tests continue to show that piece of ground outperforming all the others. It was the hog lot in rotation.

Rich was a catcher for the Nemaha Blue Jays. When he was in eighth grade Nemaha High School closed, and he had to go to school with the archrival Early Cardinals a few miles away. "The kids got along fine but the parents fought like hell," Rich says.

Like his dad, Rich started out farming right after high school. He rented ground from landlords who liked him and, like Wayne, could see how hard and smart he worked. He gathered up 320 acres, and bought more as opportunity arose. He bought the place where his son Jon now lives south of Storm Lake for three thousand dollars an acre just before the farm crisis. It dropped in value by two-thirds almost overnight.

"I thought I might lose it," Rich says.

Rich had Grandpa George's and Wayne's Great Depression mentality. He had squirreled away just enough cash to ride out the storm and save the home place. By 1988 he bought another piece for twelve hundred dollars per acre, one tenth of what it might sell for today.

"I've always been pretty tight. Maybe too tight. My wife

would tell you I should have enjoyed things more. Jon, he's a lot different than me. He's willing to do things that I wouldn't do, and sometimes maybe I should listen to him."

Such as: Jon convinced Rich to buy sixty acres along the Raccoon River. The twenty most highly erodible acres were enrolled in the Conservation Reserve Program at more than $250 per acre under a Pheasant Restoration Program. That is double what you could net growing corn on those twenty acres. Native grass, wildflowers, and a native food plot for birds were planted. Jon hunts deer and pheasants there. Rich secretly loves it. Jon is obsessed with it.

"It's just in my being. I don't want to destroy the land. I would plant filter strips and grass waterways even if I didn't get paid for it because I don't like seeing corn stalks in the ditch or in the river," Rich says. "But if I weren't getting paid for that CRP ground I probably wouldn't leave it in grass. We would plant corn."

Jon agrees. He doesn't own the ground but you can understand how the Robinsons have survived, and even thrived, amid natural and economic forces that are always trying to bury you. If those twenty acres could not be in the CRP he, too, would grow corn there.

"That's fifty-six hundred dollars lost," Jon figures, if the CRP program goes away.

Rich misses no meals. Neither does Jon. Property taxes would be maybe six hundred dollars on the entire sixty acres. That would be the only ownership cost, as there is no debt against the land. Rich never borrowed money from the bank to buy land. Depression mentality. Jon has it in the blood. The land must produce income.

"In the end, it's always about the money," Jon says.

There is just no way around it. If you want to hang on to your land, you must get paid. Almost all farmers and their heirs want to do the right thing if we provide the right incentive. For the rest, you need a whip to get them moving in the right direction.

The CRP program is exhausted. Congress talks about curtailing it significantly. The Robinsons' CRP contract expires inside ten years. If it is not renewed, that land will probably get planted in corn or soybeans. Before they bought it, the land was planted corn-on-corn year after year, draining directly into the river. The neighbor across the river to the west plants right up to the bank. The Robinsons would not do that. It violates Rich's sense of stewardship.

"I like leaving things for nature," Rich says.

But where you can farm, you will farm. He will leave a generous grass strip next to the river for protection. The other eighteen acres will go back to rows. Who am I to blame him? I can't afford to own that ground.

Father and son hope that Washington sees the value of keeping that land in wildflowers and pheasants. Jon does not want to plant it. But he would if it were his, and he watched it sit idle from income. He doesn't want to run a cow-calf herd nor does he have any idea where to start. He wants to hunt. He wants to hear the turkeys. He nearly ran over a fox on his way home. He was stoked.

The next generation moved the last generation along in its thinking. The next generation will watch over the land at least as well, if not better, than Rich did. There is a connection to the land not for what it is but for what it represents: the family Robinson. Jon cannot imagine letting go of any of it anytime. That attitude was seeded in the Great Depression and the farm crisis and cultivated by an old Nemaha bachelor farmer. You don't change horses quickly in that stream of acute consciousness.

I hate expressways for any number of reasons, the main one being that the expressway is filled with maniacs who want to drive as fast as they possibly can through throngs of traffic. So I take our county blacktops. Or IA 2, if I have to get to Fort Madison on the Mississippi, as I did recently.

Anyone but a blind man would be overcome by three things driving across Iowa from west to east:

First, the stunning beauty of the southern two tiers of counties. It's early June, the hills are lush, flowers bloom, Amish buggies roll past. Not far up the road is where Grant Wood framed *American Gothic*. The whole landscape looks like he painted it in green and blue and yellow. No place could be prettier.

Second, the stunning absence of cattle on those hills.

Third, the stunning poverty and shrinkage.

From Creston to Centerville on the undulating southern tier of counties, it's a whole different feel than from Sheldon to Clear Lake on the flat northern tier.

The soil is not as good. Farms are poorer to the roadside eye. Mobile homes are parked along the highway. Centerville hasn't had a coat of paint in a while. The old brick manufacturing haunts closer to the Mississippi cast shadows, not iron.

They had great ambitions back when they built the state's best town square. There were the coal mines. There were small farms. Ottumwa was a bustling meatpacking center for those farms. Its population dropped in half since 1980, to about twenty thousand. Most of the farmers held a second job in Mount Ayr

or Bloomfield or some other little county seat with a light manufacturing plant. Over the past fifty years the cattle disappeared
to huge feedlots in Kansas and Texas, the small manufacturers
were gobbled up and moved out or just closed down, and the
brains decided to ply their gray cells someplace else.

The populations of Taylor and Ringgold counties dropped in
half since 1950, down to five thousand or six thousand people each,
a quarter of the population of Buena Vista County. And they're still
losing people at 2 percent per year, according to the best estimates.
It's been continually depressed for the past fifty years, with poverty
rates rivaling Harlan County, Kentucky. These are Iowans who are
Appalachia poor.

Poverty and lack of opportunity trap people. You see them at
the convenience store. They will tell you they feel left behind if
you ask them. They drive down IA 2 in an old pickup. You wonder what they're driving to.

They never have been able to really grow much corn on that
ground, but they try. Taylor and Ringgold counties had the highest acreage withdrawals in Iowa from the Conservation Reserve
Program since 2008, when corn prices shot up. That means more
soil into the vales and then the creek winding to the Des Moines
River. And it means a few more people washing out with it.

You won't solve poverty in Taylor County with hunting lodges
and oak savannas owned by doctors from Des Moines.

You solve it by looking back at the heyday: when everybody
had a cow-calf herd. When Ringgold County had cattle, it had
people. And back then Iowa did not have a terrible soil-loss or
water-quality problem.

Government programs are directed at putting land into corn,
sugar, wheat, and cotton; or to taking land completely out of
production with the CRP or Wetland Reserve Program. There

is no program for a hardworking young cowboy who loves those rolling hills but can't find a way to make a living on them. Anyone with ambition must leave with a heavy heart because the entire livestock infrastructure has been ripped up and abandoned.

You can drive across the entire state of Iowa and not see a single hog or a single cow standing out there.

Cattle are the new buffalo that keep the system whole: from grass to manure to beef to jobs. If you have grass you can hold water. If you have water you can raise and process crops and livestock and create jobs. The cycle can be maintained. It takes a lot of hard work and an ability to listen to what the land is telling you.

The problem is density, according to the great conservationist Leopold. When you have too much of anything you upset the intricate balance—too much corn pollutes the rivers, too many chickens in one spot spread flu, too many hogs in one place suck up too much water and foul the air.

Nature always finds a way around the tricks we throw at it. It finds a way to reduce density through pestilence or weed pressure. Bird flus mutate as we develop vaccines. Roundup (glyphosate) is losing its efficacy and so is Bt corn, which is genetically manipulated to resist rootworms. We are running out of rock phosphorous, foundational to conventional fertilizer. Reduce the density—that is, rotate fields and among crops integrated with grazing—and you can achieve balance. You work with the land, not try to defeat it. The renewable source for phosphorous is livestock manure. The rootworms cannot survive if corn is planted in a field every third year. Weeds are controlled by the soil and other plants that crowd them out, and occasionally by human or even episodic chemical intervention.

Seth Smith is a young farmer from Nemaha who works with his wife, Etta, and his dad, Lynn, not far from Rich Robinson along the Raccoon River. Seth uses rotational practices to grow organic corn and graze cattle profitably. He was featured on the cover of *Iowa Cattleman* magazine in 2017 for winning the Environmental Stewardship Award after the waterworks lawsuit was dismissed. Seth had been building his diverse farm for more than a decade before the litigation because he, too, was concerned about water quality and keeping his costs down. Cover crops net him about forty dollars per acre by saving nutrients and feeding cattle. He has six hundred acres in organic corn fed by cattle manure composted with corn stalks. The Smiths have installed catch basins to protect the river from cattle grazing on pasture and a pivot to redirect that nutrient-rich runoff to other fields. Generally, organic corn fetches twice as much at market as conventional corn.

Yet the corn doesn't have to be certified organic by the USDA to make a difference on the bottom line. Sustainable practices can reduce chemical use and seed costs. Fred Kirschenmann, eighty-two, former director of the Leopold Center at Iowa State, returned to his family farm in North Dakota in 1976 to convert it to organic using livestock and a four-crop rotation. When he took the job in Iowa in 2000 a family moved in to manage the operation, which supports them and Kirschenmann from nineteen hundred acres of land planted in alfalfa, golden flax, hard red spring wheat, and winter rye.

Iowa's land traditionally has been considered more productive than North Dakota's. Kirschenmann challenges that notion. His farm supports a family and then some without thrashing the soil—in fact, building it to hold exponentially more water during a hard rain without drowning a crop. Fertility builds while input costs are cut by half or even more. Iowa's soil is so rich it makes us profligate; in North Dakota they have had to make do without the same level of attention from the seed and chemical industry (until more recently). They have to figure out how to make their land rich, and make it pay. Iowans are taking note. The Practical Farmers of Iowa, a sustainable ag group, is trotting the story around the state during revolving field days that are beginning to attract crowds of farmers. Thirty years ago, the organization was thought of as farmer freaks. They are becoming mainstream as more farmers see the profitability numbers year after year, explains agronomist Hatfield. He can see interest growing around the Raccoon River watershed, and that increased profitability is at the center of the discussion.

Kirschenmann wants to use his remaining time on Earth to preach about soil health. Microbials will fight the pests and weeds if we work with them, he insists. Integrated pest management is a well-studied discipline. It works.

"There are no silver bullets," Kirschenmann said. "If you don't work with nature, it fights back." He believes we can fix it with young farmers and new ways of thinking. Free-range pork producers are making a fortune in Iowa in the great outdoors. McDonald's pressed for cage-free hens after consumers pressed the company. Consumers prevailed. Now there is pressure on all ag sectors to adapt sustainable techniques. Tyson launched an antibiotic-free pork brand. Kirschenmann was at an alternative-crops conference in North Dakota where executives from General Mills said that this was the future of food production. Younger people today demand it.

Seth and Etta Smith are the future. They are figuring it out and leading the way. They don't portray themselves as the righteous ones. They're just trying to make a living the smartest way possible, and Seth didn't appreciate the whipping the farmers near the Raccoon took during the waterworks lawsuit. Most people are working hard to do the right thing in a way that they can survive.

The Smokin' Hereford BBQ in town uses only the Smiths' beef and brags it up—the state cattlemen proclaimed it the best burger in Iowa. The pace of change is quickening. The ag supply chain is fighting it, and that's a powerful force. It is not more powerful than the knowledge, now upon us, that our soil and water are in peril. It is not more powerful than nature itself. Yet sometimes our brains fool us with the pride that we can outwit everything, although deep down we know we are not really that better off today living by mining the soil.

"An ethic may be regarded as a mode of guidance for meeting ecological situations so new or intricate, or involving such deferred reactions, that the path of social expediency is not discernible to the average individual," Leopold wrote in *A Sand County Almanac*. "Animal instincts are modes of guidance for the individual in meeting such situations. Ethics are possibly a kind of community instinct in-the-making."

All the scientists I interviewed are confident that Iowa will turn things around, that we are in the midst of it. They also all said in chorus that we will have no choice. Nature will demand that we comply, or else. The good news is that the answers are at hand. We can learn again how to live with the land and survive come what may, and try to anticipate the change. Instincts are awakening in Iowa. We all know we have a problem. We know what is true and what really works.

# CHAPTER 15

# Via Dolorosa

The Stations of the Cross, the Via Dolorosa, or Way of Sorrow, is depicted in a series of framed paintings on the walls of St. Mary's Catholic Church in Storm Lake. The figures are contemporary: men in overalls with modern hammers nailing Jesus down, women in heels and dresses—the commoners crucifying the son of a carpenter, one of their own. The church was built in 1953 under the aesthetic direction of Father Edward Catich of St. Ambrose University in Davenport. He was a friend and understudy of Grant Wood's. He was a onetime Chicago jazz musician nicknamed "Catfish." He was an artist and a priest, a regionalist becoming a modernist within a religious discipline and a radical point of view inspired by the communal Catholic Worker Movement. He went on to world renown in calligraphy, stone lettering, and stained-glass illustration.

Eight years before St. Mary's went up, the Vatican admonished Catich for drawing holy cards showing Jesus as a common man, dressed in a T-shirt dead on the ground, victim of a fascist

state. Another showed a white Madonna with a black baby who
hangs on to a white mask. The bishop of Davenport ordered them
out of circulation. In correspondence about the holy cards with
Catholic Worker foundress Dorothy Day, she and Catich urged
each other on with their countercultural art. If they were to heel,
Catich said, they would be no better than the secular artists.

So Catich kept on going with more pencil drawings that were
to become the series at St. Mary's. The paintings, too, became a
matter of controversy. The Vatican continued to send letters to
the Davenport Diocese up until 1962 to put a leash on that stray,
at which point the bishop finally stood up to Rome. I'm not sure
how Storm Lake, in the even more conservative Sioux City Diocese, pulled it off other than for the power of pastor Monsignor
Cleo Ivis's formidable will to raise money and build a great
church. The clue might lie in the brilliant stained-glass windows that reach to the skies to glorify the saints, from Thomas
Aquinas to Maria Goretti to Francis of Assisi. The window
closest to the altar in the pole position leading all saints is that
of Pope Pius X, who had been recently beatified and who shared
the same name as Pope Pius XII—the genesis of those letters of
admonition.

Jesus as just a man, beneath even us as he makes his way
through the paintings. He takes on the look of the indigenous,
whose faces Catich studied as a boy growing up in Montana,
until he was orphaned at twelve. The victim's face is round and
his cheekbones high, hair black, skin dark, and chest barreled in
heroic form. In the main stained-glass window three-headed
cubist demons and gargoyles with Mayan glyphs are bounded
off from a crucified Jesus. A stream of blood and water from his
side is shed on Storm Lake. The artist ordained this a special

place with a renewing covenant. It was, after all, the only church that had the spirit to take on his work.

When you look inside you see all the people, brown and white and black, illuminated in the dapple of the stained glass. The church is the main organizing cultural institution in the immigrant community, and St. Mary's is especially so to the Latinos. It is their safe harbor, their sanctuary. They see themselves on the walls, and we are drawn to walk with them.

I t was about five a.m., she said. The sun was just eking over the horizon. A foggy dew obscured the street in San Salvador, El Salvador, as Emilia Marroquin walked with her grandmother. "Look," her grandma said, "there's a row of coconuts on the road."

As they approached it became clear it was a row of human heads lined up by the death squad.

"I remember living in that situation. You would see people hanging from the trees, women without breasts during the civil war. And it's worse now.

"I won't go back to El Salvador. I'll go to China before I would go back there. It's not safe."

Emilia, forty-six, was on the verge of tears the entire time she talked about her story and the stories of the dozens of young people she knows who live in a bureaucratic limbo without proper documents.

The Dreamers.

She supposes that as a child she dreamed of being a homemaker. That's all a girl could dream. Her mother left for California when Emilia was six. Emilia lived with her grandmother. Emilia's mother was a house cleaner for a man in California who took pity on her. He sponsored her application for permanent residency, which allowed Emilia and her sister, Patricia, to emigrate from their life steeped in terror.

She spoke a day after President Trump, through Attorney General Sessions, announced that he would cancel the DACA program instituted by President Obama for children brought to the United States by their parents. Trump gave Congress six months to come up with a plan for the Dreamers, young people brought here from Honduras who can't even remember being there. There might be five hundred, maybe more, in the school district. Marroquin knows many of them through her work. It rends her heart.

"These kids grew up in this country. They went to Storm Lake High School. They feel that they are citizens of this country. They got the Dreamer card because they follow the law. They try to follow the rules. We have to do everything we can to protect them," she said.

Marroquin came to Storm Lake from Los Angeles in November 2000 in a blizzard she will never forget. She had met her husband, Douglas, another Salvadoran expat, in L.A. They married and started a family there. One day he was walking their one-year-old son down the sidewalk and witnessed a drive-by shooting in front of their home.

"We gotta get outa here," he told Emilia.

She had just met a woman through a friend who told her about IBP hiring in Storm Lake. They were here in the blink of an eye.

She lasted about a day at the plant. Doug worked there for fifteen years, and now works at the Hy-Vee supermarket distribution warehouse in Cherokee twenty-two miles away. Emilia didn't breathe a word of English when she moved to Iowa. She buckled down and learned through Even Start, a federally funded school program that helps teach parents with preschool children.

Armed with English, she enrolled at Iowa Central Community College and earned an associate's degree in human services in four years. After another three years of study, she will soon graduate with a bachelor's degree in human services from Buena Vista University.

"You can't believe how much work it has been, especially when you can't speak English and you have four kids" (Arminda, twenty-eight, who works for the Buena Vista County Attorney; Naomi, twenty, a student at the University of Iowa; Matthew, eighteen, a senior at Storm Lake High School who wants to be a writer, Lord help him; and Briana, fifteen, also a student at SLHS).

All the while she worked at the Head Start / Even Start program as a community liaison and home visitor. She helps families get the help they need, helps them set goals and achieve them, and orients them to a new life in Storm Lake. She likes helping parents succeed, just as she was helped. That's one of the things she appreciates most about serving on the school board: helping parents figure out how things work here and explaining things to them.

She says the Storm Lake schools are working hard to help immigrant students succeed. There are before-school and after-school programs to help with latchkey kids. Those just ran out of federal funding but hope to survive on private contributions and, for the first time, fees for students. The district gets extra state funding with each English Language Learner student, but that expires over a five-year period with each student. The district seldom raises property taxes yet provides extraordinary services to students and families, Marroquin says.

"You don't see that level of concern at every school. I think it's something we can be very proud of," she said.

Her sister, Patricia, works for the U.S. Department of Agriculture in a Denison meatpacking plant. They see each other all the time. They are all citizens now, Emilia, Doug, and Patricia. Protected, Emilia can speak freely.

"Our supporters are growing. You can see it here and across the country. Microsoft, Amazon, Facebook. That's positive. Steve King is just one person. Congress is so much bigger than that. This needs to move quickly. I still dream about a big immigration reform bill."

Spoken like an optimistic new citizen who believes in the power of the people over big money and cynicism.

There is talk of aiding immigrants. They have been talking about it since 1986, the year of the last major immigration reform (supported by Senator Chuck Grassley, who now, as Senate Judiciary chairman, says he regrets it because it amounted to amnesty). And Representative King did play a role in bringing down House Speaker John Boehner over immigration reform. Speaker Paul Ryan is cognizant of the minority rumblings beneath his chair. He decided in April 2018 not to seek re-election, like Boehner before him.

Latinos avert their gaze and keep their eyes on their work in building Storm Lake. Marroquin relishes her task. This is her dream come true.

She seeks no higher office. She has no ambition for herself. She speaks only of the immigrants.

"I don't know what God has prepared for me. I'm praying to God that something good happens for all these people, for this country. I pray a lot. God makes miracles. Look at mine. His timing is perfect. It is our place to find the reason."

The ones who work get by. Many do not, so they leave.

The Latinos in Storm Lake live in shadows, afraid, Poncho Mayorga told me in 2005. His words still ring true. They fear the boss, ICE, the system. So they keep a step back and eyes askance.

Poncho left and returned to Ayotlan, Jalisco, in Mexico. He comes into the pool hall there with a big grin and greetings for all. His little pickup is parked outside with the portable welder that is his stock-in-trade.

"Work here is sometimes good, sometimes not. But this is my home," Poncho says. He worked in Illinois, South Dakota, and Iowa as a common laborer and welder. He spent some time in Sheldon, and put down a few beers at Malarky's Pub during visits to his friends from Santa Rita in Storm Lake.

"I had too many problems in the United States because I am Mexican," he said. "Too many Americans don't like us. Whatever the problem, they say Mexican, Mexican, Mexican. But it's African, Nicaraguan, Salvadoran. I work in the snow, in the hot, on the kill floor, in the welding shop. But too many Americans say, 'Hey, wetback.' This is no good. Mexicans go to the United States to work. That's it.

"In the U.S., the money is good all the time. In Mexico, we're never in good money. It's only for the big people."

One of the little people walks in. He is Cucko, seven, whose mother works in the fields all day trying to support six children. The father left. There is no child support, no welfare, no alimony.

Just the kindness of men in the pool hall. One day Cucko may join us in Iowa, if he makes it.

At 8:15 p.m. a church bell rings once. Conversation stops. Pool cues rest. Beer bottles are put down. All the men stand at attention looking at Santa Rita Church. The town is silent. Hands are folded. A minute later, the gong sounds. The men bless themselves with the sign of the cross. Revelry resumes.

What was that all about?

"We pray for Catholics all over the world," Poncho says.

Cucko prays for us.

People walk for miles from distant communities to pay homage at St. Juan de los Lagos up in the hills not far from Ayotlan. A town of seventy thousand, it is to Jalisco what Dubuque, home of the archbishop, is to Iowa Catholics. A church on every corner, including a basilica visited by Pope John Paul II.

The pilgrims approach the door and fall to their knees on the cobblestone floor. They march on their knees to the altar, where they offer a prayer to Santo Toribio, patron of the immigrants.

The stream of humanity on its knees flows all day and night.

Jesus cries tears of blood in the pictures. The Madonna looks down, sad. And there, enshrined in flowers, is the photo of Toribio, once a Catholic priest in this region.

Toribio was born in 1900 and executed by federal Mexican forces in the town of Tequila in 1928. The priest had refused government orders to quit preaching, and he celebrated Mass among thickets to hide. He was found in an abandoned tequila distillery, where he had set up a makeshift chapel, and shot to death as his sister cried out. He was declared a saint in 2000, and his day is marked as May 25.

In the 1970s, an immigrant was in the desert of Arizona lost and without water. A man appeared, gave him water, and showed him the way. The immigrant arrived at his destination safely, and returned to pay homage to the saint whose picture he had never seen.

Upon arrival at San Juan de los Lagos, he saw the picture of Toribio. It was the same man who had helped him in the desert. People say it happens all the time: Toribio gives money or water or comfort to the people dashing over the border in the dead of night.

"Do you believe this?" I asked Moises Delgado, the Ayotlan County official and lawyer.

"Yes, don't you?" he asked me.

"I am like doubting Thomas," I said. "I need to see the wounds and feel them to really believe."

He wears a cowboy hat and boots, sometimes has a red pickup truck, and ushers the lost immigrants to safe harbor. When they ask how they can thank him, the man tells them to go to Santa Ana de Guadalupe Church in Jalisco and ask the locals about Toribio Romo. The locals point to his portrait in the church, and the immigrants realize it is the man from the desert.

This man of the people was a playwright and social critic who urged his people of the Los Altos region near Guadalajara—Storm Lake's sister city, Ayotlan, is in the same diocese—not to emigrate to *el norte* but to stay and fight for freedom in Mexico. But he also acknowledged the long oppression of poor rural Mexicans.

"Hunger knows no borders," Toribio said.

The bloody pictures, the people on their knees, the sad faces, the revolutions, the dashed hopes, the woman without arms sewing with her feet, the simple poverty, the rehydration room, the poor lady with the sugarcane, the kindnesses without answer, the wounds all around, inescapable yet compelling. You are drawn to be enveloped into it.

The plane tilts over Omaha. The fields are golden in the five o'clock Saturday sun. It is beautiful. Somewhere on I-80 or I-29, a van is filled with Mexicans hoping for a future. Some end up dead, like the ones piled in the train car at Denison. Some make it, like Raul Andrade, who met his wife, Angie Stephan, in 2001 in Storm Lake.

They are happy. Raul will become a citizen. He has a shiny red pickup that he wants to deliver to his father, a campesino, at the Santa Rita festival in May. His dad's pickup is shot. He hopes to bring his two-year-old daughter, Cambrie, to see his hometown. She wears a necklace and on its end is a pendant. It holds a picture of Santo Toribio. She is blessed.

Every December hundreds of Mexicans in Storm Lake celebrate perhaps their most important holiday: the feast of Our Lady of Guadalupe. We see people dressed as mid-1500s peasants in bright red, the color of the rose. They will feast, parade, dance almost in a trance, and feast again in the St. Mary's School gym. If you want to see and begin to understand real Latino life, this is it.

Every year we chronicle the festival as if it were St. Patrick's Day, a cultural relic that is thrown into the melting pot and becomes something of the U.S., a day for drinking and drinking songs. St. Patrick drove the serpents out of Ireland (metaphor for wave after wave of foreign conquerors), and Guinness had nothing to do with it.

The feast of Our Lady has maintained its much deeper cultural significance. Mexicans take it very seriously.

"The Mexican people, after more than two centuries of experiments, have faith only in the Virgin of Guadalupe and the National Lottery," said Nobel laureate in literature Octavio Paz.

But what is the story actually about?

It goes like this: On December 9, 1531, peasant Juan Diego, fifty-seven, a widower, is walking past a hill near Mexico City where he encounters an apparition of the Blessed Virgin Mary. (In Mexico, the rich and powerful always live on top of the hill.) She wants a shrine built in her honor so that she may spread the gospel of love to the Americas. The local bishop would not believe the poor Indian. Juan Diego returns with blooming roses bound in a cloak made from cactus fiber in which Mary's image appears as Matron of the Americas. The bishop becomes a believer. The shrine gets built on that hill where five messages were delivered to Juan Diego, and millions of indigenous people convert to Christianity.

Before, the natives were subject to Aztec atrocities that involved the sacrifice of twenty thousand people per year. The Spanish came along with their own version of atrocious. And then Mary appears on a hill. She puts on a mestiza face, half Spanish and half Indian—the face of an outcast in the Latin American culture of the time. Her only message is unity, love, and dignity.

She always addresses Juan Diego as "my littlest child," or "the least of my children." For the first time, the people of Mexico had been claimed by a higher authority than an Aztec priest or a Spanish conquistador.

Her most important message:

"I am your merciful mother, to you, and to all the inhabitants on this land and all the rest who love me, invoke and confide in me; listen there to their lamentations, and remedy all their miseries, afflictions, and sorrows . . . that nothing should frighten or grieve you. Am I not here, who is your mother? Are you not under my protection? Am I not your health? Are you not happily in my fold? What else do you wish? Do not grieve or be disturbed by anything."

Natives saw in her a liberator from this veil of tears.

They still do.

The Virgin is a protector of immigrants, along with St. Toribio. You see the image of the Virgin tattooed on the backs of men or emblazoned on their jackets—she has their back.

Pope John Paul II declared her the patron saint of the Americas in 1999. That's right, a mestiza—the lowest of the low in colonial Mexico—is watching over the United States these days. It is not some Aryan queen.

She implores Juan Diego to trust her, that she can make the bishop believe. And if he can, well, there might be hope that others will see the peasant as a person of dignity. Her iconography links the old world to the new, European to native, North America to South America.

It is said that her eyes look down because she takes on the sorrows of the children. She chose roses for display because they are the emblem of a certain sadness in a perfect form.

In all her reported appearances, from Fatima to Lourdes to Guadalupe, she reveals herself to the poor and disenfranchised. She does not speak directly to clerics. Her message is always to join her in a prayer for peace and unity. It is always the same message. Can millions upon millions of people be so wrong?

Plenty of people see it as so much dancing or jumping around.

Those folks don't matter to the dancers so much. They have been called every name in the book by their neighbors here in Storm Lake and by our own elected officials. Many have crossed the Rio Grande in the dead of night or rode a freight train through Honduras in hopes of a job that will put a roof over their head. They know they could be snapped up at any time by ICE. It has always been this way. It was the way of Juan Diego.

They work day and night, they pray to a statue of the Virgin they donated to St. Mary's Church. They come together in multiple generations and crawl on their knees to church, always looking down as she does, acknowledging something greater than herself. Her name in the native language means "woman who puts serpents underfoot."

She came through for Juan Diego when the church, the only authority at the time, tried to laugh him off. Those people dancing know who got the last laugh.

Juan Diego died a happy man two years after the bishop and his court brushed him off the first time.

Myth? For you, maybe. For them, it's the one real day of freedom over the oppressive centuries. The one day when peasant is prince. When ICE cannot touch you. That's a miracle in this world.

They come from all over Latin America, even Cuba, in search of something, usually just a safe place. In my mind's eye I can see a relief from the cathedral in Old Havana from a 2015 visit. Inside the box along the side wall Mary is suspended over a boat containing three copper miners trying to get home before a storm. She stands on a silver half-moon.

Outside a Santeria woman, black, dressed in all white, with a white umbrella, has forsaken her former identity in a place where identity and structure morph and decay under sea wind and salt. They leave, and land in Storm Lake. The Santeria woman will assume a new identity, in concert with the divine, in hopes of a better tomorrow.

You cannot separate those hopes from the poverty or the reality of Latin America, which links itself to Storm Lake, nearly a continent away.

In rural Mexico, they crawl on their hands and knees over cobblestones to the shrine of St. Toribio, who watches over immigrants. He gets them across the Sonora and to Storm Lake, Iowa, where they assume a new identity in hopes of a better life.

Once here, they dance in the St. Mary's gym to the lady who came to the poor campesino Juan Diego. They venerate her statue.

And once here, from Cuba and Mexico and El Salvador, they sing for the great hero of all Latin America, José Martí, who wrote:

> *With the poor people of the earth*
> *I want to cast my lot*
> *The brook of the mountains*
> *Gives me more pleasure than the sea.*

# CHAPTER 16

# A Place to Call Home

In the late 1800s, Jim, John, and Mike McKenna escaped the oppression of the Crown and landed in Boston off the boat from Ireland searching for someplace they could be free to call home. They found their way to Storm Lake just as winter was setting in, and dug a hole into a hill near a creek that fed the Raccoon. They lived in that dugout for the winter, came out in spring and saw that all was good, and propagated all around Sulphur Springs with children and corn and hogs.

Ed McKenna, the friendly pharmacist at the Hy-Vee supermarket, derives from those hardy genes and clings to his coordinates. His cousins are still farming and raising hogs around the neighborhood more than a century later. Ed served on the school board when they built the elementary school in 2008 and was president when they expanded the high school in 2016, from which he graduated more than fifty years ago. Those McKenna brothers were looking for someplace new where anybody had a chance, and they were willing to live underground like gophers to plant their future in Providence Township, Buena Vista County, Iowa. They stuck. Ed sticks. A big reason the Storm Lake school board supports immigrants, no matter what, is because people like Ed McKenna remember where they came from.

People from faraway places made Iowa home.

Home to a pro baseball player, grandson of immigrants who eschewed the bright lights. To a tie-dyed bar owner in a village of six hundred who probably should be anyplace else, yet doesn't know where else to live the dream. Home to a trapper who sees freedom in a gun and can smell a fouled river. To a young Latina who wants to trot the globe singing opera while landing in Storm Lake. To a young Mexican American who sees hard work and success as a combined virtue. And to a coyote hunter who needs just one arrow.


L inda Torres, twenty, is a mezzo-soprano with a math fall-back position.

"I want to go around the world and sing opera," she said over lunch at Better Day Café on Lake Avenue, where she tried the new chicken, avocado, and bacon sandwich.

Linda would find out the next day why she can't hit five notes in a certain vocal register. She thinks she has nodes on her vocal cords. The doctors say they can dissolve them and return her full range. She hopes so.

"I am afraid of losing my voice. It happens."

She gets the call: It's not nodules but something else. She waits for more news.

Linda is a sophomore at Buena Vista University. She wants to teach second- or third-grade math. She and her siblings were math whizzes at Storm Lake High School. An older brother is a police officer in Denison. A sister moved to Chariton. Her younger brother, Nacho (Ignacio), is a senior at Storm Lake High School and hopes to attend Buena Vista.

Her seventy-eight-year-old grandmother, who lives across the border from Brownsville, Texas, is awed by Linda, that she actually is going to college. Linda holds that in her heart. Linda was born in the United States; her mother was born in Mexico. Attending college is something fantastic to her grandmother.

Linda worked three jobs to save enough money to go to college. It held her back her freshman year, she thinks. Since then, her mother switched jobs from Tyson to Buena Vista University to work as a custodian. That means her children get free tuition. The new college president, Josh Merchant, just met Linda's mother and was asking all about Linda. He wants to recruit more Latinos to Buena Vista, and he wants to learn what blocks them. For starters, Linda tells college officials that the dorms don't represent real life. She knows of about eight Latinos who live on campus. At Storm Lake High School, 70 percent of the high school graduating class is Hispanic.

She didn't meet her own academic expectations last year and decided she would be better off living off campus this year. She cut down from three jobs to two: waitress at Better Day and waterpark supervisor at King's Pointe Resort, all while studying for a double major.

While Linda was growing up, her mother struggled to make do. Linda's father left when she was young. Linda never saw a winter coat until she was in kindergarten. A couple of teachers, Stacey Cole and Jacquie Drey, asked her mother if it would be all right to take Linda and her brother to Walmart to get coats.

They outfitted the kids. "We didn't have much," Linda said. "That's why I want to be a teacher. Because of Stacey Cole and Jacquie Drey."

Cole's husband, Chris, is the assistant police chief in Storm Lake. Hence, Linda's brother wanted to be a cop.

Many Latinos want to get out of Storm Lake and away from the stifling watch of their parents. "Our culture is very strict," Linda explained. Her sister was not allowed to date in high school. It can chafe, so they get away. But often, they come back.

"To us, family is everything," she said. That's the tough part of opera. She would have to leave her family in Storm Lake to sing around the world. She believes she can do it. She can feel it. If she can just get her voice back.


Linda works for Topiz Martinez at Better Day. Topiz is an Aztec name. His brother is Tano and his sister is Icxiuh. Topiz's father, Guillermo, moved from Mexico City to California to the Twin Cities, where the children were born. He wanted his children to remember where the family came from, to remember their heritage.

What is that heritage?

"About Mexico, I don't know," Topiz tells me from behind the counter. "That is not my experience. My experience is as a Mexican American. And I am very proud of that. To me, it is about family."

He is twenty-eight. His dad bought the building that houses Better Day Café fourteen years ago. Guillermo's brother moved here to work at Tyson. Guillermo rehabbed and flipped houses in the Twin Cities and put his eye on property in Storm Lake. He knew it would grow in value. It has, by probably 25 percent since he bought what was built as a pharmacy and soda fountain in 1897.

Topiz lives upstairs and pinches pennies. He started his restaurant in the building three years ago as a coffee shop. He couldn't make it on that so he started making sandwiches. He can't quite get ahead on that so he is shooting to turn it into a breakfast and lunch joint with a grill. That will take cash, which he is saving one day at a time to avoid taking debt.

Topiz wants to live here to be with his cousins and uncle. It's a chance for him to build something of his own, and he likes it.

"We had pretty impressive growth from last year to this year, but last year I was barely breathing. So I'm not sure how impressive the growth was."

He has learned the hard way: how to keep the books, how to make a great cup of coffee, how to serve a lunch rush with two tiny sandwich grills. He has had his rough spots but he is proud of the food he serves. Customers like him. He is always cheerful, he learns names immediately, and he never speaks a cross word. He is a good businessman. He will thrive.

Topiz was born in Minneapolis, but he calls this place home. He wants to serve Storm Lake, maybe on a city board or a commission as he builds the business and learns the ropes. Someday he wants to do like his dad and build houses. He loves carpentry.

What is he about? "To work hard. To not let our parents' hard work go to waste. To make it pay off."

This is the future of Storm Lake speaking, young people who have nearly nothing but optimism and a capacity for hard work. Who wants to drive them off?

The main north-south street through downtown, Lake Avenue,

is full, increasingly occupied by Latino-owned businesses. That is not the case in most small Iowa towns, where you could shoot a cannon down Main Street and not hit anything. La Juanita up the street does a land-office business in five-dollar burritos *mucho grande*, declared the best in the land. Those burritos bought the owner, Victor Bautista, a farm north of town where he runs horses inside a white fence. It is painted on a mural over the dining hall. Tradesmen and women of all cultures go there for cheap food. A taco costs two dollars.

Either they are the best vegetable hawkers you have ever seen or these women just want to make friends. Nhia Yang, twenty-nine, and her mother, Mang Xiong, sixty-five, insisted that Dolores take a big bunch of lemongrass for free from their busy Storm Lake Farmers Market stand on the courthouse square in the late August rain. "You take. You take. You like."

We take. And then we buy. Some big green leafy stuff.

"What's that?"

"Spinach water." She meant water spinach.

"How much?"

"Two dollah."

"What do you do with it?"

"Stir-fry."

Beautiful little purplish and pinkish balls sit in baskets. They look like decorations. Ukrainian Easter eggs.

"What are they?"

"Eggplant."

"How much?"

"Two dollah."

"What do you do with it?"

"Boil."

There are big ones, too, and in-betweeners. And every size of cucumber you can imagine. One looks like a rugby ball.

Something looks like a scaly green sea urchin.

"Bitter melon."

"How much?"

"Two dollah."

"What do you do with it?"

"Stir-fry. Or boil it."

And so on.

The men are back home or working the pack.

They came to Storm Lake seven years ago from Thailand. Why did they come? I ask. Mang looks over at her Hmong cousin in the next booth and repeats the question. They laugh and go back and forth in their language and keep on laughing. Nhia laughs.

"Too much gunfire. Violence," Nhia interprets.

What they probably were saying:

"What a ridiculous question. That man has no idea what we have been through. The Chinese kicked us around, the Vietnamese kicked us around, the Laotians kicked us around, until we ended up in Thailand, and working in the garden right here in Storm Lake every day is a far sight better than getting shot at in Dien Bien Phu."

Interesting that the Hmong and the Tai Dam people who live in Storm Lake both originated at, and were driven out of, Dien Bien Phu along the old Asian opium routes. They lived in the forests. They were hill people. It was ground zero for the start of the French Indochinese wars that led to the Vietnam War and the killing fields of Cambodia. The Hmong never really wanted a part of any of these wars but fought the Laotian government at our behest. We are just getting around to paying them back by inviting them in.

So of course they are relieved to be in Storm Lake.

Nhia works at Tyson and she likes it. They have twenty-some cousins in town, and she guesses there might be two or three hundred Hmong in Storm Lake. There are thirty thousand in St. Paul, Minnesota. A large contingent lives in Wisconsin. They like to stick together.

A neighbor who lives a few doors up from us squats in the yard and picks lamb's quarters, the bane of every Iowa farmer. You could stir-fry it or boil it. A woman walks in Sunset Park with a basket on her bicycle that contains big bags loaded with weeds. She crouches and picks another. Mabel the newshound makes her nervous but the Hmong lady concentrates her gaze on the greens.

They eat rice and a little bit of meat with each meal. Mainly, it is the vegetables they grow. They say they brought the seeds with them from Thailand, where they farmed. They sell these gnarly little ears of sweet corn grown from that seed.

Mang picked up a purple long bean from a bunch and ate it raw while we visited. She smiled the entire time. The crow's-feet around her eyes and her cousin's in the next booth indicate that they laugh a lot, and that they are in the sun a lot. They all have dirt under their fingernails. They work together and help each other out. They will get by. Everyone is well fed. When you see how the Asians and Latinos have climbed the ladder from refugee to renter to homeowner in Storm Lake, you would make a safe bet on the children of these Hmong women getting ahead, just like Linda Torres's brothers and sisters.

Dolores took the lemongrass home as a gift. They have nothing but their seeds, and they wanted to give the lemongrass to us, just like the lady who gave me sugarcane on the street corner in Ayotlan. We could learn something from them. Instead, normally I drive past and smile. First they come from Laos, then Mexico, then Cuba and Myanmar and Sudan. And Samoa. They want to give and build, not take and tear down. They have seen plenty of that where they come from.

Fifty families, many of them undocumented, live in a mobile home park in Alta, five miles west of Storm Lake. It's owned by a company in Canada. The homes are purchased on contract by the residents, and they each pay a two-hundred-dollar monthly lot-rental fee. Teresa Villegas, twenty-five, with two little children, bought hers for twenty-five hundred dollars. She sends the children to St. Mary's School. She wants them to live the dream she is pursuing.

Many of the trailers have become run down. Residents complain. It got to the city council in late 2017. The city council would just as soon condemn the whole works but the city attorney advised them that it is horribly expensive to condemn something—and then there remains the problem of those with no place to go. The owner up in Canada claims he didn't know the score. People are being exploited but they fear being turned out. Tom called a councilman to ask about it. The councilman hung up on him. Mayor Ron Neulieb said talk of condemnation was "just rumors," even though it was discussed in public during at least two city council meetings that Tom attended where he heard it with his own ears. Neulieb was trying to douse the embers of resentment against the trailer park and its residents, while at the same time attempting to get the homes up to snuff. The city code enforcement officer, a retired construction man, tried to work with the families on meeting codes. He got to know them and they trusted his patience. The mayor and his wife, with church volunteers, turned out to help residents fix up their homes on weekends. Progress was being made.

Just as things were getting calmed down and worked out, a new mayor was elected and took office in January 2018. Al Clark, who moved to Alta from eastern Iowa a year earlier, went door-to-door and campaigned hard when the other two candidates didn't. Clark is a Trump fan. He relishes confrontation. The city building inspector who was working with the residents abruptly quit. The new mayor told local pastors that he wanted to clear out the trailer court, and that the pastors should prepare to help find new homes for the displaced. The residents rose up again with support from the pastors.

Villegas was alarmed.

"I love my job. I love my home and I love my kids," she told Tom. "I just don't want to get kicked out of here."

Eight homes in this park currently are in violation of building code. A new code enforcement officer was hired. He quit in March 2018 after less than a month on the job. Within days of his resignation, red-tag notices were posted on six homes by the city. The residents believe the mayor posted them. The notices say the residents cannot inhabit their homes. People are living in unsafe conditions. The city has a responsibility to all neighbors. But there are business owners in town who don't want to shoo them off to Storm Lake and lose the school enrollment. The Alta-Aurelia shared district has lost enrollment each of the last five years. The school superintendent was trying to stick up for the trailer court residents.

Alta was a town of eighteen hundred settled, and later mainly populated, by Swedish and German Lutherans. Now it's a town turning brown. That makes some people anxious. The Alta city council got uptight when a taco cart owner pulled his cart onto private property near the community center during Latino weddings or *quinceañeras*. Members said he wasn't paying property taxes, even though the property owner who gave the taco man permission was. The taco man was willing to comply with all permitting and health requirements, but the council still wanted him back in Storm Lake. Change is hard. But it all gets worked through, generally. People see what they say in the newspaper and realize what they are thinking and often back off, as they did with the taco man.

The residents of the trailer court cause no particular trouble other than the code violations, which they endure because they have few options. They are poor. That's why they are there.

"A lot of us here are undocumented immigrants. They can't stand up to anybody out of fear," said Desarae Morales, twenty-six, who works as a caregiver at a group home for profoundly disabled children. "I've been homeless once and I don't plan on being that way again."

Villegas hopes to move up. In the meantime, she intends to stand and fight for her home alongside Morales and others who can afford to speak. Latinos will stay in Alta because it's cheap and the town needs them. In the end it will get sorted out, as it always does. But there are issues to work through that often are beyond the residents' comprehension, and almost always beyond their control.

Villegas received a red tag on her home. She had been living with her sister briefly while recovering from surgery. She said she was unaware of an unpaid water bill that generated the tagging. In early March 2018 Villegas and her children faced the prospect of homelessness.

The new mayor refuses to speak with Tom or reveal his endgame. Mayor Clark maintains that he will not speak to us because we purvey "fake news." The trailer park residents are afraid after thinking that things would get better. The International Brotherhood of Teamsters' new community organizing arm, TeamCAN, heard about their plight through *The Times*, assigned professional organizers to the trailer park, and hired a lawyer to defend their rights. TeamCAN representatives met with the mayor and other city officials two days after the red tags were posted. The mayor agreed to allow TeamCAN help the residents draft a cleanup plan involving the owner from Canada. It still could all blow up, but the storm was calmed. The Teamsters are planting their flag in Alta in hopes of reaching out to new workers in new ways and renewing labor in rural areas. Knowing Alta, the people of the town will put a few enlarged egos in check and embrace the immigrants as they have before. Many townsfolk are speaking up for the trailer park residents and want to help. And they want to help provide for safe housing. The volunteers showed up when asked.

After all, the Alta council voted to donate five hundred dollars to a school program that packed poor students' backpacks with food for the weekend. Back in 1979, the town lifted up the Phomvisay family, Laotian refugees who landed in town when Aiddy Phomvisay was seven years old. The churches settled them and helped Aiddy master English. He married his high school sweetheart, Mindy Radke, and went on to become a school principal in Des Moines. In 2014, he was named Iowa's Secondary Principal of the Year. He gives all the credit to Alta and those church ladies and teachers. It's not so simple to say that rural white people don't have a heart for rural brown people.

The council members sometimes are ticked off that we talk about these sensitive problems. Dolores got the cold shoulder at National Night Out in the Alta city park for the reporting that our son Tom did on the trailer court. She will keep coming back to take photos, as she did the week before, when Silvino Morelos bought the old sale barn just east of Alta. They used to run hogs, cattle, and sheep through there along the railroad tracks and Highway 7. Mainly sheep from 1971 to 2004, the span during which Jerry Carlson owned it.

Silvino went to Los Angeles from Mexico thirty-three years ago, and to Storm Lake twenty years ago. He and his wife, Mayela, started Morelos Meat Market. Mayela works at Tyson pork from 5:00 a.m. to 2:00 p.m., then takes over the cash register from Silvino. He works the evening shift at Tyson. His day is done at midnight. They are expanding. They just bought a building downtown twice the size to expand. It will allow room for even more jars of squid or exotic green sauces with Lao writing on the label that I dare not try.

He missed the farm where he was reared in Mexico. He is trying to re-create it after having purchased the vacated Alta sale barn. He has gardens in the pens outdoors where the livestock were held before being led into the show ring. The ring is still there. At one time there were theater seats in it, not benches, like the Storm Lake sale barn had. The auctioneer's bench remains as goats Silvino keeps inside nose around it. His brother Gerardo helps out with the farm and at the store.

Silvino wants to build a house out there. He wants to call Alta home. He isn't going back. The sale barn is his dream as he works day and night. Everything is about family in the rural Mexican culture. The old ones live with the young ones and the young ones don't want to leave them. Our folks used to be that way.

B utch Biittner always comes home.
       He stood in the shade with his big paw on the sign carved in the shape of a baseball bat. BIITTNER PARK, it says, named after Butch (a.k.a. Larry). He was the best there was. Behind him the dirt infield was awash in July sun just after the All-Star break. This was where he got his start in baseball, before the place even had a fence back in 1964. He made it from this dusty little field to the one called Wrigley for a great five-year run in the middle of a fourteen-year big league career as a steady batsman and fielder. A journeyman who won't be in Cooperstown.

Butch was my hero. Bigger than Harmon Killebrew to me. I knew him. I saw him. I held his broken bat. What is he doing now? I hear he could be irascible. My anxiety was misplaced. He loves to visit. You shake his hand and it is concrete.

I had taken notice when I heard that he threw out the honorary first pitch for a Saturday night game on July 8, 2017, that saw the North Siders drop one to the Pirates, 4–2, a familiar story for the former first baseman born to a farm family north of Varina. The honor was coincidental to and not commemorative of forty years earlier, when Butch recorded his only major league mound appearance during a July 4 doubleheader. Let the box score show that Larry Biittner hurled one and one-third innings of the first game against the Expos. How did it go, Butch?

"I struck out the pitcher twice in an inning. That sorta tells you how it went," said Biittner, seventy, drinking iced tea at the Family Table restaurant in Pocahontas, thirty-five miles east of Storm Lake. "I remember it like it was ten minutes ago. I try like hell to forget it."

But then he is reminded by some punk who shagged balls during Buena Vista Beaver games behind the green wooden Memorial Park fence with his brothers and buddies. I was ten. Larry Biittner was a college junior who hit like a real man. The foul balls had to come back to the dugout. The homers we could pocket.

Depending on who the Beavers played that day, and how Biittner and Danny Monzon felt, we could go home with two or three new game balls in a day, with just one Louisville Slugger scuff on each. We would rummage through the broken bats to get Biittner's, then tape it up and use it in sandlot games at Bradford Field down on College Street.

He was, in my mind at least, the greatest athlete to ever inhabit Storm Lake.

His dad, Ed, came over from Germany in 1897 when he was three. The family were tenant farmers. They spoke German. That's why they have the double i in their name. It's all about the umlaut. It was supposed to be Büttner, with that funny umlaut ü. They didn't countenance that at Ellis Island so it became a double i. Nobody cared. The Storm Lake cousins dropped one i to make it simpler yet.

"When Dad died he only knew a few cusswords in German," Butch recalled.

Ed gave up farming and moved to town when Butch started kindergarten. Ed became one of the two town cops. He taught his tough lefty son the knuckle curveball. Butch didn't need any work on his ninety-miles-per-hour fastball. And he could put lumber on the ball like nobody around here.

At six feet two and two hundred pounds, Butch was recruited to play basketball at Drake University by the legendary coach Maury John. Butch hated big-time college basketball. He needed to get home. He knew he had a chance at playing pro baseball because they scouted him in high school. He came back home to play at Buena Vista, a national small-college powerhouse. At first coach Jay Beekmann was skeptical because Butch had a reputation as a party animal. But Beekmann had seen him hit, so he let Butch in on a gamble.

"I had to teach Coach Beekmann how to work with me," Butch said.

He became the Beaver ace. He led the Iowa Conference in pitching and batting. His buddy Monzon, a Puerto Rican from the Bronx, was in the three hole and Butch batted cleanup. Monzon was drafted by the Twins in 1967. Biittner knew he was next. I recall sitting with my dad and Vince Meyer of Bancroft, a bird dog for the Phillies, watching Biittner from the first-base bleachers.

After his 1968 senior season Biittner headed down to Kansas to play summer ball. He was on his way home from St. Joe, Missouri, and heard that the pro draft was on. He got to Pocahontas, where his mom, Hattie, gave him a phone number. It was the Washington Senators' scout. That fourth-round draft call put him on a path to play for the Washington Senators, the Texas Rangers, the Montreal Expos, and the Chicago Cubs.

Butch was a solid singles man who hit .270 over his career. He developed a bit of a cult following in the late 1970s in Chicago sparked by a fly ball that bounced in the outfield. He was running for it when his cap fell off, and he couldn't find the ball. The bleacher bums yelled, "In your hat! In your hat!" He found the ball and threw the batter out at third. Those lovable Cubs.

He agreed that he led a charmed life. But the dance on the road isn't all it's cracked up to be. He found that what he really missed was home: Pocahontas, population eighteen hundred.

"I don't tolerate cities," he said.

Traffic was slow on the main street leading to Biittner Park. In fact, there was no traffic at all. That's the way Butch likes it. A few classmates live in town. He golfs and fishes. He visits the grandkids down in Des Moines. If you really need to find him, you might check Ike's Bar about happy hour most afternoons. He played softball for years in Storm Lake but had to give it up at age fifty-five. That left shoulder needed surgery and killed his heater.

He speaks of Memorial Park in Storm Lake with as much, if not more, affection than the Friendly Confines of Wrigley Field. The years might do that to the grandson of an immigrant who has been under the brightest lights of all. The Beavers used to repair the wooden fence and grandstands and paint them. They mowed and raked. They sculpted the mound and bullpens. That was their spring training. Butch loves the place.

"Beekmann helped get me there," Biittner said.

He probably never would have to buy a drink in Chicago, but he feels the love back home. To us, Butch was the best there ever was.

"I'm just a country boy. Where else would I be?"

If there is anyone who should bail out of this rural place it is Byron Stuart. He is gay. He wears tie-dyed T-shirts under his overalls. Sometimes on special evenings he wears a purple tutu over his overalls. He ends every email with the word PEACE, always all caps. What is he doing in Pomeroy, Iowa, just a few miles down the road east of Varina and Sunken Grove?

Running a shrine to Jerry Garcia, of course.

Byron, now sixty-five, dropped out of Iowa State and wandered home not knowing what to do. He just stayed. He lived with his parents, German farmers, near Pomeroy. He helped out on the farm. But he didn't want to be a farmer.

So he bought the bar, built in 1893, and turned it into an oasis for traveling minstrels. Canned Heat, Todd Snider, Commander Cody, Freekbass, Kinky Friedman, the Bastard Sons of Johnny Cash. Acts from East Nashville, Austin, New York, and the King of the Tramps from Auburn, Iowa.

"I'm living the dream I never knew I had," Byron said.

His Sunday shows at 5:00 p.m. draw people out of the gnarled woodwork: bankers, hermits, doctors, Deadheads, bikers, lawyers, farmers, editors, and Leonard Olson, who makes kaleidoscopes. Leonard used to live on the fast track in the city until he had a massive heart attack. "I have been to the other side and there ain't nothin' there," says Leonard, who operates the Kaleidoscope Factory and the University of Leonard in Pocahontas. If your check is good, you can meditate in his tepee along the highway.

He carves kaleidoscopes by hand because he likes to look inside them. And they sell—by mail order and to tourists. Leonard does okay.

Byron struggles. For $10 you get a ticket and two free sodas, until just recently when he had to stop the free drinks. A pizza is $6.50. Byron raffles door prizes during the breaks and tells off-color jokes. He pays the acts $500, plus free beer and pizza and a motel room in Rockwell City. Sometimes he makes $100 on the $10 cover. Most of the time he probably loses.

"I'm addicted to music," Byron confessed. "I just have to keep doing this."

Guitarist Sergio Webb of Nashville calls it the "hipness center of the universe."

"I call it a listening room. People don't come here to get drunk. They come to listen to good music," Byron said.

The band shows up at the front door thinking it might be a scene from a bad movie—every other storefront is deserted. They get inside for a hug from Byron and admire the Grateful Dead memorabilia and get the vibe. They pencil it in on every future trip from Minneapolis to Kansas City. He says he puts up with the bar during the week to live for his Sunday shows.

People in Pomeroy like Byron. Nobody hassles him. He is free to live as he wishes. He gives the old coffee klatchers a key to the bar so they can open up in the morning and serve themselves. After they have winded themselves, they lock up and leave.

About seventy-five locals who maybe didn't like the decorations started their own "sports" bar in the town of six hundred. Byron's business suffered. Those Sunday patrons showed the love by organizing a campaign to help him fix the roof and buy some time, with more than five thousand dollars raised in a week or so.

"It brings tears to my eyes just thinking about it," Byron said.

He keeps rockin'. Byron provides a respite from the dominant culture.

You find the unexpected when you look for it off the main route. Three gay men dancing with a biker mama wearing colors on her leather to the sound of Brother Trucker covering "Bertha" by the Dead. There are people you never heard of who live for the sake of the song. How does Byron do it? He doesn't know. Somehow he makes just enough to keep the show going on.

J ohn Paulson would eat the back end of a skunk if you could smoke it right over hickory or pickle it. But he won't eat a fish out of the Little Sioux River, which starts from Spirit Lake on the Minnesota border down through Okoboji and Lower Gar Lake, wending southwest toward the Missouri past Linn Grove and Peterson. He sees what goes in. He won't eat what comes out.

"You always want to shoot a skunk in the heart and not the head or he'll spray all over," John advised. He likes to use a 9mm Ruger when checking traplines.

"I don't kill critters like I used to."

You won't find him at a Rainbow Gathering. He wonders why the deputy sheriff got upset and told him he had to quit shooting his cannon at ten p.m. on a Saturday night in Truesdale, population fewer than one hundred, five miles north of Storm Lake.

"Tell John he needs to let Betsy cool down," the deputy told John's wife, Nancy.

He blew up an outhouse as the central event of a party. He gets choked up when he talks about buying his grandson a semiautomatic rifle.

John is a great guy. If ground squirrels are your infestation, he will flush them out, trap them, and skin them for free. "They make nice little furry coin pouches," he remarked. He doesn't eat them. "Not worth the bother. Not enough meat. But they have a nice little pelt to them. You can skin one lickety-split."

John, sixty-three, and his bachelor brother Mike, sixty-one, put up drywall. They are the last of the plasterers. They learned plastering, fishing, and shooting from their dad, Max.

John grew up trapping. He doesn't like Hillary Clinton. He likes Obamacare. He likes Medicaid and Medicare. He likes Bernie Sanders. You know he voted for Trump, though. He doesn't talk about it. He eats raccoon, catfish, tree squirrels, beaver, muskrat—anything you can trap, shoot, or hook from a lake or trout stream. But he will not eat a fish from a filthy brown Iowa river for the toxins in them.

For John, the politics is about the guns. He was convinced that Obama did not respect the Second Amendment. It's why he has a visceral reaction when you mention Hillary's name.

He reads my paper. He is an environmentalist, an ecologist, truly a master gardener. He knows a lot more about flora and fauna than a person with a biology degree. He understands what motivates a walleye in warm water. He knows how to trap a fox using feral cat urine. He knows how the black squirrels drive out the red squirrels—with attacks on the crotch. "Mean little bastards," John said.

He doesn't care about Mexicans or gays or what your religion is. He says the two gays put out a pretty decent dinner at the small-town café that he frequents. He could be friends with Byron if he knew him. He thinks Topiz Martinez is A-OK, loves his sandwiches.

If you put all these buddies of mine in a room with their weapons you would have the Nicaraguan army. They have assault rifles, every caliber of handgun, shotguns small and large, and enough ammo to survive the end of the world. And, yes, even a cannon. They don't need no stinkin' body armor. They are not afraid of Muslim invasions. Nobody is taking out Storm Lake on their watch. They are afraid someone will try to take their guns away. Guns turned Iowa red. Guns took down the Democratic leader of the Iowa Senate. Guns will take down anyone who talks them down. People are more powerfully emotional about them here than they are about two-hundred-bushel corn. County Supervisor Dale Arends said he thinks that everybody should carry a shotgun into the courthouse for security.

Guns help keep the fear away.

They believe that a gun secures their freedom and protects their property.

And freedom is all they have left. Along with a house in Truesdale.

It was one of those perfect crisp fall mornings during the deer rut, when the males go berserk as huge combines roll through the golden carpet of corn. Deer retreat to the brush to lock antlers with other bucks so they can get at that doe.

Guy Colvin wants to get at them.

He has been a welder by trade the past thirty-some years, a singer of Johnny Cash songs in his Varina farmhouse–cum–bachelor den.

And a hunter by nature.

He works in a metal fabrication factory that makes grain-handling equipment. He drives forty-five minutes to work. The young guys there don't understand him. He is the Man in Black. He does not chitchat; he welds. They know he hunts. They were going out with assault rifles to hunt coyotes on Saturday.

"You and your rifles and your infrared scopes," he told them. "Take one down with a bow. I can get one within hours."

They laughed off the old codger.

Action was slow at Sunken Grove, a pothole marsh savanna timber complex abutted by Cedar Creek and enveloped in rows of grain under reaping. Deer are thick, but not this morning.

He climbs down from his tree stand with bow and quiver at eight-thirty a.m. for some "still hunting" on his way out.

Take a step and stand.

"You just use your eyes and scan the woods."

One step and stand. A minute later, another step and stand. Then a third step and stand.

"I see this big hunk of brown overtop of a fallen cottonwood tree," Guy said. "I'm hoping it's that damn mountain lion we've been hearing about running around here."

The flash of brown sends him down to one knee and into striking pose in one motion. The movement causes the critter's head to pop up to see what's going down.

"I get it right in the neck."

It's a full-grown coyote. He throws it in the back of the pickup and takes it home to hang and bleed in the garage.

As dusk draws near, Guy wants to see if he can still fill out his deer tag with a buck. He goes back to Sunken Grove. He's on the ground working a fenceline with brush and brambles.

"These bucks are known to get a little horsey on you in rut," Guy said. "They will charge and they can kill you."

He is armed with only a bow and arrow. He comes across a six-point buck, good size, good eating, mixing it up in the brush.

"He sees me. He is snortin' and stompin' and rakin' his antlers on the brush, and it's thick in there. He's pissed and he's gonna come at me. He lifts his head to charge and I get him right through the lungs.

"It was the most glorious day in my hunting life."

He took the coyote to work the following Monday to show the riflemen. A guy at work offered to skin and tan it. The pelt hangs on his wall while he strums "Sunday Mornin' Comin' Down."

The fellows he works with thought Obama wanted to take

their AR-15s. This gun is their hunting tool. Guy owns only a muzzle loader that shoots one pack at a time.

"That's all I need. One bullet."

His mother and sister moved from home down to Tennessee to be closer to other family who had moved down there. He thinks about the big river blue catfish down there. He could get a welding job and get away from the mopes who don't understand or respect him.

But he stays. He can't leave Sunken Grove.

He used to sit on the shore of Storm Lake late into the night hunting for Mr. Whiskers. He knows there is a forty-pound channel cat with his name on it out there somewhere. He catches blue gills from farm ponds, puts them on a hook to swim around on a line hooked to a pole that looks like it was used for Olympic vaulting. He casts into about four feet of water and mud hoping for that trophy.

Then he bought a boat.

"It took my fishing to a whole new level."

Out in a twenty-miles-per-hour wind amid the whitecaps that sometimes go brown as the silt bottom churns, Guy reflects on his politics.

"Give me a government grant. I'll teach kids how to work, how to weld, how to hunt, how to survive."

Eating the catfish and venison is like a religious experience for him. It completes the cycle, from corn to loin, from bluegill to cat, from rabbit to coyote. He eats with his son, who suffers from schizophrenia, just the two of them, one sixty and one thirty. Guy doesn't know how long that can last. The son has no options. Mental health isn't a rural thing. The governor just shut down two of the four state institutes that provide indigent care. Mental

agriculture, we care about farmers, and we care about clean water. These are the things that add up to a vision of a sustainable farm and town relationship where one builds off the other. I knew our readers knew that. And that we are hopeless progressives who go against the grain because it's just in us.

Michael Gartner, a Pulitzer Prize winner for editorial writing in 1997 and my old mentor, had encouraged me to enter for editorial writing in 2013. He even wrote a nomination letter for me. I did not win. I had said, the hell with it. I will never enter another contest. But these editorials were different, something told me.

I sent them off to Gartner again, but I never heard back from him this time. That, to me, was a strange sort of clue that something was going on. Call me weird.

April 10, Monday, two p.m. My hair looks great. Still gray but shorter. My mustache is trimmed. I have wrenched that column out of my bowels about how a Democrat will never be governor again. I sit at my desk, watching a live stream on my computer at www.pulitzer.org. Pulitzer Prize administrator Mike Pride is starting to announce twenty-one winners for 2017. Editorial writing is number eighteen.

ProPublica. The *New York Times*. The *Washington Post*. The *Miami Herald*. The *Chicago Tribune* . . .

Number seventeen, the Pulitzer Prize for Commentary, goes to Peggy Noonan of the *Wall Street Journal*.

Number eighteen. "For editorial writing, Art Cullen of *The Storm Lake Times*, Storm Lake, Iowa."

"Holy shit!" I shouted as I shot up from my chair and almost through the stained ceiling tiles.

"We won! We won! John! We won!"

"Won what?" John asked, thinking I'd cracked.

"The Pulitzer!" I screamed to him from five feet away.

We hugged for the first time in our lives.

Then a hug for Tom.

Dolores was shooting it.

Then I hugged her. There are no pictures of that.

"For editorials fueled by tenacious reporting, impressive expertise and engaging writing that successfully challenged powerful corporate agricultural interests in Iowa," the citation read.

We had heard stories about how the phones light up once you win. They rang off the hook. The first to call was Tom O'Donnell, who used to ride "the hot seat" as an assistant city editor at the *Des Moines Register*. The second call was from Bret Stephens, then of the *Wall Street Journal* and now the *New York Times*, who chaired the editorial writing jury. He was most gracious. He then hooked up with Tom on the phone and gave him the pep talk. The next call was from Tom Vilsack, and I broke down on the phone with him like a blubbering five-year-old. The entire Pulitzer committee would have pulled the award if that call had been recorded, I was such a fool.

The *Washington Post* called. The BBC, Japanese and Australian TV, Irish national radio, NPR and CBS. All the publicity generated more than thirty-five thousand dollars in unsolicited donations to the Iowa Freedom of Information Council from across the U.S. People value open government and a free press, even out here among the hogs and turkeys. I was invited to speak a month later at the National Press Club in Washington, DC. At the hotel bar I struck up a conversation with a man reading a newspaper.

"Hey, did you win a Pulitzer Prize?" he asked me.

"Yeah. How did you know?" I asked.

"I'm from Iowa. Of course I knew. I'm from Clinton."

We were immediate best friends. Everywhere you go you meet somebody from Iowa. Not Des Moines or Clinton or Storm Lake, but Iowa.

Back home, Buena Vista County supervisor Paul Merten (D–Storm Lake) in late April penned a letter that we published word for word saying that the Pulitzer Prize was tainted. "I guess if you tell lies long enough they become the truth in the mind of the teller," he said of *The Times*. Publishing is the only business I am aware of that invites criticism of its best efforts and prints it, verbatim in our practice, which is what the Pulitzer Prizes should be about.

John, Tom, and I went to Columbia University in New York to pick up the prize in May. At lunch I sat next to university president Lee Bollinger, whose dad was a community newspaper editor/publisher in Oregon who slept with a shotgun under the bed because the sheriff was after him. It was surreal for someone like me, who thought of himself as a bumpkin, to be among the greats of American journalism. *Washington Post* editor Marty Baron told Tom he was the future of journalism. If Tom can't live off that for a year, I can.

I connected to my kids through baseball. It's how I was reared. We learn to father from our fathers. I am not your friend, I am your father, and it is my obligation to teach you baseball and work, and to try to rein you in.

Tom and Kieran were mirror twins—they faced each other in the womb. Kieran came out first, left-handed. Tom came out second, right-handed. They toddled in circles around the house following each other. They finished each other's sentences. They made a baseball battery.

Kieran toed the rubber. Tom was behind the plate. Kieran pitched like Uncle Bill—skinny southpaw who threw deceptive junk. Tom prayed for a collision at home plate, an RBI machine in Little League. We drove all over the state—as baseball players have been hard to muster and innings hard to find in these millennial years of computer games—listening to the Twins on WCCO with John Gordon and Dan "the Dazzle Man" Gladden.

Tom liked to hit the ball—off the fence. "Yeahhh," he would growl as he rumbled toward first in a frame that would stretch to six feet six inches. He liked the crowd. He was a good-time Charlie. He drove me crazy asking questions constantly. He got too big to catch, and Kieran tired of coaches and the jock cliques that are so common in a small town, so they quit baseball in high school. Tom was so good on the tuba it earned his way through the University of Northern Iowa on a music scholarship; he majored in economics. He told the professors he wanted to be a reporter. They thought he was delusional. "You have an economics degree. You could work on the Chicago Board of Trade. You could go to law school. You could do something. Why work at a newspaper?"

Because he saw his dad buy a newspaper in every little one-horse town he drove through on those baseball trips. It looked like the old man was having fun at it.

My heart just about burst. Tom was coming home to *The Times*. I dashed off this letter to a young reporter:

Dear Tom,

We are delighted that you have agreed to work at Buena Vista County's Hometown Newspaper. We are especially delighted that you will work about 80 hours a week for next to nothing but the satisfaction of seeing your name in 10 point boldface all caps Utopia on Page One of the best community newspaper in the world.

Since you did not read journalism textbooks, we will boil it down to a dozen paragraphs (called "grafs" in the trade) or so that should serve you amply.

When James Madison wrote the First Amendment to the Constitution, he had you in mind. The reporter is the cornerstone of an informed electorate and a functioning democracy. Tyranny prevails wherever the press is not free. Stand guard.

Reporters hold about as much regard as the world's oldest profession, but we are not professionals. Nobody gives us license, we draw it from the Constitution. Nobody can require some academic degree of us to publish. All we have is our own credibility, which is called into question twice a week in our circumstance. Readers decide our future, not any branch of government.

We strive for accuracy. When you spot your mistake in the paper, it should make you want to retch. Really. This is a healthy neuroticism. Correct your errors prominently and your credibility will build. When you lose that nausea over a mistake, go be a shaman in India.

Newspapering is the most fun you can have fully clothed. If you find writing is a chore after a while, you are in the wrong business. When you are standing in the rain waiting for a murder suspect to come out of jail, think of what job you might have as an alternative. It is not an attractive thought; the rain falls soft.

As noted above, the pay is lousy and the hours can be terrible. The newspaper always comes first. If you are on your honeymoon, as Jake Kurtz was, of course you tell your bride to wait a moment while you take photos of a fire. The marriage will be there in a half-hour, the fire will not be. It is all worth it when you see that newspaper roll up every Tuesday and Thursday, and your byline leads the page. When that thrill is gone, try the monastery or actuarial sciences in Clive.

Get the news up front. Don't wander around. Get in and get out. Over-report and under-write. Write for readers and not other editors. Write as if you were telling your mother about it in the kitchen. When appropriate, make them cry.

When you think you are pretty good, just remember that when Mark Twain was your age he had already been run out of Keokuk where his brother Orion owned the newspaper. By 27, he had the notes for the book *Roughing It* and he was writing letters from Hawaii for the *Sacramento Daily Union*. When you are writing letters from Hawaii, then you will know that you done good. Until then, get better.

Twain was not the only great writer to get his start at a dirty old newspaper. Hemingway, Fitzgerald, Kipling and Swift all honed their craft in the columns of newspapers. Not to mention Ben Franklin.

A pretty good rule is that an Iowa town will be
about as strong as its newspaper and its banks. The
best journalism is that which builds communities. You
build your community by publicizing good deeds done,
by reporting on the cheats and scoundrels and other
politicians, by urging yourself and those around you
to do better, by allowing dissenting voices to be heard,
and by making certain that your town's issues are
heard in Des Moines and Washington. Use your
power to build, and the newspaper will grow naturally.

Always be honest. Again, credibility is your only
stock-in-trade.

Anonymous sources almost always want to
remain anonymous for interests that do not coincide
with yours. Beware.

Above all, rejoice that you write for a living. Well,
often it's more like slinging words together in a
semblance of order to get your point across. You can
change the world through journalism. Tom Paine did
it with *Common Sense.* Bob Woodward and Carl
Bernstein of the *Washington Post* did it with
Watergate. Associated Press photographer Eddie
Adams did it—with one brutal photo he started the
end of the Vietnam War. That's the only good reason
to get into this business. Because, when you're
looking for a friend, remember that the dog can't read.

> Love (you had better check it out),
> Dad

PS: Is that story done yet?

---

One thousand four hundred four columns. That's an "Editor's Notebook" every week for twenty-seven years, not without fail but without exception. Once I asked John if my time would be better spent selling ads than writing this no-good column on a Monday morning while suffering an acute case of chronic motivational deprivation. No, he said, I had to have a column every week. I have not missed.

Because every weekly newspaper editor is expected to write a column.

Editorials are a piece of cake. Get outraged, marshal facts and an argument by reading the newspaper and ripping off the reporter's hard work, and let your fingers fly. Outrage has never been a problem for me.

But a column. That's a different thing entirely.

It is not supposed to be an argument based on logic. It is supposed to be you writing something important in a graceful or funny way. Graceful is hard. Funny is harder yet.

The column is my most valued possession as a newspaperman. I am a reporter. I am an editor. I am a photographer and a page designer. I am a pressman. I am an editorial writer and a businessman. I write a column. I wish I were a columnist. Somebody who writes whatever he likes brilliantly, with dash and flair. But it is Monday. If I can write one or two great columns a year—and by that I mean I could read them ten years later and not shudder—then I will die a whole man.

The finest Iowa political columnist of my time was Donald Kaul, who wrote the "Over the Coffee" column on the *Des Moines Register*'s editorial page four times a week for three decades. He was funny. Brother Jim, while in high school, was honored to win the Over the Coffee Vacation Column Contest, where he got slotted in once when Kaul took a week off. I think the title was "What If They Threw a War and Nobody Came?" Chuck Offenburger created the "Iowa Boy" column for the *Register* that ran four times a week. Offenburger scoured the state for interesting characters and upbeat stories, or to campaign for causes like our statewide network of private colleges. He would poll rural Iowans from a barbershop in Audubon about farm policy, or search every greasy spoon for the world's best cinnamon roll.

I marveled at Bill Wundram of the *Quad-City Times* in Davenport who wrote a daily column about life along the Mississippi. When he got up there in years the editors would cut him back to three times a week and he would get sick. So they would put him back to seven days a week on page 2 and Bill would get better. Max Maxon wrote a daily front-page column for the Webster City *Freeman-Journal*. They were pretty good. For sure, they were there. Every day. Most weekly papers had a society columnist who could write like Erma Bombeck and was buried in the B section. Few of those grand dames are left. It was Jean Anne Seagren in Storm Lake, the daughter of copublisher Phil Jarnagin at the Storm Lake *Pilot Tribune*. In "Here on Early Street" she demonstrated that she could write better than the "Old-Timer," her grandfather Bill Jarnagin. Down in Shenandoah at the *Evening Sentinel* it is Evelyn Birkby, ninety-eight, who writes "Up a Country Lane" weekly and hosts a homemaker show on KMA Radio, where the Everly Brothers got their start. Her publisher, Willard Archie, told her to "write friendly and always include a recipe." She does to this day.

John D. Field, editor and publisher of the *Hamburg Reporter*, wrote "Country Tub Thumping," in which he thumped his rival editor, Dave West, from the *Sidney Argus Herald* ten miles away. West called Field "Old Jawn" in his column, "It Takes All Kinds."

My column changed through the years. At first it truly was a notebook of happenings, political and otherwise, involving local people. Writing ten items of interest in one column might be the toughest task of all. Those are the most highly read. But it was too much work and it wasn't me. I settled on a more free-flowing column that touches on everything, from our own dysfunctional families to butting heads with the city manager (his was as hard as mine) and often poking fun at ourselves.

I have quit my job several times in my mind but the dream always ends with John taking away my column. I wake up startled and realize how lucky I am to be alive with a deadline on Monday at 10:00 a.m.

You start thinking about it on Saturday afternoon during the Hawkeye football game and keep it in the back of your head until Sunday night, when you start to feel like you have a forty-page term paper on James Joyce due in the morning. You drink coffee and think. You walk up and down the press line—even after the press is gone, the ink globs are still on the floor—and think. You smoke. You drive around the lake and pray. You read the entire World Wide Web. You see if there are any new emails.

And BOOM. It's there.

"Why is that light on in the farmhouse?"

I drive by in the night and wonder: Who is in there? What are they talking about? How is the farm doing?

A half hour later it is in the can.

It might be the best column I ever wrote. I will eat it if I can find it. I have no idea when it was or where it is, but it was a good

one, I can tell you. It is out there somewhere. I must keep on trying to better it. It is Friday. I don't have to think about that until
tomorrow. It will come to me. I will never know how that happens. It is like one of those horizon experiences the beautiful
people describe. I would not have gotten to experience it had I
made my way up Interstate 35 back to the Minneapolis *Star-
Tribune*. I probably would not have been an editorial writer winning a Pulitzer Prize. More important, I would not have written
a column. I know where I belong.

G ood pressmen are hard to find. So I became one.
We had a six-unit Harris V15A built in 1973. It printed
fifteen thousand copies per hour and could run a twelve-page
newspaper section with full color on the front and back pages.

A former pressman taught me the basics of offset lithography.
Moses did it with grease on the Ten Commandments. Grease on
a stone. Or chemically treated aluminum plates that wrap around
a press cylinder. Argh! Just cut my thumb. I fired that pressman,
or he quit after threatening to drop a half-ton roll of paper on
me, which I probably deserved.

After that I was on my own. I learned a wrench from a ham-
mer. I learned that you never want to change an impression
blanket that rolls on a cylinder that meets the plate cylinder. It is
work. Get me the needle-nose pliers. You curse a lot. Get the
hand grinder out. You have to change a blanket only when you
are an hour off deadline and ten people are watching your every
move waiting for papers. You are covered in ink and sweat drips
down your nose and a fly lands there, and you rub ink all over
your face.

Our brother Jim, about whom you haven't heard much yet, got laid off as Austin bureau chief for the Hearst Newspapers in Texas. He landed as an editor at the *Texas Observer,* home of the ever-fun populists Molly Ivins and Jim Hightower. When the *Observer* couldn't afford him anymore, Jim in 1995 established a national version of the *Observer*—the *Progressive Populist,* a "Journal from the Heartland." It is full of clippings for left-wing zealots who live between the coasts—and we testify every October in a postal statement that there are not enough of them, just about ten thousand willing to pay forty bucks a year for a view from the Democratic wing of the Democratic Party. He edits the *Populist* in Austin; we produce it in Iowa.

Our sister, Ann, worked in the newspaper business in Omaha, brother Tom was a speechwriter for liberal Atlanta politicians and a regional playwright of note, and our brother Bill is a habitual letter writer to newspapers. The family does have this writing thing going on. Our niece is a mobile editor for the *New York Times.*

For twenty-three years we printed *The Times,* the *Populist,* advertising inserts, the college newspaper, and a paper from Cherokee. The paper from Cherokee, which John and I handled by ourselves on Saturday mornings and early afternoons, dumped us when we tried to raise the rates by ten bucks a week. So much for fraternity among publishers and thieves. We printed a good weekly paper for a woman in nearby Laurens until she went belly-up. We never sought payment for her back bills. She paid what she could when she could. She recovered, has a nice little custom publishing business, and never forgot our forbearance. She sources her printing business through us, and we find her best printer at the cheapest rate. Those small things help keep little newspapers going.

We prided ourselves on being the first Iowa newspaper to be entirely composed on a computer and sent directly to film using lasers. We upgraded from a film imaging system by sending the page image directly to the printing plate. We printed the most beautiful color of any paper anywhere on technology as old as rock.

Somebody said that owning a newspaper web press is like keeping a leopard in your apartment—eventually it will kill you. It ate money. It could take a digit off you in a flash. But it was our mark of independence—it was our press. We waited on no one.

And I loved it. The roar of the gears. Watching your byline clean up on the front page as you ramped up to speed. Seeing the four colors of a photo—cyan, magenta, yellow, and black—move into register with the nudge of a wrench on the fly. Smelling the grease and the ink and breathing deeply of the paper dust and cigarette smoke.

John ran the mailroom while I ran the pressroom. For a few years to save money I ran the press by myself, and eventually trained reporter Jake Kurtz to run it. Neither one of us knew how to fix anything. We hired an old British motorcycle Zen mechanic, Jim Robinson, to help on the press and keep the building from falling apart. Jim's daughter Whitney was sprung from college with a psychology degree and now she sells our ads.

There is never enough money in newspapers, and it keeps getting tighter. The newspaper industry was ripped inside out when Craigslist took away our classified ads and bloggers stole our news, reporting it as theirs. We chase fewer readers competent in English, or even their own native language. Civic engagement has declined, even at the small-town level. Kiwanis and Rotary clubs struggle for members. School board election turnouts can be as low as 10 percent, which might be a sign of satisfaction. None of that is good for a community newspaper's bottom line.

We always have tried to pay competitively. We want our employees (ten in all, half named Cullen) to be wealthy. We regret we cannot pay more because the economy simply doesn't afford it. We always offered health insurance to our employees at no cost to them. In the years preceding the election of Barack Obama, our health insurance premiums were increasing 60 to 70 percent per year.

Our ad manager, Mike Diercks (Hygrade Jack's son), came to us from the hospital and bankruptcy. He worked himself into a heart attack and insolvency as co-owner of an auto dealership in a struggling nearby community. He got out of the dealership but not before losing his house and everything else he owned but his car. And his wife, Linda, stayed with him, too. Mike was a beaver out on the street, suffering from diabetes and kidney failure.

He was fortunate enough to have a son donate a kidney for transplant, which took successfully. That year his medical bills were $580,000. The insurance company responded with a whopping rate increase.

Mike died of a second heart attack. He was still selling ads.

Our associate editor, Tina Donath, was a graceful writer who rarely breathed a word. When she did it was worth listening. She had a master's degree in philosophy and was a teacher reconstructed into one of the best newspaper writers I have ever read.

Tina developed cancer. She had to drive right past our hospital in Storm Lake to get treatment in Sioux City, because the cancer treatment center here was located inside the four walls of the hospital and thus outside our insurance plan. It would cover only outpatient cancer treatment, which meant it could not be administered in our rural hospital. In Sioux City she got treatment in a building next to the hospital. That's how the rules worked. She would drive home seventy miles and write about the city council meeting at night. She refused to stop. She took a break and I never saw her again. Tina died.

The insurance company raised our rates 70 percent that year.

We were going broke paying for and negotiating health care on behalf of our employees. This was all to keep happy a private insurance industry that the Republican Conference would gouge itself on a pike for.

I was writing about this and Senator Harkin caught it. He invited me to testify at the Senate Committee on Health, Education, Labor and Pensions hearing on the Affordable Care Act on November 3, 2009.

Academics to the right and left lobbed theories past one another while the state insurance commissioners defended their pals in the industry, pleading for a "level playing field" for the Blue Crosses of the world.

Quoting the *New York Times*:

"It was the small-business owners who had the last word, and it was unexpectedly powerful. 'Everybody here's talking about being fair to the insurance companies—when have they been fair to us?' Mr. Cullen said. 'Why do we have to be fair to them? It just incenses me when people talk that way. These people are legal thieves with antitrust protection, and we want to treat them with kid gloves. It drives me nuts!'"

I told the senators to get health insurance off our backs, like Reagan would have said. It apparently did not impress the Republicans because they are still trying to put that monkey on my back.

Harkin told me after Obamacare was approved that the Democrats had sixty votes for the public option. But majority leader Harry Reid and President Obama allowed Senator Chuck Grassley to help Finance Committee chairman Max Baucus (D-Montana) to write the insurance exchange financing.

Grassley outfoxed Baucus. He wrote poison pills into the state health insurance cooperatives that were Trojan horses for the public option. He told voters at town meetings that the federal government would have a death panel that could pull the plug on Gramma. All at the orders of Republican leader Mitch McConnell. Grassley obeyed, poisoned the legislation, and won the chairmanship of the Judiciary Committee. Remember Merrick Garland, the Supreme Court nominee who never got a hearing? Score that one to Max Baucus.

Chuck Grassley worked directly against the interests of our small business while saying he was our champion. He still is. He was right in there in 2016 trying to repeal and replace the legislation he ghostwrote for Max Baucus. Iowa now has one health insurer of any consequence: Wellmark Blue Cross and Blue Shield. The state health insurance exchange set up under the ACA collapsed. The biggest insurer in the state Medicaid managed-care program, AmeriHealth, pulled out of the program a year after it was launched because it said it was losing hundreds of millions of dollars. Voters across the country rate health care now as their top concern; it decided the Virginia governor's race in the fall of 2017. Iowa Democratic legislators heading into midterm elections tried to introduce a state single-payer program and were not run off with pitchforks.

We have a hard enough time trying to put out a newspaper without having to manage health care. The politics might finally be catching up to the people as talk of a public option resurfaces. Something has to compete against Wellmark. Small businesses can't afford the political duplicity much longer.

Aside from being publisher, John is worrier in chief. He worried that our computerized laser platemaking machine would get a hiccup—it seemed like we bought it yesterday but the expensive gizmo was ten years old. He worried that the old press motor might cut out for the last time. He worried that the labeling machine would wake up one day deciding not to make labels. He based his worry on long experience.

At age sixty-six, John tired of all those production worries, and he was not so fond of throwing mailbags anymore either. So we took a trip—John Cullen, our graphics man, Jon Robinson, pressman Jim Robinson, and I—to visit our longtime friends at White Wolf Web in Sheldon, about an hour northwest of Storm Lake, just to see what their press was like.

The trip convinced us that our press run had come to an end. We would send our printing to Sheldon.

It was a mind bender. It became eminently clear that technology and scale had passed us by in the pressroom. On one side of the office wall we had all the latest in digital media production. Open the door to our pressroom and you walked back to 1973. It took two of us to handle six printing units. In Sheldon, they are running a new press with twenty-four units with essentially one pressman manning a computer console with clean hands.

We could print two pages per press run in full color. Sheldon can print twenty-four pages in full color (better than we could produce) in one run. They print it, insert sections, label the addresses, and deliver our paper to the Storm Lake post office as cheap as or more cheaply than we could print it ourselves.

Ink densities no longer are left to the master craftsmen's eyes. Computers read the page and tell the pressman where to turn the ink keys, and how far. Colors are lined up by pressing buttons on a computer. Back in our cave, we slung ink with trowels and cursed broken webs of paper sotted in puddles of water.

I had to mope around for a month after John made the fatal call to shut down our press. Old pressmen get sentimental about gears.

We printed *The Times* on Thursday without a peep. The color was gorgeous. The press purred like a kitten, a large, upset kitten. I was appropriately sentimental and blew my nose into some twelve-inch, thirty-pound newsprint.

Friday the thirteenth would be the final voyage. We were printing brother Jim's national political journal, the *Progressive Populist*. We were more than halfway through the run of ten thousand copies when our cranky old folder jammed as badly as I had ever seen it jam. Steel arms that catch the papers got all bent up. Pressman Jim lay on the floor doing precise surgery with a three-foot crowbar. We got things sort of bent back into place to limp through the final two thousand copies, at which time the folder jammed again.

We shut off the power, left the folder jammed and the floor littered with shredded paper.

No ceremonies. No final eight bells tolling for thee, as the navy would do when decommissioning a ship. Just a final curse at the greasy boar and a final denial of 220 volts. We sold the press for parts to another newspaper in Iowa for $10,000. We bought it twenty-five years ago for $150,000.

_____

We are still mainly an ink-on-paper operation. We have a website at www.stormlake.com, but it primarily serves elderly snowbird readers who winter in Texas or Arizona. It is not a revenue producer. The ad revenue doesn't cover the cost of paying the internet rent on it. We try to figure out how to deliver the news digitally, but we have not ciphered a way to make it pay. What works for the *New York Times* does not necessarily work for *The Storm Lake Times*. We lack critical mass to make digital volume work.

Paper lends credibility to the news report. Anybody can tweet. Not everyone can sustain a print operation. It remains to be seen how long Storm Lake can. As long as it remains a community, and not an unrelated gathering of people. A community supports important civic institutions, like independent journalism. Tom wants to stay. We have a great staff. Our former reporter Jake Kurtz says he wants to return to *The Times* when his wife, Sabrina Martinez, finishes her medical residency and hangs her shingle in Storm Lake, a Spanish-speaking physician. It probably will take a doctor's pay to help float the newspaper boat every now and again when a leak springs.

Rural contraction and consolidation threaten community newspapers and the civic conversation in ways that roll Henry Wallace in his grave. We already can see how Facebook and Twitter can distort even Storm Lake life and rewire its conversation. That story about human trafficking that involved a sweltering trailer from Schaller? Many locals don't believe the connection, they say on Facebook, because you can't believe the Associated Press, even though the owner of Pyle Trucking told the AP that the trailer was his. Of course it was—his name was emblazoned on the side of it. Yet people still don't believe it.

It's coffee shop gossip gone digital and viral that people somehow believe. The newspaper becomes a vetter more than ever, where separating the wheat from the chaff appears vital. Amid the cacophony in even a little town, where most folks know everyone around the entire block and beyond, the gatekeeper asserts its relevance to help keep Storm Lake whole with the facts.

The value of it remains to be determined. Newspaper advertising revenue nationally dropped from $50 billion to $18 billion in the ten years leading to 2016. We feel it. So does the other paper in town. Circulation has been "soft"—a euphemism polite editors use to describe a picture that's out of focus—for three years. It declined three months in a row after we won journalism's highest honor, then started to tick up slightly. We are publishing one of the best community newspapers in America, but the bottom line often suggests we are not that good. And it is not just us. Papers across the country don't know where their next edition leads. The reaction is to cut pages, cut editors and reporters, and cut frequency, and shift your attention to digital revenue that is a penny on the print dime. It cannot be sustained. Digital revenue for newspapers is flat, when you subtract the category killers (the *New York Times, Washington Post,* and *Wall Street Journal*).

The rewards have never been that great since the days of the prairie editors showing up with a sack of type over their backs. They came to explain an expansive unfolding story. It has been a struggle for good newspapers ever since—you can make a lot of money milking a town until it runs dry, but it's not so easy when you try to serve a town in perpetuity. We just want to make a little bit, maybe a 5 to 8 percent cash flow, to put out a newspaper worthy of a Pulitzer and Storm Lake. Just enough to pay the bills is all. There's a hole in the toe of my sock. My left shoe blew out while in New York picking up the prize. Those streets are mean indeed.

As long as people will put a value on that conversation, as they have in Iowa by dint of 289 community newspapers putting ink on paper, *The Times* should be able to tell the Storm Lake story.

There is no explaining away the fact that our Anglo readers are dying. It will be another five years, I would guess, before we can see the sort of readership gains we need from our new neighbors. The interim is a tremendous challenge.

No, it's an existential challenge.

Unless communities support journalism, all the prizes in the world are worth what you can melt them down for. No matter the medium, journalism must be fed. It is being starved at every level, from Storm Lake to Salt Lake, by citizens who think they can operate in a bliss free of the weight of adverse facts.

The newspaper will keep at it. Somehow we will convert new arrivals into readers, someday. We will sell just enough ads to pay the bills. We will make it. I don't know how. Maybe with sales of this book. We will report on the health of the river and the lake. We will raise hell over health insurance. We will love our town. Brother John always believed from day one that if you report the news unflinchingly, no matter the cost, it will work. And it has, so far.

This thing might hang together after all, if John and I can dodder out of the way at a convenient time. Someone might give us a clue.

# CHAPTER 18

# We Wish to Remain What We Are

Every Sunday morning Dolores puts on her dancing shoes to work the pedals of the organ at St. Mary's Catholic Church. She is ever dutiful. She also has control. She sets the tempo. She nods to the cantor. She dictates to the priest, of all people, his pace without him even knowing it. An attuned ear hears "Go, Cubs, Go" disguised as a communion dirge for Ralph Flowers's funeral, or "Whiskey Before Breakfast" played slow and light for the offertory.

She is the product of a humble farm family in a little Luxembourgish hamlet whose motto is "We wish to remain what we are."

That cloister shaped her to be self-effacing and self-denying—two cookies only at 4:00 p.m. lunch—to defer in conversation on an opinion offered pending further consideration, while at the same time dreaming of being noticed and loved and expressing herself amid the crowd of nine children stuck on a farm.

She learned at her mother's hand how to leave your thumb-print signature in a perfect pie crust made with West Bend lard. She learned with the slap of a nun's ruler on her hand if her form was improper on the keyboard in the choir loft when she was twelve. Her brother Paul accompanied the Notre Dame Glee Club to exotic foreign places. She accompanied the church choir with the loud tenor.

She plays a dozen instruments or more, accordion to zither, and inspired our daughter, Clare, to major in the clarinet at Drake University. Like her mother, Clare worked at it. She practiced so much her teeth went wobbly from the reed and she had to give it up. Her education prepared Clare perfectly for a career as a newspaper copy editor, as unflappable as Benny Goodman on deadline. Dolores led Tom's twin, Kieran, to an interest in soil and growing things. He wanted to pursue a graduate degree in sustainable agriculture but the fellowships in Iowa all got eliminated in the agribusiness purge of universities. He works as a scribe to doctors in Marshalltown, another Iowa meatpacking town, and as an emergency medical technician on the ambulance crew. He might try medicine, because his sort of agriculture is practically foreclosed for the moment in the halls of Iowa academia.

Dolores had a rabbit, a small substitute for that pony she always wanted, given to her for Christmas by Aunt Irene Bormann, eccentric enough to make Dolores's dream come true that someone would give her an animal in a home where they were not welcome. Dolores awoke one morning to find her rabbit dead in the basement. It was reported that her brother Steve was in the vicinity with his friend Jerome Kohlhaas. Years later, there were several Bigfoot sightings around St. Joe, Bode, and Ottosen. People came out with guns. In the dark of night a girl screamed when she saw the hairy beast's shadow from a shed light. The family rushed outside. "Anybody know what time it is?" the voice from the shadow said, and was not heard from again. Jerome swore to me that he does not know who Bigfoot was. Sasquatch might have claimed her rabbit that night, but who could pin it on him?

She cried and cried and one day recently assuaged that memory with a new rabbit, Milhouse. After Sunday Mass, Dolores gathers pieces of cardboard that the rabbit has nibbled from oatmeal boxes. She arranges them into images on greeting cards and thinks it might be her break into the Museum of Modern Art: Who else creates in collaboration with a white rabbit in memory of those sacrificed to Bigfoot's fumblings? When she holds the rabbit it can feel like a baby but better, because it doesn't cry and it poops in a box.

When I met her she was rummaging through abandoned farmsteads and pilfering broken glass, barbed wire, and pieces of wood. She made batik backgrounds for the items assembled in boxes using beeswax from candles pocketed from the church, repayment for years of service and abuse.

She perched on the Storm Lake St. Mary's organ bench after having just delivered sixteen pounds of twins one August morning. She listened to the homily on the sin of birth control. She pulled out the stops and plowed into the next song for an exclamation point that might obscure what the priest just said. She returned the following Sunday. And the one after that. The priest later was found wandering a mall naked. She will outlast them all to the final coda.

On Monday morning Dolores is back to shooting pictures of a two-headed calf or a blind bowler who rolled a perfect game at Century Lanes in Alta. Those sold some papers. Or that Tea

Party patriot who was impersonating Patrick Henry going spas-
modic in the Sunset Park Band Shell in front of a huge rally of
angry whites on Labor Day. "'Give me liberty, or give me death!'"
he cried, because the Tea Partiers were too cheap to bother serving lunch. Gangsta rappers sent her roses after she featured
them at Malarky's Pub.

The stories that got away from her—Dwarf tells story of his
life: "The Lord done it." His brother, who had power of attorney
over him, spiked the story. Or: Baby born in Porta-Potty. You
might understand why the mother who didn't realize she was
pregnant until she really had to go got cold feet on that story.

Dolores patrols days, nights, and weekends with Mabel the
newshound in the black Chevy with "Buena Vista County's Hometown Newspaper" stenciled in white on the side. In the dark night
near Newell, delivering mailbags to the post office, a huge, lighted
cross shines over the town from the top of a grain elevator. It
barely illuminates the hog manure tanker kicking up a cloud of
dust and stench that permeates the car. She recalled the other day
the morning we lay in bed and I said, "Come on, let's go home to
Storm Lake. It'll be fun."

"It has been fun, for the most part," she said.

*Fun* was not the first word in the St. Joe lexicon. She didn't
really want to remain what she was that much.

She occasionally helicopters over Tom, making sure he sees
the dentist and has clean socks, until he starts shaking his head
at her in front of the entire office. She returns her attention to
an illustration of Uncle Sam picking the pocket of a veteran in
the hospital, for the next cover of the *Progressive Populist*. Start
to finish, including a ten-minute fuss over Tom, the art is done
in an hour. She fills the paper with pictures. She keeps it all

together. She carries the weight of Luxembourg gracefully on her shoulders.


I worked so much I didn't know my children that well. Dolores was handling all the load. Joe, our oldest, was a happy boy who preferred the company of adults to other children. He took up the fiddle and charmed crowds with his mother and a dog in a little Irish band. Joe had a hard time making friends. When I could not reach inside and beyond the savant to try to save him it would rip me to shreds. We had our bouts. He was bullied and mocked from junior high school to stints in college. Joe is different from the rest of the world, certainly from the expectations of what makes for conformative behavior in a small midwestern town. Some people don't fit in small places. I learned that. I had to let go of Joe.

At age thirty Joe fiddles on street corners for spare change in his violin case. He busked in Kansas City, Nashville, Memphis, New Orleans, and Seattle. He lives where people will take him in. He is a lamb who wears the affectation of a streetwise cynic, and he takes a piece of my soul with him wherever he goes. I pray he makes it through the night, pray to my father and to Uncle Joe Cullen, the departed Linotype operator, editor, and wit. And I think that I could have, should have, might have, done something more or better. No matter what you accomplish, no matter what problems you solve, no matter how much cash and advice you lay on him for his next destination unknown, there remains the dilemma of father and son, as old as myth itself. But it doesn't feel like myth to me every day I think about Joe, who becomes a spirit to me in his and my absence. Where is he? How is he? I feel as helpless as Dad did when he was slipping away as I was slipping away from him.

Joe calls from the Sioux City bus depot. He is just in from Seattle, over the Rockies and through. He is on his way to Nashville with a story of when he lit in New Orleans:

It was June. A friend had a house that was being remodeled. They could crash there. A monsoon poured outdoors. They had no money or food. It was about midnight. A man walked out of a back room.

"I have lasagna," he said.

His name was Lee. He wore a bandana around long gray hair and a wisp of a chin beard.

"Joe, go get the forks outside on the table," Lee instructed.

Joe had never seen Lee before. How did he know his name? He also mentioned Joe's friend Tommy by name.

Tommy didn't know him either.

Joe does as ordered. He went outside and found forks on a table.

Where did Lee come from? The lasagna was hot but there was no oven. They ate it.

"It was excellent," Joe said.

Lee showed up a few more times, seemingly out of nowhere. He didn't tell Joe much other than to "be yourself and don't let people mess with you."

Joe was sitting on a street corner fiddling about three weeks later. He had weathered the storm that landed him at the mouth of the Mississippi. The Presentation Sisters, the same order that taught me in Storm Lake, operates a soup kitchen and homeless center there. He had enough to eat. He had a place to stay. Lee came up from behind and put a hand on his shoulder. "I'm leaving now," he said.

Joe hasn't seen him since, for more than a year.

Lee showed up when Joe was living in an abandoned house

not knowing where his next meal was coming from. It came. Other wings have folded around him. Bar owners and musicians look out for him. One called Dolores several months ago to let us know that Joe was all right. That he was being looked out for.

Joe played videos for us of him fiddling with hot jazz bands. He really is good. He was lost, but maybe he is found now.

Joe left again on the Jefferson Line out of Sioux City, just a week's visit home, and then back to the beat of the French Quarter. He reached out to hug me for the first time as I dropped him off at the depot. His guitar and fiddle were in cases slung over his back. Everything else he owned fit into his backpack.

I could not reach all the way around.

"I'm proud to be a freak," Joe told me.

And I am proud to be the father of a man who admits it.


A hot September breeze sweated through the corn trying to dry on the south side of the St. Joe cemetery one Saturday noon. Daryl Baker stood lone sentry in a dark suit waiting for the crew to lower Helen Gales, eighty-seven, into her resting place.

Dolores's mother, Helen, died in her own bed of pancreatic and liver cancer with her family surrounding her, without pain. It was beautiful, by all accounts. All good-byes were bid. Would that each of us go that way.

It was a huge and lovely funeral with family from Alaska to Arizona. Father Merle Kollasch offered a wonderful homily that included colloquy with Helen's widower, Ernie, who wore his sixty-three-year-old wedding suit. The children and grandchildren played the music, and it was a celebration.

Over two days the people flowed past, mainly my age and older. Hunched-over widows silently prepared dinner in the basement during the wake. Men in short-sleeved shirts, tanned arms, and pressed blue jeans processed past. There wasn't a pretentious soul in the house, other than the few who might have been shipped in.

St. Joe is pure Iowa. You don't have to ask for milk at dinner, they serve it to you cold. A woman from Bancroft told me that she knew Grandma Bessie and sold her, a diabetic, illicit sweet rolls and candy. A man from Whittemore blew past and declared that he revered J. S. Cullen, my banker grandpa who got wiped out during the Depression. And then he disappeared off into the crowd somewhere.

They roll with the ebb and flow of the Des Moines River. Some years are up, some down. Dr. Jerry Shey sat in the back row of church. He says you make money by sticking with it. Buy low and sell high, says the man who had one pair of shorts at Iowa State Vet Med and washed them in a sink above the dairy barn every night.

Helen was reared to think first of others, of community and church and family. Never yourself first. Always the last to sit down at supper. Her parents, Mike and Minnie Bormann, were the first to be called in St. Joe when they were raising funds for any Catholic school or church project. She embraced their spirit of generosity and stewardship.

Hers was a generation of feeding the men, of rearing a brood of nine with the help of her parents, of slaughtering chickens and teaching your children decency and modesty. Of mending overalls and making dress wear out of scraps. It was her expression of love and fulfilling obligations that was all part of the order of

things. I know her best through Dolores, who in many ways is
her expression in patience, sincerity, and tolerance. Or daughter
Clare, who exudes her calm.

The river's up. The corn is tall. The Capesius cousins, who
run the Pioneer seed dealership, think it's going to be a tremendous year from Storm Lake to Algona. We're in the sweet spot.
But Chris cautions that this year will shake a few more guys out.
It wasn't that easy stashing cash on seven-dollar corn because
most of them couldn't afford to sell at that price. He is the pro-
verbial bachelor farmer who knows everyone. He is always there
with more common wisdom than most great prelates.

Caroline Bormann, at ninety-four, with no college education,
at the wake sang the praises of Senator Barbara Mikulski for
providing the clinching vote to secure a nuclear deal with Iran.
Her daughter tried to move her on as she analyzed Joe Biden's
chances in the Iowa caucuses with too late an entry. She is why
Iowa deserves to be first in selecting the leader of the free world.

Her nephews are farming part of Helen and Ernie's land.
They're using more sustainable techniques, trying to reduce the
load on the Des Moines River.

The old farmstead where Dolores was reared is vacant. Tall
grass leads up to the shed where Ernie and hired man Clete Salz
were nearly crushed by a combine head set on blocks one gray
November day. We heard the thud and walked out of the house.
Ernie and Clete stood with their fists on their hips looking and
laughing. Ernie had been under it just a minute ago. Farming is
the deadliest profession.

Up on the hill overlooking the village of St. Joe and the river
bottom, the house where Ernie was reared is there only in its
foundation rubble. The old place was razed when a controlled

burn went out of control. The south breeze was cool under the catalpa tree where Dolores and I spent our first summer together. No prettier place exists.

St. Joe is ten miles south of Algona and Catholic. Hanover is five miles west of Storm Lake and Missouri Synod Lutheran. The names in town remain the same over the centuries in St. Joe: Bormann, Thilges, Becker, Reding. And a McGuire for diversity's sake. The same German names—Hinkeldey, Winterhof, Radke, and Friedrich—endure in Hanover. Most of them have the first penny they ever earned, those who lasted this long. The St. Joe annual soiree is the Mulligan Stew, which Hanover would have as a Polka Festival. The rest of the year they spend going to church, attending to school activities, and working. My father-in-law wears hand-me-down clothes from his white-collar sons.

Everyone in St. Joe and Hanover is getting older. The farmsteads go vacant. The cemeteries get fuller. Iowa is the most elderly state. Its farmers are the oldest in the land, with most of the landholders being over age sixty-five—the guys who survived the farm debt crisis. The generational transfer of wealth is under way, much of it flowing to heirs on the coasts. Those who survived and have no bred-in farming successors post an auction ad and the land goes into fewer, stronger hands.

Those who left return to find what shaped them and hold on to it. Patty Gales spent her summers in St. Joe on breaks from her home in suburban Chicago. Now she lives in Ozark, Missouri, about ten hours south of this wide spot on U.S. Highway 169, with a steeple. Patty lived with my cousin Mary Beth in college, and her sister Kathy was pals with my sister-in-law Teresa McClain Cullen in Dubuque, and it's just such a small world on top of the hill in St. Joe. We descended, and Daryl Baker stood there in the breeze next to his old friend.

Since I met him shelling out that corn crib more than thirty years ago, nobody has done more to inform my view of rural Iowa than Ernie Gales. He is eighty-eight and alone now. I drove over the Varina road and up to St. Joe to visit on an August morning, to ask him about how he looks at it all now. He views the present through an objective and not nostalgic lens of the past. He is nostalgic mainly in the sense that progress isn't always so when it is masquerading for conspicuous consumption and waste. I have more credit hours in that topic from his lectures than anybody but perhaps his own sons.

We ride low past the four-feet-tall grass and wildflowers slunk in a four-door Buick near the Des Moines River at St. Joe. An arm clothed in a shirt worn gauzy comes under my mustache as the finger stump points to a purple petal on a tall plant with a broad leaf. Ernie thought it might be a weed but on closer inspection determines it must be some sort of wildflower.

The Buick rumbles along the river around the Ray Gales farm. Ernie is driving, of course. "Got stuck in a low spot with the tractor mowing. It's around here somewhere. There's a log in here somewhere, too, I gotta get it pulled out, we might bottom out but I don't think so."

We are in the bottomland abutting the Upper Des Moines River circling the 125 acres put into native prairie plantings through the Conservation Reserve Program. We work up to the top of the bowl near the old abandoned corn crib covered thick in green grape vines. "That'll get torn down," he said of the pastoral icon.

He shuts off the car and talks about what tremendous land this is for corn. In a different age and a different situation he might be growing it. His entire worldview is built around avoiding financial risk and cost. He gets paid about three hundred dollars per acre from the government to just drive around it with his Buick and scout weeds.

"There's a cocklebur. Gotta get after that. I see a cottonwood. They come up and you don't even notice. That has to come out. There's a thistle, I think."

It might be a coneflower of some sort. He wants to keep it clean and looking good.

He would plant it if he were younger and assured of a crop. He could play the odds of not getting drowned out by using crop insurance and more often than not he could get a bin buster out of these bottoms. At his age the risk is not worth the potential reward, and he would rather drive around in his Buick than plant.

"I like the growth, definitely, but if it were profitable we would farm it," Ernie declared. "It is just so superproductive. But you could lose money farming it now.

"It used to be there was very little risk farming it. You could throw some of your own soybean seed down there. Now you have your expensive seeds and inputs and taxes and you got your . . ." He keeps on the Ernie Monologue Tour—you can try to navigate for him but it is pointless, especially for a son-in-law.

Ernie says he is not sentimental about the land. The place with the square house where Dolores grew up does not dwell in his heart so much, but the bounty of the land around the house does. His sentiment rests up on the hill overlooking the village of St. Joe where he was reared, and on the Ray Gales farm. It's for the family memories.

"I do think of Ray Gales when I'm out here," Ernie said of his father's brother. "We came out here every Sunday for dinner. We had a lot of good times and you were dealing with a smart man, not an ambitious man, sort of a lackadaisical man, I guess a guy could say."

It's lackadaisical on the bottoms on a Friday in mid-August. The river is low. We ford the thicket to the river and stand on an exposed sandbar. Coon tracks. Turkey tracks. Deer, fox, and coyote. So dry, no mosquitoes. Too dry for the corn on a hill, for sure. It's burning up. Not the tall grass. It's as thick as a sponge and smells green. It holds what little water hit the slope and the soil with it. Grazing is not allowed on CRP ground. You can see how it could feed you in the toughest year if it were allowed. But it is not. That's how interest groups write a farm bill. Those decisions are made far beyond Riverdale Township no matter how it votes: It used to go Democrat, but now it goes Republican primarily because of abortion. Ernie was a member of the National Farmers Organization as a younger man when the NFO was radical, but he came in later years to speak in favor of a more religiously conservative view as articulated from the pulpit. He attended Mass daily until they cut it back to just weekends a few years ago for lack of clergy.

Ray's son, Sonny, was a gadgets guy. Ernie is a mechanic. They were born engineers. They spent childhoods together along the river, and retirements together. Sonny died. Ernie misses Sonny.

He wheels the Buick past Dwight Bormann's place, where he has planted a patch of aronia berry bushes. It is one of those superfoods. Ernie hears Dwight will make good money on them. Up the blacktop P-56 where the family square house stands vacant, and across to the west, is a field that used to be owned by Louis Merkel, one of the few Protestants Ernie related to regularly. Louis did not work on Sunday because it would make your crops fail. Louis is long gone. The Apostolic Christians took over and planted rye there. They are going organic. The Catholics call them "Coffee Dutch" from West Bend. Ernie has video of them threshing the rye with new, bright green John Deere machines. The Coffee Dutch stick together. They help one another with land and machinery. They do not drink or smoke or dance. They profess not to watch TV, so I do not know what those antennae were for on some of their houses, maybe lightning rods. They go to church for several hours on Sunday interrupted by coffee. And they work. And they make money. If the Coffee Dutch are going organic, Ernie respects it because they know what they're doing.

We rolled over the Upper Des Moines River and up Highway 169 to the place on the hill. About half the 112 tillable acres are planted in lush green soybeans by his nephews, the Capesius brothers. They are five sons of Ernie's late sister Margie. A couple are bachelors. They work hard, made a lot of money raising their own hogs, and with the Pioneer dealership. They look out for Ernie. The slope running down to the river is "government acres" exploding with wildflower color—purple and yellow and green. "When we planted it first it was all alfalfa. It was perfect growth, a green sweep. It was loaded with pheasants. They went out and shot a round and got thirty birds in one hour, the Capesiuses and them guys," Ernie said.

He thinks that mare's tail standing five feet high is a weed but isn't certain. Managing nature is complicated. At first you mow and then you burn and then you leave it alone. It's hard to leave it alone when you spent a half century with a moldboard plow in the fall turning over clods. He started behind a horse when he was about nine, Ernie thinks.

"Some people are animal lovers. I never was. Guys who were

good with horses, they could make some really good money. They had big stud horses and raised colts and trained 'em like pets. You sell those to the guys who don't know horses so they'll work good. Then you run the cheapies. A good team could be worth two to three acres. Dad was good with horses. He would drive a team down to the train in Livermore in the morning and come back with supplies for the St. Joe store. He made money from horses."

The oats powered the horses that planted the corn and fertilized the field along with the cows and hogs. A twelve-hundred-pound steer can put out seventy-five pounds of "nutrients" per day for the land. It was all a family needed.

They got their first tractor in 1936, an F-12 made by International Harvester. It had steel wheels and a dirty burn and a corn planter. They used it to make hay, too. But they still used horses for most chores. Ernie planted beans in 1945 with horses. In 1946, at the age of forty-six, Ernie Senior told Junior that he would be planting alone the next year, which Junior did with a tractor. The horses were goners. Sorry, Dolores.

He became more interested in how machinery could make him money than how the land could. "I never bought much land to speak of. Your whole life changes when you buy more land. They assume it goes on the same but it don't," Ernie said.

Tractors and combines allowed farmers to take on more acres but they found their limits with weed control. A family could work only so many acres and keep the weeds down. Ernie Junior was among five children fed by 150 crop acres. They canned and slaughtered. "You could eat meat, milk, and eggs to no limit," he said. They had three hundred chickens, ten sows, and ran seventy to eighty cows along the river. Rotating crops controlled weeds: corn, beans, alfalfa, oats, sorghum.

"Everybody did work, even if you were two to three years old you could haul cobs," he said.

In 1972 he bought his first International Harvester combine alone, having shared previously with Rich Kohlhaas. It had a 13.5-foot bean platform. Now the platform is 40 feet wide.

The introduction of chemistry following World War II allowed farms to develop scale. Finally, herbicides developed for the war effort could take out weeds and reduce cultivation that had been done with horses and small tractors. The postwar boom helped lead to a period from 1940 to 1960 where St. Joe could support its own Catholic high school with fifteen students in a class. As farm sizes grew with chemistry, the children disappeared with the weeds. The St. Joe school closed in the 1980s.

"Jiggs Kollasch used to run five miles with the bus and he would have a full load," Ernie recalled.

He farmed about five hundred acres between his family's land and that of Helen's family, the Bormanns. He harvested corn with his combine for a fee and shelled corn, the dirtiest job in agriculture, where you tie up your pant legs so the rats won't run right up your leg to your you-know-what. He made money with gears and wheels.

"You could make a living here on a farm. If you were a good farmer you could make money," Ernie said. "I made money by spending less than I took in."

He conserved. That's why he has all those shells of Chevy pickups in the grove up on the hill. You could buy them for two hundred dollars each and run them like hell, then you had spare parts in the grove. He still has the old Ford rig that Benny Thilges smashed up hauling a load of corn to Algona for Leo Thilges forty years ago. You never know when you might need a manifold.

He has a Farmall tractor from 1938 with a 1946 hydraulic loader attached. I ask if it still runs. Wrong question. He uses it all the time. He springs into action. The carburetor hasn't worked right in decades. He drains the flood into a tin cup and pours it back into the tank, then flies up into the iron seat. He wears Big Smith overalls, shoes with Velcro bindings and duct tape holding them together, and a Murphy Farm Drainage cap. He always parks it running downhill so he can pop the clutch on the fly, and kaboom she chokes out smoke from beneath a dented Folgers coffee can shrouding the exhaust pipe.

Ernie parades it around the yard up on the hill, around the burned-out foundation of the home in which he was delivered. He slides it beneath a tree with a dying branch and lifts the loader arms to a forty-five-degree angle to display how he trims branches. He could show you how he climbs up there foot over foot on angle iron eight feet above the ground. He likes to shoot videos of the harvest by climbing grain bins for the panoramic view. He shoots video with one hand on his tractor, mowing while steering and running the shifter with the other hand.

Agriculture has hit its limits as he understands them. Why do they plant at the margins? Why do they deny what they see before them?

"They read too many farm magazines and attend too many conferences," he said.

Minds are fed with free food offered by the company selling the chemicals.

"We were a lot better off. We were all equal, and we weren't competitive with each other. Now we are."

The Luxembourgers took on their statist motto of wishing to stand pat because Germany, France, and Belgium kept horning in on the grand duchy. Over here across the pond in a tiny village their wish is denied by the interlopers of industry and monied politics who have put them now at odds. Something Ernie said that rings true, from a thoughtful man with just a country high school education, born of that mind-set: "Capital scours the globe looking for a slave." Ernie believes we often enslave ourselves by wanting to get sucked in.

There are foxholes in the grass along the hills. There are wild turkeys at the edge along the river. There are river swallows, who live in the mud banks, flitting all over the Buick. And grasshoppers and monarchs thick about the windows. He lumbers around looking for any signs of velvet leaf or cocklebur. It's four years in prairie now. You would think it were one hundred. The idea of planting corn there still tugs on him. But for someone who says you want to take the old route until you can't take it anymore, this is a minor revolution. Does he like what he sees?

"Any good crops look good to me."

Gray-headed coneflower. Wild bergamot in its bed of purple, plus purple clover. Canadian wild rye. Big bluestem.

"I'm well occupied," he said. "If you love your work you never have to work a day in your life."

# CHAPTER 19

# Where Is That Song Coming From?

Before the prairie was the ice. And before that it was sea that retreated to the Great Lakes of Superior, Michigan, Erie, and Huron, the font of the Midwest. The migrations traced across by boat, foot, and horse between north and south long before Henry Lott or the surveyors.

Before Inkpaduta and the Dakota were the Sac and Fox, who drove out the Ioway, the sleepy people, with an assist from Uncle Sam. The Ioway were descended from the Oneota people, a democratic and egalitarian lot who divided themselves into agriculturalists (buffalo) or predators (bear). Before the Oneota were the Mill Creek people, who lived among the Little Sioux and Raccoon rivers and no doubt around Storm Lake. We have found their traces of settled agriculture that would move around depending on weather and landscape demands. They planted corn and squash.

Where did the maize come from? Not Iowa.

The North American and Latin American indigenous people met at what is now East St. Louis, where the Missouri and Mississippi rivers join. It was the biggest indigenous city of the land, called Cahokia. Historians suggest that this is where the North American Plains people first got corn, through that intermingling.

The Mill Creek people left northwest Iowa without explanation about AD 1300, archeologists believe. It coincided with a great warming period that lasted from about AD 1100 to AD 1300. Droughts lasted decades. People had to move where the landscape would sustain them. One theory is that they went up to the Dakotas and became the Mandan tribe.

The Goddard Institute for Space Studies projects that, given current warming trends, northwest Iowa could return to the weather that might have driven out the Mill Creek people.

The Oneota people followed, down from the Great Lakes near Green Bay, and then the Ioway emerged from the Oneota as the landscape recovered. They were master farmers, practicing sophisticated resource conservation by planting corn in hills with squash vines running up the stalks. They put land fallow by letting the elk and buffalo roam. They managed large plots of land, perhaps two hundred acres or more, to support villages. They worked the land around their village at what is now Des Moines, and left it fallow to recover while they moved upstream with intentions to return. The Sac and Fox came up from behind and took it from them. An 1837 map in the Ioway hand shows their trail running from Fort Dodge to Storm Lake, what is now Iowa Highway 7. It shows the Raccoon and Des Moines rivers—their place, an idea contested by the other tribes who drove them out.

The idea of "the beautiful land," or "The Land Between Two Rivers," as the Ioway called it, was central to their very notion of identity. The Ioway refer to this as "our place." How could it ever not be theirs? They lived easily on the land and, looking now from Oklahoma or the Kansas-Nebraska border at White Cloud, wish they could return.

It might have been that the Oneota and their heirs, the Ioway, were more successful at community than the Mill Creek people, who were related to the more militaristic and turf-conscious Mississippian people who dominated Cahokia. It is in times of stress, when crops are poor and the creek runs dry, that people come together to persevere. Or to turn against one another.

"It's not the climate change that kills you, it's the people," agronomist Cruse says.

It has been mainly easy and mostly sleepy here. At times it hasn't been.

The Ioway and Dakota people had to confront the place as it was and move with its contours. The men and women who sought to dominate and subjugate the lands and people they encountered are beginning to confront the limits of the place and themselves. We watch the old worlds wash away and run down the Mississippi to the gulf, and new worlds take shape incomprehensibly right before us and around uncertain turns. New, flexible people who eat lamb's quarters come to confront the place and make it their own. Most are indigenous people reclaiming their stake along ancient routes where their ancestors once met. Ioway blood courses up and down the Mississippi and into Mexico, and the mestizo carries it back up to Storm Lake today. Like the Mississippi, that flow is relentless and cannot be bounded. You can bend it only for a while. It takes its course.

As the data play out in corn yields, land sales, and migrations, we will be reminded how the land and water and air will dictate how we respond. It will not be with the crude dredge line along the Raccoon or near Sunken Grove. It will come from GPS (invented in Cedar Rapids, and the computer was invented in Ames) devices that can tell you precisely how many pounds of ammonia to apply to a twelve-square-foot grid of ground, and how many corn seeds will be placed in that grid through real-time soil analysis. That is already happening.

The cattle will come. The corn will move north, or so it seems charted. The grass will return in this century. Rural infrastructure will be buried by time and wind and rain, and the soil with it. The Kansas City Federal Reserve Bank will tell you that the rural places with potential to grow have natural amenities that attract people. Who else would want these places but those seeking freedom or just a safe place to survive? Not the expatriate in Des Moines or Minneapolis. An epitaph writes itself for rural places far from the urban crowd, that critical mass, and the fortunes that follow it, except for those places with the resources and an open-enough mind-set to embrace new ways. Storm Lake will transform itself as it has through millennia, and each generation will learn to adapt, or so we would think, as the Ioway did until other humans drove them from their place. They think of it and remain drawn to it.

The Latina at Iowa State who lives undocumented with her parents might be the one who figures out how to process beef using less water. Or that Sudanese boy once lost might find the key to restoring topsoil to Iowa at a faster rate than it is being regenerated through improved soil tilth techniques—which might save the people in South Sudan suffering from their own climate-related soil degradation. Linda Torres will teach them. She will shape them to succeed as she has.

That has been the story of Iowa, from hybrid corn to the Green Revolution that fed billions of people in India and saved them from starvation. Either technology will quickly kill us through an engineered monoculture or it will save us by introducing us to a future that is based on what Storm Lake actually can support.

Aldo Leopold, the great conservation philosopher, said: "We end, I think, at what might be called the standard paradox of the twentieth century: our tools are better than we are, and grow better faster than we do. They suffice to crack the atom, to command the tides. But they do not suffice for the oldest task in human history: to live on a piece of land without spoiling it."

We learn from the Ioway about how to live in a place without spoiling it. Or from Ernie Gales or Aldo Leopold. Their wisdom resonates, if you listen, and can be in harmony with modern technology.

The cardinal's song rings with the Methodist church bells, sitting in the backyard at 125 Irving Street. It's half a block up from the lake. The yard is shrouded by trees, including a walnut we transplanted from the Des Moines River bottom twenty years ago. It provides a leafy, shady stage for red squirrels to put on their show before the green globes fall.

He is brilliant red, the cardinal, but you cannot squint hard enough to see him in the blur of green and backlight. You cannot help but hear him speaking from the other side, as many think. Today, it says that things are all right.

It's the Fourth of July. I rolled up and down the parks on my bike through the afternoon. There are people—young people— from all over the world living in Storm Lake. This is the one day a year when they all step out of the shadows to come together. In the backyard we have new Latino neighbors. They were having a big family party with the loudspeaker playing these tremendous Mexican songs in a voice that sounded distinctively like Linda Ronstadt's. There is only one voice like that—who could be imitating her? Turns out Ronstadt recorded *Canciones de Mi Padre (Songs of My Father)* in 1987, and my new neighbors were introducing me to an entirely new genre of mariachi from the greatest female voice of my generation. *Muchas gracias.* Two cultures come together over a song that a fence cannot contain. No fence can.

The song might be from Inkpaduta tracking a cougar down Cedar Creek. He never saw that great inland sea of water that gave way to grass. But he knew it. It was water all the way. The Vikings left traces to tell. They came all the way down to Sioux Rapids, legend says, and left their marks in guide stones.

The sea and ice that preceded the prairie left their underground infrastructure. A buried river runs beneath my house. Our lake bubbles up from springs pressurized by that river.

The Ioway hear their ancestors call them home from the reservations. The young ones bring the old ones back to see the black soil and recall the stories. They forgive—for the loss of everything, they forgive the other tribes and even the white man—and dream of coming back, perhaps just one acreage at a time. To this very place where they feel bound, to Spirit Lake north of us, which they considered sacred.

They came up the trail from Cahokia and mixed with the

natives from Mexico. The trail long preceded ours, north and south, sharing seed and blood. They found the beautiful land but could not hold it.

The prairie was something to conquer, Storm Lake something to build around for my people, my world. We turned it upside down and gouged it. We used the stones the glacier mason laid along the banks to build the foundations of the town. We shipped it out to be crushed for roads. And then we stepped back and looked at what we had done. And we tried to fix it.

Art Murray's song was to behold it, to drain it and clear it and reap it. To control it as he could. Those men, too, had a sense, enough to stop and leave Union Slough National Wildlife Refuge to remind us of the blue heron and goldfinch, oak and wild rose, a goose nesting on the muskrat den. Yet 98 percent of the rest of Iowa remains under the claw and tile, our own underground rivers enriched with our excess.

It's the song of the wind on the waves on the rocks that never stops all night long. It laps and shapes and washes away what every generation comes to know. We have to relearn.

Except for the song. It goes up as an Angelus from the bells of Santa Rita Church in Ayotlan for us all.

It beckons us to be with one another. That's what the song is about, that river that guides us or wind that draws us or spirit that binds us.

To be in a place and of it, swaying with the breeze off Buffalo Ridge through the big bluestem shadowed by wind turbines.

To be in a place that heals. If you leave the land to itself, the native grass always pops back. The seed is always there. The soil grows back. The pasqueflower blooms. You may touch it lightly. A place that opens, where you can be free to create your identity or find it lost in the Ray Gales bottom along the East Fork of the Upper Des Moines in the wild turkey tracks not yet washed away. We write its history. We come to it and know it is home, where you hear the song from our fathers and mothers calling through the wind rustling the dry corn.